M000286514

Fourteen Friends

By the same author

ROMAN MORNINGS, 1956 (Heinemann Award)
EARLS OF CREATION, 1962
ST PETER'S, 1967
ANOTHER SELF, 1970
ANCESTRAL VOICES, 1975
PROPHESYING PEACE, 1977
HAROLD NICOLSON, 1980–1 (Heinemann Award)
CAVES OF ICE, 1983
THE LAST STUARTS, 1983
MIDWAY ON THE WAVES, 1985
THE ENIGMATIC EDWARDIAN, 1986
THE BACHELOR DUKE, 1991
PEOPLE AND PLACES, 1992
A MINGLED MEASURE, 1994

Fourteen Friends

JAMES LEES-MILNE

JOHN MURRAY
Albemarle Street, London

James Lees-Milne 1996

First published in 1996
by John Murray (Publishers) Ltd.,
50 Albemarle Street, London W1X 4BD

The moral right of the author has been asserted

All rights reserved. No part of this publication may be reproduced in any material form (including photocopying or storing it in any medium by electronic means and whether or not transiently or incidentally to some other use of this publication) without the written permission of the copyright owner, except in accordance with the provisions of the Copyright, Designs and Patents Act 1988 or under the terms of a licence issued by the Copyright Licensing Agency, 90 Tottenham Court Road, London W1P 9HE. Applications for the copyright owner's written permission to reproduce any part of this publication should be addressed to the publisher.

A catalogue record for this book is available from the British Library

ISBN 0-7195-5594 9

Typeset in Garamond on 12/14 pt
by Pure Tech India Ltd., Pondicherry

Printed and bound in Great Britain by
The University Press, Cambridge

To
DIANA MOSLEY
and a friendship of
over seventy years

Contents

Illustrations   ix
Preface   xi

1. Kathleen Kennet   1
2. Paul Methuen   18
3. Vita Sackville-West   41
4. Sacheverell Sitwell   67
5. Rosamond Lehmann   79
6. William Plomer   88
7. Patrick Kinross   103
8. Henry Yorke and Henry Green   122
9. Robert Byron   132
10. John Fowler   158
11. Osbert Lancaster   169
12. Everard Radcliffe   179
13. Richard Stewart-Jones   194
14. James Pope-Hennessy   201

Acknowledgements   231
Index   235

Illustrations

(between pages 114 and 115)

Kathleen Kennet, taken by the author, *c.*1935.
Paul and Norah Methuen, 1956
Vita Sackville-West, by Jane Bown, 1958
Sacheverell Sitwell, by Francis Goodman, 1951
Rosamond Lehmann in the early 1980s
William Plomer
Patrick Kinross with his mother and two sisters on the Isle of
    Lismore, 1932
Henry Yorke, by Cecil Beaton, 1949
Robert Byron
John Fowler in his garden room, *c.*1970
Osbert Lancaster, self-portrait, *Cornhill Magazine*, 1948
Everard Radcliffe
Richard Stewart-Jones
James Pope-Hennessy in the Second World War

Preface

THE FOURTEEN SKETCHES of friends which make up this book
are not biographical, although I must concede that they contain
a few biographical data, without which the reader might not
know who some of the friends were. In fact the sketches cover
mere fragmentary days of their lifetime, those spent in my
company, some over many years, some over a few. Length of
friendship, however, has no bearing upon its depth.

One of my intentions has been to show these friends as they
appeared to me, as they related to me. But what does 'as they
related to me' mean? In their birth, procreation and death I
played no part, nor in the most noteworthy moments of their
lives. I had no specific influence on their thoughts or actions.
The achievements they left behind, by which they may be
remembered by posterity, would have been no different had I
never existed. What justifies my presumption in touching upon
their lives at all? It is that if I had little measurable effect upon
the fourteen, they clearly had a good deal upon me. I do not
give particulars of how they did so because, with one
exception, I cannot put a finger on the occasions. I cannot
assert that Kathleen did or Patrick said something one day
which arrested the whole pulse of my cognition, deflected me
from one path of my philosophy into another, or changed my
character instantly from bad to good (or at least for the better).
Nor was I consciously aware, while they were alive, that their

attitude to any parochial or cosmic issue might lead to such a mutation. William Blake wrote in *Jerusalem* that 'He who would do good to another must do it in Minute Particulars ... for Art and Science cannot exist but in minutest organized Particulars and not in generalizing Demonstrations of the Rational Power.' The fact is that particulars are seldom noticed actually happening. They work away like the minute pebbles of Chesil Bank to cast up a firm and enduring bulwark against encroaching oblivion. While these friends were alive I took them for granted. Now that they are dead I am able to see them for what they outstandingly were, strongly focused against a clearer background. Such is the vision afforded by death.

If anyone asks me why I have selected these fourteen from all the friends I have had – at least ninety per cent of them must now be dead – I can give no answer. They seem to have selected themselves. Of the fourteen, three were country squires, three poets, two novelists, four travel writers, two painters, one a sculptor, one a cartoonist, one a decorator, one a horticulturist and one a conservationist. If the total adds up to more than fourteen, it is because some of them come under more than a single denomination. No two of them were alike. Yet all of them may be called aesthetes, and their interests were mostly esoteric.

Another intention is to express my gratitude to the fourteen for having existed, and having bequeathed me most memorable delights. Of some I may appear a trifle defensive, because time has not been kind to them. It is sad that unless an artist be literally a saint – which is rare indeed – he or she is seldom credited with saintly endeavours. After all, most people have in their make-up the interchangeable attributes of both saint and devil. But the devilish attributes will be sure to catch the limelight. It is the chronicler's duty to curb a natural tendency to sensationalism and contrive to render his subject's good deeds no less patent than his bad ones. It may be a difficult job in all conscience, but is one not to be shirked. On the other hand, a too kindly author may so gloss those failings which in his subject's lifetime were almost past enduring that the reader will deem them endearing. I trust there is is nothing to mislead the naïve in these pages. Yet the reader as well as the author has to play his part and keep his head.

J.L.-M.,   1996

Kathleen Kennet
1878–1947

MY MOTHER AND her sister, my aunt Doreen Cuninghame, were great friends of a strikingly handsome Victor Campbell, captain in the Royal Navy during the First World War. My mother admired him much and my beautiful aunt may have done more than that, I fancy. My mother, who had always longed for me to become a sailor (an idea that was obnoxious to me from the very start), sent me one holiday from my preparatory school to stay with Victor on his destroyer. The crew were tolerant of me on board, but I suffered from sea sickness, and from terror lest I might be called upon to climb to the mast head, or to distinguish port from starboard and in failing to do so might reveal the colour blindness of which I was deeply ashamed. To this day I have detested all sailing and being on the ocean wave. With Victor Campbell, I need hardly say, I was not a success. Yet the one thing I vividly remember about him was a casual reference to his close friendship with both Queen Maud of Norway and the widow of Scott of the Antarctic; the latter was shortly to marry his best friend Edward Hilton Young, like him a gallant sailor. Queen Maud duly impressed me, but Kathleen Scott intrigued me. Had she not triumphed over her husband's glorious death near the South Pole and brought up their son Peter to run around London naked and shoeless? About the nakedness Mama and Aunt Doreen were slightly sniffy. I now suspect both of them thought Lady Scott a bit of a show-off.

I

But their attitude did not diminish the fascination this celebrated and romantic woman held for me.

It was certainly not through Victor Campbell that I met Kathleen. Probably it was when she was sculpturing my employer George Lloyd's head, in the early 1930s. In the first (undated) letter I have from her she wrote that she must show me Lord Lloyd's head, adding, 'It's so tiresome meeting people year after year in crowds and never knowing a single real thing about them. Come again, ask yourself. I'd no idea how close a link we had in the Campbells. Rum world.' I may already have been to her house or seen her at parties. She was someone whose presence in a crowd could not be ignored. At that time she was a woman in her fifties, even older than my father. No great beauty, she was distinctly handsome: with a silhouette like carved granite, her face was more masculine than feminine. She was totally unconcerned with her appearance; her clothes were abysmally dreary. She wore sack-like garments with no adornment of any kind beyond a straight band across her abundant iron-grey hair, close-cropped at the back of the neck like a man's. Her rugged countenance radiated satisfaction with her lot and the confidence of one who had through sheer guts made a way in the world. She knew her own mind, and her dedications, of which sculpture was ostensibly the foremost. That for friendship with leaders in politics, literature, music and the arts closely followed. There seemed to be no public figure with whom she was not on intimate terms. Indeed Asquith, Lloyd George, Bernard Shaw, T.E. Lawrence, Hugh Walpole, J.M. Barrie, Max Beerbohm, Gordon Craig and Isadora Duncan, to name only a few, were at different times her constant visitors for tête-à-tête confidences. She had stacks and stacks of letters from these celebrities. There is no doubt that each found he (or she: mostly he) was able to communicate with her uninhibitedly, for Kathleen was absolutely direct and trustworthy. Profoundly interested in human beings, she ignored the irregularities in her friends' behaviour and kept her own counsel. The great poured in and out of Leinster Corner, the Hilton Youngs' Bayswater house

2

which faced the northern boundary of Hyde Park. Leinster Corner was like a cosy early nineteenth-century house in the country, say a vicarage, with garden and studio at the rear. Kathleen made no more attempt at decorating her home than she did her person, and like so many artists displayed a sort of aggressive non-taste.

And there was Captain Scott's shade hovering prominently in the background of the living lady. She was never shy of talking about him, and quite naturally held him firmly on his pedestal. Nor was she guarded in her assessment of his associates and companions in the Antarctic débâcle. She would talk subjectively about the 1910–11 expedition to the South Pole and the abortive return journey as part of England's history, in which she had played a rôle. The impression I got was that she had never been deeply in love with Falcon Scott whom, when she was no longer in her first youth, she had scrupulously chosen, in a sort of Norse, mythical way, as the fittest father available to sire the paragon son she was determined to bear. After a free-and-easy and decidedly Bohemian life *en garçonne* in Paris and elsewhere abroad, she was well into her thirties before she took her first matrimonial plunge.

On one occasion she was very outspoken to me about Ernest Shackleton (whose failure to reach the Pole in 1909 was indirectly responsible for Scott's ill-fated expedition), describing him as rotten, of bad blood, no good, and disliked by Scott; about Cherry-Garrard – too rich by half, and besides he dared to criticize Scott; about Oates – just all right; about Bill Wilson – he had an impossible wife; about Ted Evans – a drunkard, incapable of speaking the truth; and about Birdie Bowers – although very ugly indeed, staunch and wonderful. All seemed to dislike one another, but so disciplined and controlled were they that tempers never flared and they never sulked.

If Falcon Scott was her chosen man, Peter Scott was her very own son. Each became a national hero to his own generation; each owed much of his promotion to her – an important point of which no question was permitted, even by imputation. In her eyes Peter, her created, could never do wrong; everything he did was right. You could not see her without having to listen to deafening blasts of trumpet-blowing on his behalf. Her letters were packed with his praises. His portrait drawings were better than anything Augustus John could do. (They are indeed excellent, and he had a true eye for a likeness.) The record-breaking sales of his duck and geese in flight were proof positive that he was the greatest artist alive. During the Second World War Peter earned very well-merited renown at sea. He was the first (if not the only) officer in the Royal Naval Volunteer Reserve to be given command of a destroyer and one hundred and twenty men. He was twice awarded the DSC and Bar, and thrice mentioned in despatches for gallantry. He had previously been appointed MBE (and, at the very end of his life, was made a Companion of Honour). When he was given a week's leave he would spend it at his mother and stepfather's house in Suffolk. He would rise at 4 a.m. for goose shooting until luncheon and sedulously paint throughout the remaining hours till bed at 8.45 p.m., prompt. Peter's brand of heroism, Kathleen asserted, was of like quality to Scott's,

> and with the same sort of undefined drive – the drive to defy inertia, the longing to set oneself the most exacting & courageous & exciting task. The instinct in both is astonishing in its un-self-regarding quality. I doubt if that kind of man can tell you just why he has this urge to risk his very full life. Con used to talk of England & his Navy, Pete of a chance to be able to do something, but they seem to me to mean the same thing.

Eventually Peter was given such important and secretive jobs by the Admiralty that he could only mention them to his mother in cryptic language.

Kathleen's second husband, Sir Edward Hilton Young (later 1st Baron Kennet, and known as Bill), who on the outbreak of the Second World War was sixty and no longer fit for active service – he too had been in the Navy, and lost an arm in the blockade of Zeebrugge in 1918 – nevertheless became chairman of numerous war committees in London, where he spent the week. Temporarily driven out of Leinster Corner after a bomb came through his bedroom ceiling, he was obliged to sleep wherever he could lay his ageing head. Every Sunday he would join K. in the country, sometimes at his own cottage, The Lacket at Lockeridge outside Marlborough, but usually at Fritton Hithe close to Yarmouth, the house he and K. had bought jointly. Throughout the war Yarmouth was so subject to intensive German bombing and machine-gunning as to render that part of the coast no haven of peace, yet Hitler's interruptions never drove K. away from Fritton and the meres she dearly loved. 'I think I am rather depraved,' she wrote to me in February 1941. 'I almost enjoy it, but not when I see the lists at the Town Hall.' A few months later she wrote that four London concerns of which Bill was chairman had been blown out of their premises. 'But work continues as usual. The more difficult the more fun.' That was her attitude about all disagreeable happenings: not grin and bear, but smile and bear them.

Bill's and her son Wayland, sixteen when war broke out, was scarcely less prodigious than Peter. He would in the school holidays immerse himself in the lives of Chateaubriand, Metternich and Liszt. At seventeen he won a history scholarship at Trinity College Cambridge and 'gave a really exquisite ninety minutes' organ recital in the Trinity Chapel.' No wonder K. could write, 'Rearing of sons has been by far my greatest preoccupation for the last 30 years & by far my highest ability has been that of a father chooser.' And she added gracefully, 'But you are ill & that does just a little darken my day.' The next day she was launching a ship with champagne and proudly watching Pete reading warrants to his ship's company and 'sending a man to gaol for going to sleep standing.'

I am almost, but not wholly, ashamed to confess that the perfection of K.'s menfolk nearly drove me to hate them. Whether it was their or her doing, or my not doing, I cannot really explain. Certain it is that their clannish meritocracy struck me as priggish and self-righteous. Moreover it made me, when among them, feel excluded. The sense of inferiority which as a family they induced, aroused my lowest instincts, which were and are to be suspicious of other people's ostensible vainglory. Could such shining exemplars of every virtue not host even one toe of clay? At first I found Bill Kennet morose and supercilious and, when he made an essay at amiability, ungracious and condescending. I sensed that he disliked me, for which I now bear him no grudge whatever, but I must once or twice have shown that I then did so, for it drew down a well merited reprimand from K. 'Bill took the trouble to bring up subjects of conversation at meals that might interest you... and then you only held your head and moaned!' Why, I thought at the time, did he have to choose subjects that might interest me? When he read poetry aloud after dinner, as though to show by this concession that his was a forgiving nature, I liked him no better.

As for Peter, my matured feelings about him are more ambivalent. I never got to know him well, or was in his confidence, although for some reason or other I was an usher at his first wedding. He was always jolly with me, while knowing full well that I was not his sort. Nor was he mine. Yet he made and generously gave me a drawing of myself. It is very good but reveals certain traits of which I am not proud, and I wonder whether he himself recognized them. There was nothing cosy about his extraverted wardroom bonhomie, his 'Cheerio, old boy!' approach, which meant nothing at all. He was a high-minded, conventional, successful leader of men; and as a conservationist of wild life, without an equal. But he was a self-centred philistine without a glimmer of humour, and with a heart as cold as stone. The same cannot be said of his mother.

Hers was a contradictory character, a mixture of some infuriating (though never malevolent) qualities and many super-abundant virtues. To take the infuriating qualities first: she always looked upon the bright side of things in a set determination to be happy. She gloried in making the best of the worst. This led to a certain winsomeness which was not always appreciated or reciprocated by her friends. In the icy summer of 1937 she wrote from Northumberland: 'We bathed by moonlight at 2.30 the other night. It was nice. Also we've been sleeping on the lake in a punt. Altogether things have been pleasant.' And again, in 1941, 'We sat in the Temple gardens & ate peanuts instead of lunching' – not because she preferred peanuts to a three-course meal, but because it was 'doing one's bit' in the war. In the same way, by not referring to this world as lovely, she 'would really be allowing Hitler a victory if his nonsense should make me "falter more or less in this life's task of happiness".' She could be dismissive of members of her own sex, including very young women whom she deemed frivolous and silly. For instance, she found 'Ran Antrim's chaste wife . . . too shy and gigglesome to judge much about her.' And her treatment of her beloved Pete's nineteen-year-old bride during the war was ill-considered. 'At long last Pete has decided to marry little Jane & I am now hectically trying to fix it up . . . at Christ Church, Lancaster Gate,' she wrote to me in 1942. But why should she have fixed it up, when 'little Jane' anyway wanted, in wartime, not a pompous society wedding but a simple one limited to her and Peter's families and favourite friends? 'She is very sweet & very talented. I have only one small anxiety; but I won't write about it [she certainly talked about it] and it will probably adjust itself.' It didn't adjust itself, for K. had met her match in this sensitive, clever and gifted girl. After the wedding K. gave vent to: 'Jane looked rather a duck (Oh *no*, no reservations) only her age, she is only 19.' It was not only her age. It was fear lest Jane might take Peter away from her, Kathleen.

Like all successful people, she was accused of snobbishness. Sibyl Colefax complained of her self-advertisement, and of her dramatization of her Scott widowhood. Sibyl even claimed to know that Scott had been rendered unhappy by his wife's 'cheapness'. Also, her alleged vamping of distinguished men came in for a bashing. These charges were rubbish. Famous men sought K. out, chose to go to her house and studio, even those who were not being modelled, to partake of her sympathy and understanding, she being the best listener any man could find. The thousands of letters these people wrote her were mostly about themselves. She disclosed that Scott's and Asquith's correspondence ran to two volumes: Shaw's, Max Beerbohm's, Barrie's, Colonel House's (President Wilson's envoy) and Nansen's to one volume apiece. I do not believe that her relations with men other than her husbands were, as her detractors implied, ever physical. On the contrary her philosophy, which today may strike people as absurd, was strict monogamy despite any temptations to stray from it. When she admitted to me, of one of her faithful cavaliers, Keith Miller Jones, that 'his exterior delights me', it did not imply that she infringed her sacred precept, or even wished to. She was far too Draconian with herself for that. And when another friend of mine protested that as a very handsome young man he had been lured to the Lacket cottage for bed purposes, I am convinced that he was simply misinterpreting her motives. That she loved many men, however, and gloried in their bodily attractions, was often manifested by her unguarded words and behaviour. She was extraordinarily naïve and innocent.

The simple truth is that K.'s besetting weakness – and that a pretty venial one, however irritating – was a child-like vanity, a quality which she may have transmitted to her sons. It did not, by the way, concern her looks, to which (as I have indicated) she was completely indifferent. It concerned her mind and her art. Her mind she set much store by.

By some odd chance I was asked in 1937 to write her obituary for *The Times*. It is customary in the case of obituaries that the subject, even if he or she is privy to the writing of the record, should pretend to know nothing about it. Now, Kathleen never let the matter drop until she had seen and corrected and amplified my draft. I don't suppose many obituarists are silly enough to submit to their subjects what they have written. But Kathleen both knew what was intended and had a lot to say. I was the recipient of a spate of letters giving interesting particulars, which I was glad to receive, of

8

her achievements: also of what she wanted to be included in her life's story. In June of 1937 she was telling me that she was sure I was leaving out a lot of things she had passed on in a previous letter. One was that in 1909, 1910 and 1911

> I used to do a lot of flying. I was actually the second woman [the first being Kathleen Drogheda] to go up in an aeroplane in 1909 with Graham White, and a year before the War I flew with Immelmann in Germany. All the early crowd of aviators, Charley Rolls, Gustav Hamel, were great friends of mine. I flew with double controls with Sopwith when that was a brand new invention. In the days when one first flew one sat on a board, like a seat of a swing, holding on to two struts – Nothing between one's feet and the earth. *Those* were the days!

They were indeed.

Then there was her relief work for the Bulgarians in Macedonia in 1903 and 1904. She had contracted typhoid while succouring refugees from Turkish slaughter, and nearly died. 'Shall I send you a postcard a day until the end of the month?' She pursued me by letter to Naples where I had gone for a holiday in the late summer. 'I must see the obit,' she wrote – and her sons were winning races, 'very gratifying to the maternal heart.' Again, as late as 1941, 'Do send it. I won't tell a soul.' She enclosed an amusing tribute to her in verse, which she transcribed for me. 'Isn't it neat and witty?' It was; Stephen Gwynn had written it in 1919. For a woman of her sort, not college-educated, not trained, to have held a civil service post in the Ministry of Pensions for a year or two during a world crisis was, to put it mildly, unusual. The poem, entitled 'The Bureaucrat', begins with the following stanza:

> The world is most amazing with Duchess VADs
> And masquerades in khaki of uniformed MPs
> But the strangest transformation we've yet assisted at
> Was when the Lady Kathleen became a bureaucrat

to finish with:

Just for a demonstration that she's alive and free
She'll maybe take the high road with some austere CB.
But till the bomb explodes & lays the building flat,
Oh what a happy Bureau with Kathleen for its Crat!

'It's all I need for an obituary, or even a biography,' she went on. 'Will you design me a plaque to go somewhere in St Martin-in-the-Fields or in its crypt?' And when I did send the obit, all hell was let loose, figuratively speaking.

' "She does not pretend to be an intellectual woman",' she quoted back, piqued.

Forgive me, she *does*, or if she doesn't pretend it is because she is that self confident about it. Ah, if you only knew the depths she has plumbed in Spinoza, Descartes, Lamarck & Aristotle, etc., if you only knew that she passed her exams for Cambridge when she was 15, that she *taught* Latin and Mathematics & that last night she stayed up till 1 a.m. reading Dean Inge's final round up. Do you read the clever old man, he is about 80 but writes like a 30 year old?

Seriously I am very interested in your rendering of me! It's a nice creature you depict on the whole. Of course really the only thing I've cared about are young male objects & and much most about my sons, but that doesn't seem a bit interesting.

Caustic? She was a deviator from the ordinary, a non-conformist, and that is what I loved about her.

In opening an exhibition of her sculpture in Heal's shop after her death, G.M. Trevelyan spoke of her as a woman devoted to the arts. She hated fraud, he added, sentiment, lack of courage. She loved beauty and the young. True enough. Only, like his, her sense of beauty was rudimentary and conventional. Sir Sydney Cockerell, who was her friend and admirer, told me she was no artist and he knew she was aware of it. That she *was* aware of it I very much doubt.

And here I must interpolate that I was exceedingly fond of K. I can never forget her kindness and generosity to the young me. Twice before the war, when I was rat-poor, she paid for me to join her and Wayland at the Swiss resort of

Villard-de-Lans where we spent the days on the ice rink and the nights on the ballroom floor. Skating and dancing were her favourite recreations, of which she never seemed to tire. And when she returned to London they were resumed on the Paddington ice rink, and at the Savoy Hotel or on any available dance floor. It did not greatly matter that when no glamorous young creature was available, an obliging but mere 'little man in the Indian political service' partnered her. Dancing, she maintained, established morale. I often accompanied her in this pursuit in London. In December 1935 she wrote: 'Of course I shall come and dance again. We might dine here [Leinster Corner] and dance afterwards; if you like; or anything you like. Ever yours K.' Memories of these escapades delighted her later years, long after she had been obliged to give them up.

> I remember you skating past the onlookers at Villard one day [she wrote], and with loathing, ejaculating, 'How glad I am I don't look like any of those.' And your loathing for the posterior of Sheila [whoever she was] ... An unusual and tortured creature I believe you to be. I only once knew anyone like you (& he wasn't); his name was Freddy Manners-Sutton & then Lord Canterbury & I believe his reputation was not above reproach. [She makes me sound quite odious.] You are a kind dear Jim to ring, to come, to bring & to send ... You are not unimportant.

Important is what she wanted and positively urged her young friends to be. 'Your two telegrams & your divine letter & most of all the poem [sent to her when I was twenty-five or six] were great fun to get. A lovely poem, now you must publish a book for me to stick the poem into the fly leaf. If possible make it a readable book so that it is intrinsically an adornment to my bookshelves. You'll see about doing that for me, won't you? Of course I was cross over Cardiff.' Cardiff, like Sheila's posterior, has escaped me.

We would go to matinées for the ballet and have tea afterwards, seated on the old green velvet sofa at Leinster Corner. Frequently during the war we met at the National Gallery for snacks and Mozart supplied by that stalwart pianist

Dame Myra Hess. Occasionally it was politic for me to make a presence at K.'s al fresco tea parties, which I never much enjoyed and would slip away from when charades began. On leaving London for National Trust expeditions I would often telephone her from a station kiosk just to say good morning and goodbye.

We would meet under Watts's *Energy* in Hyde Park for walks to the Round Pond and then the Serpentine, where she vouchsafed that on warm days she was wont to hire a boat for 6d. an hour and row herself once round the lake. I am reminded of a blood row on one of these Hyde Park walks, after a Beethoven concert in the Albert Hall. She let fall that she had sent a letter to *The Times* stating how gladly she would countenance the total destruction of Rome by the Allied bombers in exchange for the lives of her two sons. I furiously rebutted these sentiments and doubtless expressed some unorthodox opinions about the war objectives. Extremely shocked, she threatened not to see me again, and to report me to the police for subversive views. A distinct coldness ensued for three months. Suddenly I was forgiven. K. never bore resentment for long. 'I was angry with my friend. I told my wrath; my wrath did end.' She was fond of quoting these lines of Blake. I was invited to the theatre, and after tea at Leinster Corner was given, by way of olive-branch, tulips and lilies-of-the-valley. In spite of her bragging that Peter's book on battle boats had sold 20,000 copies I noted in my diary, 'Adorable woman'.

Frequently before, during and after the war she asked me to Fritton Hithe for weekends. The house, thatched, long, low, nondescript but *gemütlich*, overlooked a lake which afforded the family infinite recreation with boats and other aquatic delights. K. would drive me in a little Austin Seven from and to Yarmouth station, where she greeted or dismissed me with a fond motherly hug. After breakfast in bed I might pick raspberries with her in the kitchen garden under a net cage, or punt with her leisurely on the water. When I was still in the army, and indeed during my prolonged and ugly intervals in hospitals, she was unsparing with concern and solace. And come to think of it, I was only one of a multitude of her friends. 'I realise that if you were hurt, not being a next-of-kin I should probably never know – so please do not get hurt,' she wrote. Her letters were punctuated with enquiries. 'Are you better?' 'Are you going to be quite well? Bill said you looked very well and decorative but he wouldn't really know.' 'Dearest Jimmy, that was a nice letter for a feller to get. Sad about your having to go on with Luminol.' She strongly recommended an alternative drug – Epanutin. I changed to it on doctor's orders but it was no less potent and nearly drove me insane. And when I was assailed with shingles, 'Are your bugs enduring creatures?' Her sympathy was very heartfelt. 'Pain', she wrote to me in a Farningham hospital, is 'the one thing that my philosophy cannot manage . . . If you told me that you were unhappy or terribly poor I should say, "Well, well, does that matter?" You must come to Fritton & get quite well.'

She took a keen interest in my National Trust work. When I was organizing two groups of British country house owners to visit French and Belgian *châteaux* in 1938 and '39 she was forward with advice as to what celebrity ought to head the deputations. Her first recommendation was Sir Sydney Cockerell. But no, he was seventy. 'Would Keith Miller Jones fit? No. Or John Pentland? Or Sir Richard Paget? . . . Why not Lord Lothian? He would be a perfect person. Try him. Say I said so. Or Rob Holland Martin (say I am going). What a lark it will be.' She came on both excursions even though she owned no historic country house, enjoyed herself hugely, and was liked and admired by all. On the Belgian trip her impatience with etiquette raised not a few eyebrows. Bored stiff by the guide conducting us round the Hôtel de Ville in Brussels, she leapt from an upstairs window into a flower bed at the feet of the famous First World War hero who was preparing himself to greet us at the exit, Burgomaster Max.

When I was discharged from the army she insisted that I should return to the National Trust without pricks of conscience. 'The National Trust is the thing you've been trained in. You know more than any of them about it, & in fact England needs you!!' Soon she was complaining, 'James, are you dead? Or is it only that half England having fallen into your keeping you have no thought for the more ordinary occupations of life, such as me?' When I became acting secretary for a short spell (the duties of which I did not care for, and fulfilled rather ill) she claimed that 'It was really God justifying his ways (for I was a little vexed with him for having let you get ill) . . . I hope you may keep control, why not, for after all you're getting quite a big boy now.'

I kept (or endeavoured to keep) K. away from my sophisticated – and by this I do not necessarily imply intellectual – contemporaries. My worse reason may have been jealousy. My better was a fear that they might mock her. Indeed, to the ultra-cynical post-Twenties generation her dated values, views and utterances were rather comical. They were not comical to the inward me. But the outward me was often too snobbish to admit the fact. Were, say, Nancy Mitford and Eddy Sackville-West to have read a letter from K. in which she exhorted me 'to see, please,' that some friend she had introduced to me, 'is the nicer for his association with you, because I think with good fortune he might be a valuable citizen (I hear hoots of ribald laughter at which I snap my experienced fingers),' they would assuredly have hooted. And this I would not have liked. It so happened that I was through pressure on their part obliged to introduce both Nancy and Eddy to her. Evidently I had parried the pressure for some time, much to K.'s amusement, for she wrote, 'I don't the least know whether I shall find my soul's mate in Nancy, never having seen her . . . but I am very ready to try.' The three of them lunched with me one November day in 1944.

The meeting was a qualified success. After Nancy's remark that she was 'simply mad about Captain Scott' and K.'s rejoinder 'So am I', a temperate sympathy between the two women, so disparate in every thought and gesture, not least in clothes, was arrived at following K.'s revelation that to her Con, any unkindness to animals was absolute torture. That touched dog-loving Nancy. 'She was fascinated by me knowing so much about the Antarctic,' Nancy wrote to her sister Diana Mosley. 'She was dressed from head to foot in pale blue hand-woven, but I thought her heaven.' To me K. wrote: 'It was enchanting of Eddy to appear to know me quite well... Then Nancy. I wanted to ask her as many embarrassing questions as she asked me. I wanted to ask her just how bad it was being Peter [Rodd]'s wife and how Unity was and how Tom. We might have the same party over again, only at Leinster... I want an open avenue from St Paul's to the river.' At a later date I got her to meet for dinner two other even more incongruously unsuitable friends, Bridget Parsons [sister of Michael Rosse and Desmond Parsons], whose lethargic choosiness did not appeal to her, and the MP Malcolm Bullock, whose trenchant and mischievous yarns slightly bewildered and shocked her.

Under the surface, Kathleen was a well-bred Victorian lady imbued with the traditions and prejudices of her paternal vicarage. Her straightforward values of honour, loyalty, decency and courage did not conflict with her slightly Bohemian tastes. These last were simple. She cared nothing for luxury and ceremonial. For absolute truth she cared absolutely, and yet had no truck with religion. She was a blithe agnostic who wanted to leave her mark on the world. She was satisfied – she nearly always was satisfied with events – that her immortality lay in that most endurable medium of artistic creation, sculpture. She took her sculpture extremely seriously and professionally. It had been her vocation and her career ever since, as a teenager, she absconded from school to London in order to learn painting at the Slade School under Henry Tonks: then to Paris in order to learn modelling in clay under no less a celebrity than Rodin. The great sculptor became not merely her teacher but her colleague and admirer.

Kathleen's allegorical compositions, her *Laus Deo, The Kingdom is Within, These had most to Give, Progress* and so on, are mostly represented by naked figures of very young men, with outstretched arms. Their exclamatory gestures and strivings towards the sublime are fairly commonplace, sometimes even verging on that sentimentality which Kathleen deplored in others. She lacked the startling genius of her contemporary Epstein ('an amazing egoist'), whom she dismissed as totally unable to carve the bold images which his virility and vitality conjured up. If she was not quite as great an exponent of the medium in marble and bronze as she aspired to be, she was unquestionably a competent delineator of character. Her portrait busts were lifelike indeed. It was her good fortune to manage, either by request or commission, to sculpture most of the leading statesmen, writers, artists and composers of her day. Her images consequently endure as faithful and pleasing pointers to a critical era in the nation's history.

K. did not reach old age. She did not labour under years of second childhood. In late middle age she suffered from *angina pectoris*, but it scarcely halted her activities. Finally came pernicious anaemia. In February 1947 I called on her at Leinster Corner, which had been reinstated after the bombing. To my surprise I was guided into her bedroom. I was horribly depressed by her condition. She could eat only fruit, and could read only in short spurts. But she spoke of the wonderful life she had enjoyed. 'The best of this illness is that there is no suffering and I do not become disgusting, at least I don't think I do. I don't decay, become horrible, or smell, for instance. I just linger and gently melt away.' On leaving I knew that she was going to die.

My next visit, towards the end of March, was to St Mary's Hospital, Paddington. She said, 'When young men like you come to see me I feel that I shall get well again; and that there is still a future for me.' When I next went at the beginning of April I stayed a bare quarter of an hour. Her voice kept trailing into speechlessness; and I spoke little. Yet it did not somehow matter. We seemed to be communicating in fervent silences. I realized then that she had been a part of my life, a part that could never be taken away, although I was unable to determine precisely wherein our intimacy had lain. I just knew that I loved her in some special way, in which one person rarely loves another – or, I should perhaps say, as a man rarely loves a woman. With her there were no obliquities of any kind, and only occasional obfuscations through which one could see, at the moment of their projection, the daylight. Of course I reviled myself for having squabbled with her now and again in the past. Towards the end of the month I took her a small present, the idea of which gave her pleasure. She said she was begging the family and the doctors to let her go. I walked home across the Park sick at heart. In May she said the effort of keeping alive was killing her, and gave a wry little laugh. I wondered why she had to make the effort. In June I insensitively handed her an illustrated art book, which I soon realized she was too feeble even to hold. 'Don't give it to me,' she pleaded. I could not take it away. So I left it; and her, for the last time.

On 25th July I woke up at 4.45 in the morning – unusual for me in those days – with a presentiment. The next day I read her obituary in *The Times* and was appalled by its inadequacy.

---

* Her granddaughter Louisa Young's excellent *A Great Task of Happiness: The Life of Kathleen Kennet* was published early in 1995 by Macmillan.

Paul Methuen

1886–1974

WHENEVER I PICTURE Paul Methuen in my mind's eye I see someone who was not all there. Let me hasten to make myself clear. By no means do I imply a man not of right mind. Very, very far from it, for he was singularly gifted mentally as well as physically: indeed he was, in the Goethian sense, a man of parts. But he struck me as a natural loner, drifting through the duties which his social obligations obliged him to fulfil – seldom, be it said, fulfilled in vain – yet drifting as though with reluctance; not so much positively evading as negatively and sorrowfully pursuing them when his thoughts were far away, engaged in pursuits that really mattered to him. No leader, no follower, he was a dreamer. Not a philosopher, but a creator. An artist in fact, first and foremost a painter. That is what he had always aspired to be, and ultimately became. No amateur painter either, but a professional, if an artist can be so denominated who is not obliged to make a living out of his creations. Sir John Pope-Hennessy succinctly defined Paul's situation by stating that for him 'the odds were loaded against creativity', in that he was born with a large silver spoon already in his mouth. I doubt if he was any more temperamentally suited to be a nobleman and owner of a large estate and historic seat than the composer Lennox Berkeley, who would have inherited the Berkeley Castle estate had his father been born legitimate. However, since Paul Methuen was the heir apparent to Corsham from birth, he knew all along what was expected of him and acquired a peculiar and endearing skill in carrying it out.

The Methuen family derived from Scotland. John, the first ancestor of note, fled south in the sixteenth century in consequence of the political part he had played in promoting the Reformation in the northern kingdom. In his nonconformity to established thinking there is some resemblance to that of his remote descendant, the subject of this essay. He had a son, the Reverend Paul, who became Prebendary of Perth Cathedral before following his father to the borders of Somerset and Wiltshire.

By the seventeenth century the Methuens had the status of well-born upper gentry who had edged their way into the ranks of the old squirearchy. In the mid eighteenth century a later Paul Methuen bought the Corsham property near Chippenham in Wiltshire, re-edifying and extending an existing manor house. In anticipation of inheriting from yet another Paul, a bachelor cousin and godfather, Sir Paul Methuen, a great collection of pictures (mostly sixteenth- and seventeenth-century Italian and Dutch) and furniture, he set about providing a suite of worthy state rooms. This Sir Paul, like his father the Rt Honourable John Methuen, had been Ambassador to the King of Portugal; he had in fact helped his father negotiate the famous Methuen Treaty of 1703, which raised Portugal to trading parity with her oldest ally, Great Britain, and incidentally brought about several generations of port-drinking and gout-ridden Georgian squires.

Sir Paul, who held various other high offices of state, died in 1757 and Mr Paul Methuen, squire of the newly-acquired Corsham, duly inherited his cousin's works of art. Not immediately but eventually he moved them into the finished state rooms on Corsham's east front, overlooking the park and lake which he had commissioned the well known landscape-gardener Capability Brown to lay out. Brown also designed the palatial picture gallery with raised stucco ceiling, the coves decorated with undulating S-scrolls. Here the principal and certainly the largest canvases – notably the Van

Dyck equestrian portrait of Charles I, the *Betrayal of Christ*, and other masterpieces – were hung, and have remained till this day, in the company of exquisite furniture supplied by Robert Adam and Chippendale. Mr Paul's grandson, likewise Paul, was created 1st Baron Methuen in 1838. By the marriage in 1844 of the second baron to the daughter and heiress of the Reverend John Sanford (our Paul's great-grandfather) the Corsham collections were greatly augmented. Sanford's contribution included many important Italian primitives and quattrocento canvases (Filippo Lippi's *Annunciation* among them), besides more furniture, notably some rare cabinets of Italian *pietre dure*.

Our Paul, subsequently the fourth baron, was born at Corsham Court in 1886, the eldest of three brothers and two sisters, to Paul Sanford Methuen, the third baron, a distinguished soldier who became a general in the Boer War and a field marshal after it. Paul Sanford was a kindly but conventional man, lacking culture and imagination. It is easy to understand how his first-born's tastes and bents perplexed him. The Field Marshal's wife, Mary Ethel Ayshford, also born a Sanford and his first cousin, was scarcely more at ease with her son than was the father. Young Paul's education was in the usual run of his class, preparatory school (Horris Hill), Eton and New College, Oxford. At Horris Hill his extra-curriculum speciality was drawing, under a Miss Sinclair. This was continued at Eton under Sammy and Sidney Evans, members of a long-established dynasty of Eton drawing-masters. Paul also became interested in natural science, and while still a schoolboy at Eton had a letter published in *The Times* about a frog which he was dissecting. At Oxford he read Natural Science and took a second-class honours degree. It did not follow that this preoccupation meant neglect of his painting. He also worked at the Ruskin School of Drawing, studying under the Slade Professor Sir Charles Holmes, who encouraged him in architectural sketching.

In no way did Paul get involved at the university with the social–intellectual, Soul-ful, slightly raffish circle of *jeunesse dorée* of his generation, young men like the Grenfell brothers, Patrick

Shawe-Stewart, Raymond Asquith and Duff Cooper. The tastes
of the Field Marshal's earnest and reclusive son were not exotic
and his manner was not conducive to the pranks and witticisms
of the *coterie*, as they called themselves. Nor was Paul the least
tempted to follow in his father's military footsteps. Instead he,
not unwillingly, allowed himself to be sent to South Africa,
where through the Field Marshal's influence he was offered in
1910 the job of assistant in the Transvaal Museum at Pretoria.
From Pretoria he extended his scientific researches into
Madagascar and Namaqualand. At this time he reckoned that
his career would be zoology.

Then came August 1914, a brutal date for young men of
Paul's generation whose temperament and inclination were in
no sense compatible with fighting or military camaraderie.
Nevertheless Paul at once enlisted in the Royal Wiltshire
Yeomanry. He was soon transferred to the Scots Guards. As a
lieutenant with that brigade he saw active service in France, and
the trenches. It was an experience to which in later years he
hardly ever referred. His only solace was his courtship of
Eleanor, daughter of W.J. Hennessy, a painter of Irish
extraction with French connections, in fact French-speaking,
and then resident in Normandy. They married in 1915 and it is
no exaggeration to state that they lived happily ever afterwards,
until her death in 1958. Throughout the war she served in the
WRAF, becoming so dedicated to the service that she wanted
to accept the promotion offered her after the Armistice. She
declined only at Paul's urgent request when he was about to be
demobilized, for he longed for her to be with him all the time.

Norah, as she came to be called, was a highly intelligent
woman, precisely the same age as Paul, a lover of the arts,
dignified, with a sweet manner that belied her astuteness. She
spoke with a faint French accent punctuated by short spurts of
laughter. She shared Paul's very pronounced liberal sympathies,
and his ideals. Of the latter the chief was the preservation of
Corsham, for which she too cared passionately. Her knowledge
of furnishing and decoration was extensive. Trained at the Arts
Decoratifs in Paris, before Paul inherited she ran her own

business on a very selective basis. An expert needlewoman, she supervised the restoration of the fabrics at Corsham, with her own fingers repairing the red damask curtains and Chippendale sofa- and chair-covers in the Picture Gallery, protecting them with a fine net dyed to match.

Whenever the couple were apart during the First and Second World Wars, and whenever Paul was away on business, they corresponded at least once and often twice a day. On New Year's Day of 1919, before he was demobilized, Paul wrote from Headquarters, Fourth Army, sending her his good wishes for 1920 and 'plenty of them and in time with patience and care lots of little Norahs and Pauls to follow.' Alas, this was never to be, and Norah's inability to bear children was a terrible sadness to them both. Their letters contain repeated references to this disappointment, and Norah tried every known expedient to become pregnant. In July 1921 she resorted to the celebrated Dr Aarons, who was reputed to have vicariously sired the eldest sons of many of the highest in the land. At his recommendation she underwent surgery, to no avail, a fiasco followed by endless make-believe and delusion. In May 1924 she kept to her bed in ill-founded hopes of pregnancy, while fretting and reproaching herself. Paul tried to convince her that her inability to conceive did not matter a scrap: she alone meant everything to him; no one else, least of all his parents with their clamour for an heir, need concern the two of them. However, the consequence of repeated disappointments was that Norah tended to become petulant and overwrought by domestic problems. Occasionally she wrote Paul scolding letters, which were instantly corrected by adoring little missives. She protested, 'I do enjoy life and in a way of speaking you are life to me, darling, and it's only when you are unhappy or preoccupied by troubles that the LIGHT is obscured for me.' I surmise that although she may at times have been terrified of losing him, he was never unfaithful to her, in spite of the strong attraction pretty women had for him. Not even when in 1930, on his own in London, he took dancing lessons, the tango, foxtrot and waltz

– the vision is somehow an incongruous one – from countless ladies.

Paul certainly had his worries, of which the principal one was lack of money. The Field Marshal was stingy with his eldest son. He gave him Beanacre Manor, on the estate, to live in, but no provision for its upkeep. All the time Lord and Lady Methuen in their unthinking way nagged at Norah, even positively rebuked her for not producing a son. Paul was obliged to forbid his father mentioning the subject to her, on pain of never speaking to him again. Meanwhile the Field Marshal, short of money through his own silliness and the ineptitude of his agents, began indiscriminately selling silver and works of art, even threatening to rid himself of the house and estate, and clear out. To Paul it seemed that his father derived a sort of ghastly pleasure from brinkmanship, for he flirted with and withdrew from sales to art dealers like Herbert Cook and Duveen. Paul, on the other hand, in his devotion to Corsham, was racking his brains how he might save these treasures for the family. Their preservation was, after Norah's welfare, his dearest concern. On his demobilization in March 1919 the first news to greet him was that his father was on the point of selling the Chippendale furniture. Evidently Lord Methuen's situation was becoming precarious, for Paul felt obliged to consent to the sale of a hundred and twenty-five pictures. He did so on the condition that the Field Marshal would never split up the Chippendale suite or sell any of the Adam mirrors. On these terms his father decided that he would make a go of it, and continue to live at the Court.

There was little love lost between the two men, although the Field Marshal's letters to Paul at this date are ostensibly affectionate, if slightly condescending. Whereas Paul's manner towards his father was always respectful, his letters to Norah frequently contained very disparaging remarks. He referred to the old man's 'maudlin sentimentality and cynicism'. His own struggle to maintain a barely comfortable home life at Beanacre and the resentment of his father's parsimony made him occasionally bitter and complaining of both parents.

To make ends meet Paul decided to take over the farm at Beanacre himself. He even went in for an intensive course on agriculture at Oxford University. His letters to Norah became full of talk about bullocks, crops, yields and the usual hazards of a struggling farmer's existence. He was very earnest, but it is questionable whether he had the right temperament for farm management. His father was sure that he hadn't, and made sarcastic comments. However, there is no doubt the experience proved of benefit to Paul when he eventually inherited the Corsham estate. Meanwhile he made copious notes and detailed sketches, not of fetlocks, udders and horns, but of windows, cornices and chimneystacks of old buildings throughout the ages. He suffered periods of disillusion with agriculture when he suspected that he was barking up the wrong tree. In January 1922 he told Norah that he was bored stiff with everything to do with personal property. He was getting on for forty and asked himself what he had so far done beyond possibly postponing Corsham's break-up for a further twenty years or so? – nothing. Two years later he was nearly desperate. Evidently, although he had passed an exam and won a diploma in agriculture, the Beanacre farming enterprise was not proving lucrative. Was his caustic father right after all? In 1925 Paul took a sadly wrong step; feeling that it would be as well to know what the future held, he asked his solicitor to ascertain the contents of his father's will. His father got to hear of the manoeuvre through his own solicitor, and was understandably displeased. Yet he was commendably forgiving of an impertinence which might have made many fathers tear up their existing will and cut out the errant son altogether. On the contrary, he disclosed that the Corsham estate was entailed upon Paul. This truly was heaping coals of fire. But Paul's sentiments were still not very charitable. 'My father's obsession that he is someone of importance', he told Norah, 'is about the funniest thing I've come across for a long time. But it is a tragedy that my mother should ever have taken it seriously.' And again, 'He is only a rabbit disguised as a Field Marshal.'

In fine, Paul had to find a job that would bring him an income on which he and Norah could survive at Beanacre Manor. It was a wretched state of affairs for a middle-aged man in his position who was – we must bear in mind – a born artist, through and through. By virtue of his recent diploma he managed to get a job with the Ministry of Agriculture and Fisheries, at first as livestock officer, then as marketing officer. Initially he was on a year's probation; after that he held the job for another five years. In other words, until 1932 his work was that of a peripatetic inspector, 'mostly visiting farms and pubs in Derbyshire, Nottinghamshire and Leicestershire', and sending in reports to the Ministry. For weekends and brief holidays he dashed home to Beanacre. On his travels he developed a meticulous interest in weather conditions. In neatly ruled columns on foolscap he kept weekly readings of meteorological observations. He also kept up a daily correspondence with Norah, regaling her with comments about his work and the people he met, who for the most part were very ordinary and rather limited men, farmers, commercial travellers and local auctioneers. Paul took every man he came in touch with at his face value, was absolutely not class-conscious, and was merely surprised by his colleagues' embarrassment when they discovered that he was an honourable and would one day be a lord. An easy frankness with strangers overcame his naturally abstracted manner (a manner which was entirely unrelated to any feeling of superiority) and eventually broke down their shyness with him. They soon found that this gentle, cerebral and observant man was perfectly harmless and friendly, albeit slightly eccentric. In the flood of correspondence with Norah Paul sought her advice how to resolve the day-to-day problems that confronted him.

Paul's work had plunged him into contact with a very different world from the one in which he was brought up and educated. Being a man of simple pleasures, and a natural abnegator of luxury and material privileges, with strict standards of what were the moral obligations of his class, Paul became more and more disapproving of what he considered the hedonistic, sybaritic upper crust. 'All my family', he wrote to Norah in 1929 from Castle Howard, his sister Kitty's home, 'are anathema to me. They roll in luxury and don't do a hand's turn.' This indictment of the Howard family was a bit harsh. After all, his brother-in-law Geoffrey had been an active MP, a junior minister of state in several ministries, and Lord-Lieutenant of the North Riding. Neither he nor Kitty, the hard-worked chateleine of an enormous palace, were exactly idle lay-abouts.

In the last years of his long life and owing to failing health, the Field Marshal felt obliged to shift the management of Corsham estate to the shoulders of his son and heir. When Paul inherited the title in 1932, therefore, he was already virtual master of the property. He and Norah were in their late forties. Although their responsibilities had increased rather than lessened, they were sweeter. Although the estate was embarrassed, Paul at last had a little free money at his disposal. His training in scientific farming, though never a vocation, made management of the estate easier than would have been the case had he previously led a life entirely preoccupied with the arts. He foresaw, eventually, a blessed surrender to his first call, painting. Over and over again Norah's letters testify to her protection of his work from interruption by outside distractions, the endless demands of a country house, in other words maintenance, lack of adequate labour and heavy taxation.

But the first thing that simply had to be settled was Corsham's future. What ought he to do, and what could he do, in the best interests of Corsham, which he loved? When I first met him in 1936, on joining the National Trust staff, this question was uppermost in his mind. Should he hand the whole place and the collections, worth millions of pounds, over to the Trust, with an endowment which he hadn't got? The endowment apart, there was the entail of the estate on his brothers and their progeny to consider, and the tiresome necessity of having to break it by private Act of Parliament. Of our conversation at luncheon one October day in London during the war I recorded, 'He was very charming. We talked about Corsham's future. We have done this for many years now.' I eventually became one of his trustees, and we were doing it right up to his death.

The pros and cons were of course dubious and daunting, caused not so much by the size of the estate, house, gardens and grounds, as by the importance of the collections. These required perennial care and expert attention for which the under-staffed National Trust was not adequately equipped in its early amateurish days. And, although their care of the collections was beyond praise, Paul and Norah were not specialists or experts in the museum sense. To my mind they represented the ideal country house owners, such as the National Trust envisaged its own future custodians emulating as the donors and their descendants died off. The Methuens got experts from the national collections to reassess the provenance and authenticity of the Corsham pictures and furnishings. The paintings were re-catalogued by Tancred Borenius, the furniture by H. Clifford Smith, the silver and bronzes by Christie's and the decorative items by Edward Croft-Murray and Margaret Jourdain. Fabrics were repaired by Norah and her band of helpers. The contents of the state rooms were rearranged. After the Second World War Paul had the splendid picture gallery carpet woven by the Royal Tapestry and Carpet Factory in Madrid to his design, contrived to echo that of Capability Brown's serpentine ceiling. In their day Corsham was all improvement and movement.

Before and after the Second World War the Methuens entertained art lovers and artists on a generous yet never lavish scale. Their food was basically simple and good – roast mutton and steamed puddings in traditional old English style – although surprised guests might on occasion find themselves wrestling with Polish eggs and rissoles. Both Methuens were blissfully indifferent to *haute cuisine*, if appreciative of its niceties when laid before them by others. Life downstairs at Corsham always seemed to be in a state of happy flux, abounding in friendly, untrained servitors from the immediate neighbourhood. And cats were everywhere, stalking among the ducks and peacocks when not nestling on Chippendale sofas or even in empty Chelsea porcelain bowls and Imari dishes.

Over big issues, Paul was incapable of taking any hasty, irrevocable steps. He prevaricated, procrastinated, and did nothing, trusting that something would turn up. With him, it usually did. Corsham never came to the National Trust, and this I think was an unspoken grief to him. He happened to die just at the time when means other than the National Trust were being devised by which the future of country houses might be guaranteed for several generations, if not for ever, such as semi-private family trusts, which protected endowment funds from penal taxation.

However, I have said that good things were apt to turn up for Paul. One of these was his scoop with the Bath Academy of Art. The Avon County Council agreed (with some reluctance) to rent from his trustees on a 99-year lease all that part of the house which had been rebuilt either outside or within for his great-grandfather by the Victorian architect Thomas Bellamy. Paul retained the Georgian state apartments under his administration, and the Nash quarters for his and Norah's dwelling. From his angle it was the perfect arrangement practically, financially and aesthetically. Furthermore, it soothed his conscience that his beloved Corsham should become a background and seat of learning for the aspiring young; students were to have full access to the grounds, which remained under his control. I verily believe it was his charm which brought about an arrangement to suit everybody. I well remember dining in October 1946 with him and Norah at number 6 Primrose Hill Studios in Fitzroy Road, Regent's Park to discuss the clauses to be inserted in the long lease to the Bath Academy. There was a distinct gleam of triumph in Paul's eyes that evening.

After his death, for various reasons besides a reduction in public funds for maintaining a college of art in the country, the Bath Academy of Art packed up. While it was at Corsham, Paul delighted in the young people who were privileged to learn art history and practise their own talents in this place of tradition and beauty. In fact, few took advantage of the free admission to Capability's superb rooms and the classic collections, for fear lest their inspiration be impaired. I once asked Paul how many students among the hundreds who must have passed through Corsham he considered to have shown signs of becoming artists of distinction. Ruefully he held up the fingers (but not the thumb) of one hand. 'No more,' he said.

His concern for Corsham led him after he inherited to play a prominent role in the preservation of country houses generally, and not merely those in the United Kingdom. Besides sitting on the Trust's Historic Buildings Committee (where I recall him at meetings, a solitary figure, either amused and chortling to himself, or disapproving and frowning, speaking seldom and then rather inarticulately; and sometimes, because of incipient deafness, getting hold of the stick by a wrong end, or muttering more to himself than the assembled company) he was also a power for good off-stage. He it was who persuaded the Trust to collaborate with the French and Belgian *Les Demeures Historiques,* and before the Second World War pressed for their members to visit some of our country houses, and our country house owners to visit theirs. In fact the Methuens were in the same parties as Kathleen Kennet abroad and in England. During these gatherings the presence of Norah, forthcoming and bilingual in French and English, was a great help towards fostering friendly relations and understanding. She acted as unofficial hostess when the French-speakers came over here. Paul's presence was that of a benign and distinguished but remote sage, his appearance not untypical of the absent-minded stage professor. His trousers were baggy, his coat shabby and lacking a button or two. A large loosely knotted yellow tie might be suspended below a half-open shirt collar, for his neck had developed a slightly goitre-like swelling, which it was uncomfortable for him to constrict.

Among the letters from Paul to Norah after their marriage in 1915 there is, curiously, no reference to his own painting until 1929. In April of that year he told her he had just seen what he described as 'a masterly picture of a drunken huntsman' by Walter Sickert. Richard Shone assures me that the portrait is of Sir Nigel Playfair in the role of Tony Lumpkin in *She Stoops to Conquer*, dressed in full and mud-splashed hunting-gear. It now hangs in the Garrick Club, to which the actor bequeathed it. When first exhibited it caused a stir. For Paul Methuen it was an inspiration.

It happened that during Paul's bachelor years in Pretoria he had sketched and painted to his heart's content. But his return to England, coinciding as it did with the threats to Corsham, the differences with his father and the outbreak of the 1914 war, caused him to abandon painting temporarily. In 1927, while he was working for the Ministry of Agriculture but itching to devote his full rather than his spare time to painting, Paul met Dorothy Warren, an impresario famous for her gallery where she exhibited avant-garde artists, including D.H. Lawrence. She said to him, 'Why don't you get in touch with Sickert? He is taking pupils again.' So Paul found himself attending Sickert's studio in Highbury Fields, early in the mornings and late in the evenings, even during weekends. Sickert not only inspired but entertained him. Paul wrote, 'He was well read in French and English and, I fancy, German. He had a wide and shrewd knowledge of the Old Masters. He was essentially a traditionalist as a painter and was impatient with methods and schools of painting that ignored the rules of sound technique.' It was several months before Sickert would allow his pupils to use more than one colour – hence the unduly monochrome underpainting of some of Paul's canvases at this time. At all events, his immature style was strongly affected by his new master's economy with colour. In due course Sickert conveyed to Paul a dash of the sparkle and virtuosity which he had derived directly from his masters and friends, Whistler and Degas, who had made Sickert study the interaction of waves and skies in the pictures of Veronese and Canaletto: Sickert's schooling had been as Gallic as it was British, and as Venetian as it was Gallic. Thus Paul Methuen imbibed through Sickert a free technique from the French Impressionists, in addition to a clarity in the rendering of light and shadow from the great Venetian masters. What he eschewed was Sickert's Hogarthian down-to-earthiness, a quality which, however English it may be, was not one sympathetic to Paul's fastidious nature.

Paul was essentially a more delicate and less realistic artist, lacking Sickert's sensuality, gusto and panache. In a eulogy of Sickert he conceded that his master 'faithfully recorded in paint contemporary life as he saw it in its many facets and which he depicted free from social and sentimental frills' – which was far from Paul's way. Yet, he went on, 'in his lovely harmony of colours and choice of tones Mr Sickert has made as great a contribution to our knowledge of painting as any other painter of our time.'

Paul's own work is perhaps best exemplified by his highly observant and evocative sketches in pastel, ink and water-colour of domestic buildings, gardens, plants and blooms, rather than by his landscapes and figures. His botanical paintings are not the least bit akin to the naturalistic colour-plate illustrations of exquisite flower books, by a Redouté or a Thornton. They are very much on-the-spot snatches, yet based on a trained understanding of botany. Botany was indeed another of Paul's intensive studies. He became a skilful grower and highly respected propagator of orchids in the hothouses at Corsham. He produced oil paintings and coloured chalk drawings of rare epiphytic orchids which he brought back from expeditions to Rhodesia (in 1961) and other parts of Africa. Like those by Edward Lear they were, to quote Edward Croft-Murray, 'observed both scientifically and aesthetically, with planned manuscript notes again playing their part in relation to the pictorial composition.' His paintings of animal life, notably the cats, peacocks, swans and guinea fowl which strutted and preened upon the lawns of Corsham, are further evidence of his serious studies of natural history.

In 1928 Paul's pictures were exhibited with those of three other painters at the Warren Gallery. Subsequently he held one-man shows at the Leicester Gallery, Colnaghi's and Agnew's, and at the Royal West of England Academy in Bristol.

After the outbreak of the Second World War Paul rejoined the Scots Guards, in 1940. Being fifty-three he was of no use for active service, but was at once commissioned to the War Office with the rank of Captain, rising to Major, and drafted Monuments and Fine Arts officer in the London district 'A' Branch. No more suitable and sensible decision could have been taken. He soon became one of a small group of conservation experts under Sir Leonard Woolley, the well-known archaeologist and digger of Carchemish with T.E. Lawrence, and of Ur. The appointment obliged Paul to live in London throughout the bombing, with only occasional dashes down to Wiltshire for the night. He was allowed leave of absence to attend meetings at the Tate and the National Gallery, of both of which he was a trustee.

In 1944 Woolley selected Paul, on account of his architectural knowledge, and his ability to draw and to write vivid and lively prose, and his French connections and knowledge of the language, to be one of two Monuments, Fine Arts and Archives officers attached to the 21st Army Group. The business of those officers was to protect works of art in the wake of the Allies' recent invasion of and drive through northern France. For a man of his age it was a glorious experience, and gloriously he carried out his duties. These included reporting on the condition of the historic buildings damaged or destroyed during the fighting, and tracking down as far as possible those Germans who had looted works of art and archives, and the destination of the spoils. While compiling his reports for Sir Leonard, Paul also kept in his private journal a day-to-day record of the invasion operations. In 1952 the amalgamated reports and journal were published as *Normandy*

Diary, 1944, with an introduction by Woolley, who called it the first book in which a Monuments Officer described his experiences in the field.

It was a pity that this large and rather expensive volume did not have a wider circulation. Although in one sense it covers a specialized subject – war damage to buildings, chiefly medieval churches, and treasures in a particular region of France – *Normandy Diary* gives a fascinating illustration of what was going on all over Europe at the time. Moreover, it is accompanied by numerous drawings made during the author's tours of inspection, chiefly in Calvados, very much off-the-cuff, so to speak, in coloured chalks and rapid outlines, and all very vivid and meaningful. Paul's comments too are brisk and pertinent. They testify to the quickness of his observant eye and brain. To take one example: at St-Aubin-d'Écrossville he wrote,

I have a good view of the château [from his bedroom window]...
and can study at my leisure the care with which the brick-work has
been thought-out, patterned black bricks being here and there
interspersed with the red ones to form regular diamond
designs. This touch, characteristic of much of the French work
of this period, gives the surface of the walls great elegance and
finish.

Only a close student of architecture would have noted such niceties.

Paul interviewed government architects of the *départements* with which he was concerned; discussed with owners of *châteaux* what instant repairs had best be carried out and how, and was invited to dine with them; applied to local authorities for tarred felt protection to roofs; placed damaged carved figures in cupboards for safety; interviewed abbots and nuns, whom he often found to be the most impartial people to check his reports; by means of his official status got local mayors to reinstate old ladies into their commandeered houses. On 16th October we read that he 'Interviewed Monsieur Homo, chemist, about a permit for him to photograph' an important

monument on the verge of collapse. In November a typical
entry was, 'picked up M. Prieur [architect-in-chief for the Eure
département] whose house was totally destroyed and his two
daughters were killed in one of our raids.' The French, stunned
by prolonged suffering and often dazed by the sequel to enemy
occupation, namely what was tantamount to an invasion by
their so-called allies, were extraordinarily forbearing with the
English *milord* sent to order them about. But Paul did not boss.
Gently he suggested in his fluent French what they could most
expeditiously do. He disclosed to Norah, rather touchingly,
that, often somewhat shy in his own language, he did not feel
so when talking in their tongue to unsophisticated Norman
countrymen. He enjoyed the privilege of a free truck and
almost limitless petrol allowance, to visit and assess damaged
buildings unreachable by French officials. Paul readily
understood the delicacy of his relations with the Normandy
natives, and marvelled at their kindness and open-handed
generosity to him with help and hospitality. He genuinely loved
France and the French, and begged the local authorities to
co-operate in financing their national monuments, which he
claimed formed the firmest bond between his country and
theirs. In fact he gave great praise for what he received from
these highly civilized people. He grieved deeply over the
lamentable destruction he everywhere witnessed. His
description of the ravage of Rouen is heart-breaking. His
appointment as *Chevalier du Légion d'Honneur* was a source of
great pride to him.

Normandy Diary abounds in delightful asides. It notes the
families who have owned the *châteaux* he visits; the food and
wine provided by his hosts, whether rich or poor; and
comical encounters, like that with the caretaker of an old
building he was sketching. This worthy individual pontificated
about the hands of the Old Master painters, as though he had
made a life's study of them. To judge the merits of a modern
picture, he declared, he had merely to look at the artist's hands
– quickly glancing at Paul's and, with a 'Phut!', turning on his
heels.

Normandy Diary also reveals the author-artist's sure sense of tone in colour. On a visit to the Château de Tremblay he commented that the

> paintwork in these fourteen rooms is for the most part in three shades of colour, well balanced and harmonised and of a soft pastel quality. One of the rooms we saw is done in a blue-green and hung with eighteenth-century chintzes. Greys predominate, usually blue, green or salmon greys. The panels themselves are invariably of a light grey, the mouldings white, cream or stone colour, and the surrounds a grey similar to that of the panels, but a shade darker. The most successful room had a subtle combination of pink and blue-greys. It was Madame's bedroom.

A subtle commingling of various grey shades is typical of sophisticated French taste. No ordinary civil servant (certainly no English one), reporting on his official investigations, would have observed these grey shades, or have written in the terms Paul used. Sir Leonard Woolley had clearly picked the right man for the job in hand. 'It rains all day here,' Paul complained ruefully. 'No wonder Frenchmen call Normandy *"le pot de chambre de la France".'*

Having recorded the devastation of Normandy, Paul was shunted in February 1945 to Belgium and Holland. And on 18th June he received his demobilization papers.

Before this actually happened I went down to Corsham for a night in May while he was home on brief leave. I was met at Chippenham station by Paul wearing battle-dress and a beret. He drove me in a ramshackle old car to Corsham. At once it was clear that his mind was still concentrating on faraway Calvados; from the station he started off on the right-hand side of the road in a very dashing manner. He looked remarkably young for a man in his sixtieth year, with a clear and healthy colouring that was no doubt due to his habitual temperance and vegetarianism. Once, when asked whether his abstention from meat was not a fad (for there was a faintly raffia-hat-and-sandal side to Paul), he replied testily, 'If you had seen the abattoirs that I have you would be a vegetarian too.' And when pressed to say whether he noticed any difference between carnivorous and vegetarian people he replied, 'Well, frankly, you all smell to me.' Altogether he was a very handsome man, tall and upright, with a distinct presence. My mother told me that in his early twenties, with his straight Grecian nose, sad eyes and fair hair, he was the most beautiful young man she had ever set eyes on.

In 1945 Paul and Norah withdrew into the west wing of Corsham Court, the greater part of which was occupied as a military hospital. They lived and ate in Nash's green Gothick library, its windows draped in the sumptuously embroidered trappings from Sir Paul Methuen's state carriage. I strolled around the requisitioned apartments, watching orderlies banging the legs of furniture with the backs of their brooms. The Chippendale chairs and sofas had, mercifully, been put away. The object of this fleeting visit was to discuss some aspect of Corsham's proposed transfer to the National Trust, but Paul, though very kind, was so floating in clouds of Low Countries problems that he could not give me his undivided attention. I found it difficult to pull him down to earth, and when I succeeded he was like a captive balloon, straining to be released.

This habit of distancing himself from a companion seemed to accentuate with age. Increasing deafness may have been one contributary cause: the tedium of the companion another. You might put a question to him and receive no immediate reply, indeed no indication that he even wished to consider it. Had you posed a subject too trivial, too boring for him to bother about? Then lo and behold! twenty minutes later, when conversation had reached a subject totally unrelated to the topic apparently spurned, a smile might dawn in his eyes – seldom upon his lips – and he would give the matter his attention, just as though there had been no interval. This made quick, transient communication sometimes awkward. He was totally uninterested in gossip, or in the behaviour of friends. He was only interested in their ideas, and of these he could be critical, even censorious. His standards of what was morally right and what wrong were clear-cut. Oliver Esher told me once that Paul had refused to allow a neighbour, one of the Hobhouses of Hadspen, to publish some love letters between Byron's friend John Cam Hobhouse and a Lady Methuen, written early in the nineteenth century. It was, Lord Esher protested, an example of an intelligent man's silliness.

Paul was very interested in psychical research, although he claimed not to countenance spiritualism. He and Norah believed implicitly in the need of those 'over the other side' to get in touch with sympathisers here on earth. However, although they may have been ready to elaborate upon their own communings to like-minded dabblers, they must have sensed that I was not one of the number. I daresay and indeed like to suppose that he kept in touch with Norah after she (as her gravestone expressed it) 'passed over' in 1958. Undoubtedly her death was only rendered supportable by his faith in an after-world.

He had another sixteen years to endure without her. To relieve some of the nagging sadness, he commissioned F.T. Kormis to carve, on a tomb chest in Corsham church, his wife's recumbent effigy in gleaming white alabaster. A small angel nestles at her feet, writing. It is an ambitious tribute to his adoration of her – 'Most Beautiful and most Wise.'

Paul certainly had a refreshing disregard for what others might think of his behaviour. Staying just after the war at nearby Westwood Manor with Ted Lister, I was once taken to a large luncheon party at Corsham on an extremely hot June Sunday. As we rose from the table Paul, who had been quite animated during the meal, proposed: 'Let's go into the library and sleep.' While we guests lingered and politely chatted, Paul darted ahead. When we reached the library he was already curled up on a sofa amid a pile of cushions, fast asleep and soundly snoring. He was still there when we left. Norah in her well-bred way made absolutely no reference to the incident. She neither woke and reproached him, nor apologised to us. A neighbour told me of another occasion when having been invited to luncheon, he arrived punctually at the front door, to be met by Paul in shirtsleeves pushing a huge wheel-barrow of manure and greeted with, 'You are too early. The gardens aren't open till two.' The truth was that both Paul and Norah were worn out by coping almost servantless with the enormous house and garden. At that time the military hospital was about to quit, and the Methuens were in process of letting to the Art College, which involved much shifting and rearrangement of contents. One day, visiting an historic house in Somerset, I was directed by my host into the garden, where I was surprised and delighted to come upon Paul seated on a stool at his easel. On returning to the house and telling my host he exclaimed, 'What, Lord Methuen here? I haven't asked him.'

Paul acted on impulse and would, if the notion came into his head, have given the shirt off his back had he thought the recipient in need or deserving of it. Once as he arrived to lunch with us he slipped into my hand a Georgian silver dog collar, clearly intended for a whippet – we owned a couple – and engraved with the original owner's initials (P[aul] M[ildmay] Methuen) and London address. He warded off my attempts to thank him for this unsolicited gift, which I assured him would be returned to Corsham on my death.

When engaged upon a task, no matter what it was, Paul became totally absorbed and could not easily be disengaged from it. My wife and I accompanied him and Diana Kendall, then his secretary and indispensable companion, on a tour to Russia in 1966. The Russian guides were extremely strict about group obedience and adherence to the timetable, but Paul was invariably late for the departing bus and had to be forcibly brought to heel from stool and sketchbook by Diana. He was indifferent to our wardress's impotent rage.

Although Paul Methuen never dissociated himself entirely from public duties in his native environment – he was President of the Royal West of England Academy at Bristol, for which he worked untiringly for over thirty years, besides holding honorary degrees of Bath and Bristol Universities – he spent the greater part of his later life painting. He thought he might be in the running for the Wardenship of Wadham

College. 'It would not allow me to paint,' he concluded emphatically. Whether it was actually offered him, I do not know. Yet Paul was not so unambitious that he would not have welcomed the Presidency of the Royal Academy, of which he became an Academician in 1954. That he never got it he attributed to the machinations of Sir Gerald Kelly the Past President, jealous of his talents, prestige and peerage.

Sickert's death in 1942 had set the seal upon Paul's conviction that after middle age life was too short to waste on hours of dross. On a cold February day he had attended Sickert's memorial service at St Martin-in-the-Fields (at the unfashionable hour, even in wartime, of two o'clock). 'Not many people,' he noted sadly, 'but saw Lutyens, Sir Ian Hamilton (his wife admired Sickert's work), Gerald Kelly and others. Priest said he was an outstanding man,' which was magnanimous. There is little doubt that whereas Corsham – the house, treasures, garden, grounds and park – was the begetter and cradle of Paul's art, the Franco-British Walter Sickert was the galvanic formulator of his style of painting. Gallic though Paul Methuen's cultivated tastes became, his native qualifications and the media of his work were best suited to the English scene. There is an integrity and total lack of rodomontade in all his painting. In that of the 1930s Sir John Pope-Hennessy saw signs of an artist in oil even greater than Sickert emerging, a painter of a more specialized and individual 'turn of phrase' like, we may surmise, Sickert's exact contemporary, the loner post-Impressionist Pierre Bonnard. To Pope-Hennessy's wonderment, as I indicated earlier, he overcame the liability (if it may be so termed) of his inheritance, but perhaps not quite to the extent of achieving greatness. As it was, by consistently bearing in mind his master's injunction that 'unless you can draw well you will never make a great painter', he has won for himself a highly respected name in twentieth-century painting. Particularly in his water-colours, his pen and rich brown ink, and his pastel sketches, Paul's spontaneity broke loose. These sketches are remarkable for their dark outlines and dappled surfaces, where characteristic flecks of light catch the high ground of landscapes and the tops of buildings, often under threatening skies.

Let me conclude with a passage from John Pope-Hennessy's introduction to the catalogue of Paul's memorial exhibition, held in the Fieldborn Galleries in June 1975.

> To the very end he retained his buoyancy and youthfulness and for that reason the paintings and drawings he produced will continue to be sought after by collectors of British art. 'This is a Methuen,' they will say, and we shall look at it eagerly, straining to catch the sound of Paul Methuen's voice and the savour of his very individual artistic personality.

Optimum Fecit (he did his best) is inscribed on his gravestone, beside Norah's, in Beanacre churchyard.

Vita Sackville-West

1892–1962

AS AN UNDERGRADUATE at Oxford in the late 1920s I was particularly green, very provincial, almost retarded mentally: ignorant. But full of romantic notions. And with an inborn love of poetry, which, so long as it was what I will describe as old-fashioned, I devoured. Poetry, that is to say, measured, scanning, rhythmical, which in a bookshop today would be shelved out of reach under the heading 'Classical': in other words poetry traditional, down to the sort that qualified for Sir Edward Marsh's *Georgian Poetry 1912–21* and was, come the late Twenties, despised as derivative by the literary avant-garde. The avant-garde sort was beyond me and left me cold. I struggled with *The Waste Land* because it was compulsory reading. Now I find harmony and emotion in it in addition to intellectual meat, just as now I can listen with a degree of pleasure to Bartók's music, which I used to dismiss as farmyard cacophony. My intellectual superiors, on the other hand, recognized *The Waste Land* as marking the indisputable parting of ways between the archaic, worn-out stuff which had met a pallid death with Rupert Brooke in 1915 and the T.S. Eliot kind. Needless to say, I worshipped Rupert Brooke. I could just about stomach Edith Sitwell, while deeming her fairly buffoonish. However, one afternoon in Blackwell's poetry section I alighted upon a very small, very slim grey-blue volume with, on the cover, 'Hogarth Living Poets, No. 11: *King's*

Daughter by V. Sackville-West, author of *The Land.*' This I
bought. In it I scrawled my too-large and untidy name, with
'Oxford' and the date 1929.

Before deciding to risk three shillings and sixpence I had
however read and approved the first canticle, beginning

> If I might meet her in the lane
> Riding a raven horse
> That trailed his golden halter loose
> And snuffed the golden gorse;

In all there were eight stanzas in the subjunctive tense, of a like
passionate yearning, before the canticle terminated in a ninth:

> And should I see her glide away
> Into the fir tree's night,
> Then should I know that I had read
> Her changeling soul aright.

Here was something that I could really comprehend – or
supposed I could comprehend, because on being re-read today
all the quatrains seem to mean little or nothing. In truth –
although I did not know it then – *King's Daughter* is the least
good of all Vita's published verse, although poem VIII contains
four lines which still echo in the memory:

> Keep thy straight strings, musician!
> And, shepherd, watch thy stars.
> She's more to me than Jupiter,
> Or Mercury and Mars.

Nevertheless I was thrilled by *King's Daughter*. To a recently
matriculated undergraduate of limited understanding it seemed
verse out of the usual, heterodox, passionate, inexplicable,
wonderful. The occasional highfalutin words like agrimony,
hewel and cantrip did not detract from the esoteric message. It
was about love. And I was all for love. My upbringing had been
so remote from literary circles that I knew nothing about
V. Sackville-West. I am not sure that I even cottoned to the

fact that V. Sackville-West was a woman. I would have been greatly surprised to learn what is now universal knowledge, namely that *King's Daughter* was Sapphic verse, addressed by one woman to another, namely Virginia Woolf who, with her husband, was the publisher. I cannot remember who eventually enlightened me. The disclosure, although it surprised, did not upset me in the least. On the contrary, it excited me. I then read *Orlando*, the book that was written for and about V. Sackville-West, who was in fact the thinly latent hero-heroine, by the recipient of the *King's Daughter* canticles. I was thrilled again. *Orlando* was for me what Nigel Nicolson was to describe it years later, 'the longest and most charming love letter in literature'.

On a visit to an uncle and aunt in Argyllshire that autumn and happening to be in the Glasgow Art Gallery, I came by chance upon a coloured postcard (about the only one on sale) of William Strang's *Portrait of a Lady in a Red Hat*. I was very much taken with it. When I discovered that the portrait was not exhibited but was kept under lock and key in a cellar, I wondered why. I still don't know the reason, nor if it remains below ground or is on show today.

It was not until I got home and made enquiries – for in those days the Glasgow Art Gallery was practically empty of visitors and certainly of officials to vouchsafe information – that I discovered the unknown lady in the red hat to be V. Sackville-West, the author of *King's Daughter*. And what was the painting doing, unappreciated, in faraway Glasgow? The answer is that VSW's maddening mother, Victoria, Lady Sackville, had commissioned Sir William Strang to paint a portrait of her daughter. One afternoon in the artist's studio, while his back was turned, Lady Sackville seized a paint brush and took the liberty of tampering with the mouth. Strang was so incensed that he refused to part with the picture, and it remained his property until his death. This was a great shame, because if ever Knole Park, the Sackville seat, lacked a good likeness of one of its most interesting family members, Vita in Strang's portrait is it.

In the portrait Vita sits slender and upright in a bottle green striped jacket with open collar, her right hand on hip, her left holding a morocco-bound book across a mustard-coloured skirt. The brim of an enormous bright red felt hat shades her dark eyes and eyebrows, long fine nose, sensual lips and cleft chin: the likeness of a young woman, strikingly handsome and noble. Her husband Harold Nicolson described it rather absurdly as 'so absolutely my little Mar. She's all there – her little straight body, her boyhood of Raleigh manner and above all those sweet gentle eyes.' There was nothing *sweet* about Vita, and the whole pose is swashbuckling, Orlando-like, determined, almost challenging. Yet Harold was right about her gentle, doe-like eyes, which in the picture are so shaded by the formidable red hat as to be barely visible. The almost aggressive pose of the figure, never apparent in Vita's middle age when I first met her, may explain the arrogant image which some acquaintances who did not know her well mistakenly conceived. Although proud she was an extremely shy woman.

If I had been a little mystified, and fascinated, by *King's Daughter* I was bowled over by *The Land*, which Vita had published three years previously (1926). Even I had the intelligence to realize that *King's Daughter* was nothing to it, nothing at all. No wonder that when she told Harold the Woolfs had accepted the latter for publication he was shocked, not as she at first feared because of the lesbian overtones, which indeed the discerning were shocked by, but by the indifference of the poetry. Vita had pretended to Harold that the poems were artificial, which they were not. Had they been so, they might have been better. As it was, they were precipitate love poems in a derivative nursery-rhyme bounce. Harold's misgivings were in vain because the volume was already in print. Yet *King's Daughter* did not imply a declension of Vita's literary powers, although it was followed in quick succession by *The Edwardians* and *All Passion Spent*, two novels which were deservedly popular best sellers without being of outstanding merit.

The Land, begun in Vita's thirtieth year, was of a very different calibre. It is a bucolic on husbandry in the Weald of

Kent, inspired one may suppose by Virgil's *Georgics*, which incidentally Vita had not read. It is interwoven with rhyming lyrics of which several are of great beauty, notably the one beginning 'She walks among the loveliness she made', addressed to Dorothy Wellesley, a poet who was very close to Vita when they were young women together. Moreover *The Land* was composed at a critical stage of that social and agricultural revolution wherein nearly all traditional methods and instruments of farming were to be discarded to make way for the prairie field system and mechanical substitutes. Here was a woman who had been born and bred in the country when the land was still cultivated by methods that had endured since the Norman Conquest, if not Saxon and even Roman times. In blank pentameters, which in 1926 were still as acceptable as in Milton's day, VSW was recording, as she was well aware, the end of the millennia of tillage of the soil. Even the farmers and farm labourers to whom she referred were recognizably of the same stock as Thomas Hardy's, as 'Turnip' Townshend's, as Piers Plowman's yeomen and peasants. Things agricultural, although on the very balance of change, had not quite tilted over the brink. Vita knew the change was about to come, the revolution she so much deplored, the abandonment of horse, plough-share and the sower's hand in favour of the petrol-driven digger, the tractor and the machine tool. 'I sing once more', she declared, 'the mild continuous epic of the soil, / Haysel and harvest, tilth and husbandry... / I tell the things I know, the things I knew / Before I knew them, im-memorially.' She has been mocked for her use of archaic terms relating to the soil, words like shippon, sneath, stelch, pannage, gavelkind, and corredy, boggart, yoes and yelms. But these terms were not archaic in her youth. They were current among country people. And she, patrician though she was, knew them as well as did the craftsmen and workers who bandied them naturally. *The Land* is a great poem. It sold a hundred thousand copies. It will be read by future generations, not merely for the chronicle of a subversive upheaval from rural to suburban living but as an enduring work of descriptive literature. Geoffrey Scott, author of *The Portrait of Zélide* and *The Architecture of Humanism,* and one of Vita's lovers at the time, referred to it as 'our poem'. He assured her that her poetry was 'your very rare gift', and that her reputation would stand by *The Land,* intimating that with it she might possibly have shot her bolt. But she hadn't.

It is very much open to question whether, as some of her contemporaries maintained – notably the exclusive Bloomsbury group on the perimeter of which she was a conspicuous adornment – and as her biographer Victoria Glendinning has endorsed, Vita was no great writer – a view which I shall dispute. A remark of Clive Bell in 1924 summarises what Bloomsbury thought of her: 'dear old, obtuse, aristocratic, passionate, grenadier-like Vita'. Unfortunately Clive's mockery of her, although not unkindly meant, has persisted to this day in academic circles. Admittedly her literary style was traditional; her views on art were conventional and her taste in English architecture stopped short at the Jacobean. She frankly disliked the classical style. Palladian and baroque buildings were anathema to her. In Venice she pronounced the Salute church to be displeasing, but the Doge's Palace to be of a nice colour. Critical and supercilious Bloomsbury considered that her lack of a classical education, and also the exclusiveness of her late-Victorian upbringing by ill-qualified governesses, were evident not only in her judgements but in her poetry and prose. Admittedly like all girls of her class she had not been sent to school or college. Yet because her half-Spanish mother's first language was French, she grew up bilingual and bi-cultured. As a child she got to know every square inch of her old home from the garrets, bedrooms, passages, state rooms and servants' quarters to the cellars and outbuildings. Knole was as much in her blood as were the genes of her Sackville and Andalucian ancestors. She worshipped Knole, clung to it, and in childhood believed it to be hers and no one else's. Knole may have been faithful to her. Like her dogs in later life, it never, she averred, let her down. Not until she was grown up did she come to grasp that under the territorial system which she so much respected, Knole would never be in her possession. It was a tremendous shock to be told that Knole's heir in her generation was her puny little first cousin, Eddy Sackville-West, the male son of her father's younger brother. She was obliged to discard the conviction that in every respect but sex she was the equal of any man whomsoever. Even so, through some peculiar permutation of nature, might she not become a male if she put her mind to it? Since the protective but constrictive walls of Knole had determined her feudal perspective, is it too far-fetched to surmise that they had also determined in adolescence her sexual instincts and urges?

Twice only after her father's death in 1928, when she was already married with a house and children of her own, did Vita return to Knole, although her uncle Charlie, who succeeded as 4th Lord Sackville, gave her a key to the garden. This key was to be her most cherished possession. Once she made use of it by night. When she came to write *Knole and the Sackvilles* she poured her very heart and soul into the book. When Knole was transferred to the National Trust and I asked if she would write its first guidebook she did so in considerable detail, room by room. But she would not go there to check that the contents were in their same old places.

Like most creative people, painters, composers and writers, Vita could never escape from her past. And what an astonishing past hers was! Sole child of an English peer of medieval lineage and reared in one of England's largest emparked seats, outside more like a walled village than a country house and inside a labyrinth of long galleries and tiny closets. If her father was easy-going and indulgent, her mother was a jealous termagant. Lady Sackville's treatment veered from spoiling to reviling her daughter. She was an extremely tiresome woman in that her strong prejudices were dictated by society and fashion, but in fact she did not live up to the codes she was a slave to, thus causing scandal in her own circle. Before she was launched on the world Vita not only witnessed but was obliged by her mother to play a role in two astonishing public dramas. In both Lady Sackville defended her own interests to some purpose. The first, in 1909, known as the Sackville Legitimacy Case, was brought by her brother Henry, who claimed the Sackville title and inheritance. Lady Sackville set out to prove (what was the case) that both Henry and she were the illegitimate children of her father's elder brother (the previous Lord) by a Spanish dancer, Pepita from Malaga. She succeeded, and her own and her brother's illegitimacy were confirmed. Her husband, who was her first cousin, retained the title and property and she her position as chatelaine of Knole and its collections. The second law case, which like the first attracted enormous public interest, was brought in 1913 by the family of Lady Sackville's late lover, Sir John Murray Scott, who had left the better part of his fortune and works of art to her in his will. The Scott family accused her of having pressurized Sir John in his dotage. Again Lady Sackville was successful.

These sensational cases had their effect upon an extremely impressionable and lonely child, who withdrew into a world of her own imaginings. Feverishly Vita composed plays and tales of romance and derring-do, in all of which she played the conspicuous role of dashing and picaresque Lothario. In childhood Vita's only contacts were the little girl children of her parents' friends, who under her strong personality were made accessories in her magical scenarios. Over them she exercised an extraordinary authority, so that they became her willing and adoring slaves.

Taking into account that she was driven by intense literary ambition and a dynamic will to work, we may well ask, was Vita's accident of birth a disadvantage? In other words, was the surface Bohemian woman of letters merely the outer skin of a counterfeit core composed of aristocratic privilege and prejudice? Bloomsbury certainly intimated as much, deeming her hopelessly upper-class. Even her two sons were embarrassed by her ties to traditional values. The elder, Ben, when he had grown up, deplored her entrenched conservatism. When he was twenty-seven and she forty-nine he wrote to his brother Nigel that 'she will never again learn any new fact. It is terrifying to witness this premature senility. Her moral code is based on utterly arbitrary premises, taking no account of the one branch of knowledge in understanding – the science of psychology.' She believed, he wrote in shocked tones, that theft, disloyalty and untruth were crimes, and that crimes were evil and not the consequence of social deprivation; he thought that she was forty years out of date.

It is possible that, but for her ingrained 'moral code', Vita's passionate nature might have precipitated her, like several women of her background and generation, into a militant Fabianism intent upon abolition of the hereditary principle, even into a suffragist smashing of windows in Belgrave Square and throwing herself in front of race-horses. After all, she was a convinced feminist. But I feel that, her moral code apart, this would not have happened, because she was married to Harold Nicolson. His sane, sensible dislike of political enthusiasms, allied to his wit and humour, would surely have restrained the most belligerent partner from committing excesses of that sort.

After the explosion, if that is not too strong a word, upon the literary scene of her great poem *The Land*, Vita's subsequent reputation as a writer maintained an even keel of excellence which nevertheless became, although she never reckoned it so, subordinate to her other reputation, as a garden creator and horticultural journalist. However, by the time she was forty her best writing was by no means over. Of future novels there was to come, in addition to *The Edwardians* and *All Passion Spent* which I have already mentioned, *The Dark Island*, an astonishing revelation of the sadistic practices of love-making. It was a theme which much disturbed Harold, who saw in it a manifestation of Vita's maternal inheritance from the dark, unknown strains of her Spanish grandmother. He had already been alarmed by *The Dragon in Shallow Waters*, written as early as 1920, before Vita's obsession with Violet Trefusis had run its course. In fact it was her passionate love for Violet which begat that book. No other of her novels was to rival in horror the ruthless savagery she imparted to the ghastly Dene brothers. *The Dragon* is a story so terrible that in the climax, when the brothers are locked together in mortal struggle (over a vat of boiling, seething soap) like the incarnations of two unmitigated evils, the reader's heart practically stops beating. (Incidentally, this book anticipated *Lady Chatterley's Lover* by nearly a decade: D.H. Lawrence must surely have read it and been influenced by the proletarian Silas Dene's ambivalent affair with Lady Malleson.)

When compared to *The Dark Island* the subsequent *Easter Party* and *No Signposts in the Sea* are as milk is to vinegar. Of biographies there are *Saint Joan of Arc*, the much acclaimed *Pepita*, *The Eagle and the Dove* and the ill-fated *Daughter of France*, a life of the 'Grande Mademoiselle' whose publication had been forestalled within a matter of months by another biographer. Several books on horticulture she wrote, and some more poetry, none of which, apart from *The Garden*, matched *The Land*.

By the time I was working in London in the early Thirties Vita's social life was pretty well over. She seldom came to London and when she did it was out of duty – to broadcast, visit her doctor, dentist or publisher. Her married life with Harold was no less rock-like, indeed rather more so than before her famous elopement with Violet Trefusis in 1918, but it was on a different plane. Emotionally and sexually each went his and her way. Harold had resigned from the Foreign Office to become a journalist and commuted daily from Sissinghurst Castle, which Vita had bought and they both moved into in 1931. In that same year Harold allied himself to Sir Oswald Mosley's New Party and stood for Parliament in the General Election. Having just come down from Oxford, without a job and excited by Mosley's aspirations for a new political order which promised a better world for all mankind, I volunteered my services. Through my Aunt Dorothy, who was also Tom Mosley's aunt, I got myself attached to the headquarters of the constituency he was contesting at Stoke-on-Trent, and spent the month of October in the humble capacity of canvasser. This involved going from house to house in the back streets, during a time of acute depression, begging for votes from impoverished and bemused citizens, usually wives in soap suds up to the elbows with babies clutching their pitiable skirts. It was an odious task, although I was then convinced that supporting Sir Oswald would be to their immediate benefit. I see canvassing now as an act of gross impertinence, and wild horses would never induce me to do it again for any cause. Needless to say neither Tom Mosley, nor Harold, nor a single New Party candidate was elected. But Harold came once or twice to Stoke to support his leader; and there I met him.

Harold was already a friend of my Oxford contemporary Christopher Hobhouse, a highly intelligent youth shortly to be the precocious biographer of Charles James Fox. Christopher was also standing for Parliament as a representative of the New Party. Dubbed by the press the children's champion – he was just twenty-one – he was no more successful than the other candidates, most of whom had absolutely no qualifications whatsoever for legislating, being an ill-assorted lot of starry-eyed intellectuals and ragamuffins. So Christopher was a kind of link between Harold and myself during those brief moments of relaxation with the party helpers in the bar of the Midland Hotel after an arduous day's work at the hustings. After his defeat Tom Mosley immediately dissolved the New Party, turned Fascist and thereby forfeited the allegiance of at least three quixotic supporters, who anyway had minimal political experience or influence.

At Stoke-on-Trent I was very shy with Harold, the distinguished man of letters, in spite of his notorious affability towards the young, and he must have found me, unlike the bright and thrusting Hobhouse, oafishly unresponsive. I met him again after I got my first job, as private secretary to George Lloyd – an active right-wing statesman in the House of Lords, companion-in-arms of Winston Churchill and like him in the political wilderness, both fighting the India Bill, championing the Navy League and hopelessly endeavouring to rally Stanley Baldwin's England to the armed services and face up to the European dictators. In London Harold was a regular frequenter of the famous Café Royal in Regent Street; and by 1933 he may have mentioned my name to Vita, to whom he wrote daily letters throughout the week.

Today a young person of modest means, or for that matter of practically no private means, like me in the 1930s, cannot realize what a boon the Café Royal was to the impecunious aspirant to hobnobbery with the literary and artistic élite. There night after night the poor young person, if he had not been invited out to dinner beforehand, might in the upstairs gallery assuage hunger and thirst with a sandwich and glass of lager in the company of his elders, betters and sometimes worsers. Even if he had previously dined at the rich man's table he might still end the night in the Café Royal. In other words, he would wander around until he recognized or was hailed by a friend, at whose elbow might be sitting daedal and fuddled Augustus John, spry and jolly Compton Mackenzie, or tousled, loquacious Jack Squire, come straight from the *London Mercury* on his way home for a final tope and gossip; or, among musicians and composers, Constant Lambert, Willy Walton or Malcolm Sargent. The old stagers would grumble about the tasteless Art Deco redecoration of the room, with its jazzy stalactite chandeliers the colour of sick, and would lament the good old Art Nouveau fittings of *La Belle Époque*, which had recently been done away with by officious improving hands. Nevertheless it was still a real café, that marvellous continental spur to conviviality and conversation so curiously ignored by the British. If I recollect rightly, the tables of the Café Royal were still marble-topped, the banquettes upholstered in red plush, and the chairs gilt, with caned seats – not made of detestable sweaty plastic. In these surroundings my contemporaries or very near contemporaries such as Peter Quennell, Cyril Connolly, Patrick Balfour, John Betjeman, Alan Pryce-Jones, Osbert Lancaster and Jock Murray mingled with the Tom Eliot–Stephen Spender–Auden lot. During these nightly vigils I may have remained inordinately mum, even anonymous, but I listened, watched and observed. The tragedy is that I have remembered so little.

I came to know Harold well; and, like all his young friends, to be devoted to him. In the Thirties he had rooms at number 4 King's Bench Walk in the Temple, between Fleet Street and the Thames embankment. The locality was eminently suited to both his semi-Bohemian tastes and his notions of domestic seemliness. Actually, he had no right to live there, because they were lawyers' chambers, but number 4 was in the name of his eldest brother, Freddy Carnock, a qualified barrister-at-law who seldom if ever practised. In the evenings KBW, as we referred to it, was tranquil as the grave. The neighbouring chambers, bustling by day, had emptied. The tree-dotted quad between the Walk and Middle Temple Hall and the famous circular Templars' church was reminiscent of Harold's dearly loved Balliol College. At the back of number 4 could be heard at night the whirring of the type-setters from Reuter's international press agency. Dr Johnson's Gough Square and The Cheshire Cheese were within a stone's throw of the lodge through which, after dark, residents and visitors alike must seek entry and obtain exit from and to the Strand.

Harold's two bedrooms and panelled living-room, minute bathroom, and kitchenette behind a curtain off the entrance lobby, were on the first floor, approached by a flight of bare oak treads and stout Caroline balusters. Like a man's room door at university, the door was immensely solid – a sported oak indeed. For favoured guests, who were welcome at all hours, even in Harold's absence, admission was by means of a great key at the end of a string, reached by a hand through the letter-box. The chambers were always filled with armfuls of flowers, which Harold laboriously brought by train from Sissinghurst every Monday morning. A familiar scent of roses and honeysuckle was mingled with that of cigarette smoke and an Edwardian brand of hair lotion from Trumper's.

Through these hospitable portals Vita seldom ventured, although Harold always longed for her to spend the night on the rare occasions when she deigned to visit London.

Early in 1934 I accompanied Harold to Paris for a few days before he joined Vita and his sister Gwen St Aubyn in Italy. I had let fall that I had never been to Paris. He was my introduction to it. A better one I could not have had. He knew the historic streets backwards. He took me to Montmartre and Montparnasse, showed me where Proust had lived and the streets and *hôtels* in which the prototypes of the Guermantes, M. de Charlus, the Swanns and the Verdurins had their town houses or *appartements*, and the environs of Balzac, Sainte-Beuve, the Goncourt brothers, Rimbaud and Baudelaire. We went to Versailles, which on a February day was practically deserted. In the Galérie des Glaces he pointed out where at the signing of the Peace Treaty of 1919 Clemenceau, Lloyd George and Woodrow Wilson had sat, and he, a young diplomat from the Foreign Office, perky and quick, had stood, pencil and notebook in hand at the ready.

For me the highlight of this expedition was a visit one evening to James Joyce in the rue Galilée. Harold has described the occasion at some length in his diaries. My chief memory is of a subfusc, bourgeois apartment with lace curtains, lace doilies, upright piano discreetly covered with a dangling crocheted cloth, skyed little pictures, and an atmosphere of mustiness, stuffiness and French soup. While Harold was engaged in conversation with his host, I was left facing the son, a younger and coarser replica of the father in build and features, wearing similar round steel spectacles with thick concave lenses. I remember that although the temperature of the apartment was warm the son wore a buttoned overcoat down to the ankles. We sat stiffly, making little effort at conversation, I smirking from time to time, he scowling throughout. And all the while Joyce purred at Harold in a nervous manner, working his slender fingers. 'He was very courteous', Harold wrote to Vita, 'as shy people are. His beautiful voice trilled on slowly like Anna Livia Plurabelle [of *Finnigan's Wake*]. He has the most lovely voice I know – liquid and soft with undercurrents of gurgle.'

Long before she came into my life – it would be presumptuous to suppose I came into hers – there hovered in the immediate ambience of Harold, markedly sensed by all in contact with him but as yet uncast upon me, the mysterious, the lovely, the highly romantic shadow of Vita. Vividly I recall first setting eyes on her. It was at Sissinghurst. I was staying at nearby Somerhill with the d'Avigdor-Goldsmids and Harry, my Oxford friend, motored a party of us there one fine Sunday afternoon. We went presumably by pre-arrangement, although Vita was none too pleased by the invasion. Their two boys Ben and Nigel, home for the Eton holidays, were swimming in the placid lake. As we approached we overheard one say – no doubt he thought *sotto voce* – to the other, breast-stroking beside him, 'Who is the little pansy [it was poor Hamish Erskine] in the yellow pullover?' 'Oh!' said the other disdainfully, 'presumably one of Daddy's new friends.' This was a lesson to me that sound amplifies across still waters. We were given tea and Vita, needless to say, was charming to us. She spoke little but always attentively, kindly. Her reserve was not the least forbidding; and obviously not a manifestation of superiority, but of shyness and diffidence. Her mien was that of a statue by Canova, if a statue by Canova can be imagined deprived of its polished white surface, for her complexion was sanguine. Her eyes were hooded when she spoke and glowing coal when she focused them upon the interrogator. Her voice surpassed James Joyce's in softness. Indeed hers is the most beautiful voice my memory retains, richly modulated, clearly articulated, resonant, grand, sweet, and with a tremulous quaver, denoting amusement and sympathy, that marked it as utterly individual to her. I call it an Edwardian voice, because the nearest approaches to its patrician tonality I can think of were those of her two contemporaries, Diana Westmorland and Diana Cooper. Unlike theirs it had the suspicion of a French accent thrown in, which denoted Vita's rather cosmopolitan upbringing and, I daresay, derived from her bilingual mother.

In the mid Thirties I still had no inkling whatsoever that Vita in her early wedded years had had a hectic and traumatic love affair with Violet Trefusis which brought her marriage within an ace of disruption, only prevented by Harold's adoration of her and determination to get her back. In conversations he constantly mentioned her to his friends, lauding her great qualities and joking about her little prejudices. He referred almost reverently to her poetry, of which he was extremely proud without, I surmised, having deeply pondered it. He spoke of her always in the most protective manner, which was very touching. He explained to me once, as though it were for my good to know, that theirs had become the perfect marriage because, unlike the majority of husbands and wives, they kept no secrets from one another; that everything they thought and did they mulled over, even if the matter was distressful to one of them. Consequently their relationship was devoid of squalid little deceits, pretences, rancours and jealousies. This I now know to have been absolutely true. It was in fact the consummation of the rules for a perfect marriage which, in a famous broadcast discussion together in 1929, they formulated before a million listeners.

True it was that Vita and Violet's elopement in 1918 caused Harold enormous distress. But even then Vita was not devious with him. She made no bones about what she was doing, and throughout the escapade they kept up a loving correspondence. The Violet incident – and how Harold hated her, and let Vita know it – was the determining factor of their marriage. Never thenceforth was there the slightest hint of their separating. On the contrary, each made a point of liking the other's lovers, and when Harold fell for Raymond Mortimer in 1924 Vita adopted Raymond like a brother, and they became bosom friends.

True again it also was that Vita and Violet's elopement was widely known and talked about in the social and intellectual circles wherein they moved – but not beyond. Today it would have leaked to the press, become a national scandal, been blazoned in every newspaper and distorted and hyped by every gutter editor, before being magnified as a major issue on world-wide television. It must be admitted that the affair gave rise to some comical as well as bizarre scenes: Vita masquerading as a wounded Tommy in the streets of London at the end of the First World War; Vita at Dover saying to herself, 'Shall I elope or shan't I?'; Vita histrionically dining by herself at a table in the

Ritz Hotel while Violet was sitting at another table with Denys Trefusis, whom she was to marry next day; and later the two husbands, Harold and Denys, together chartering a two-seater aeroplane for Amiens, there to exhort their respective spouses to return to them. As Harold subsequently pointed out to Vita, her sense of humour was not highly developed. It was a deficiency which led to further amatory misunderstandings, verging on the ludicrous. These in turn gave rise to untruths, not between Vita and Harold but between Vita and those in love with her. Harold called them her 'muddles'. There were dreadful 'muddles' with Mary, wife of the outraged poet Roy Campbell whom the Nicolsons had befriended. Campbell cruelly pilloried the Nicolsons in a vicious broadside, his long poem *The Georgiad*. Then came a further 'muddle' when Geoffrey Scott and Virginia Woolf were both in love with her at the same time. And then – for oh! what a tangled web we weave – there were Virginia and Hilda Matheson, also simultaneously. These and even further muddles required much sorting out. Vita was sadly grieved by the pain she caused people emotionally entangled with her, and invariably penitent. Plaintively she averred that she was incapable of making anyone happy – not Mary Campbell, not Dottie Wellesley, not even Harold. Inconstant in love she was, perhaps, but in friendship valiantly steadfast, as many testified. And Harold, instead of upbraiding her, exalted her virtues and like a society lady shaking a finger at her pekinese for lifting its leg against the drawing-room curtains, scolded her in too docile a manner. He would merely exhort her to avoid getting into another muddle – in vain.

Hilda Matheson, a close friend and valued support to both Vita and Harold until her premature death at the beginning of the Second World War, was different from most of the other woman lovers. She was not sentimental, adoring or cloying. She was clever, sensible, practical, kind and stable. When her affair with Vita petered out she acted as a sort of unofficial, unpaid secretary–confidante, financial adviser and travel agent to both Nicolsons. She saw them into Sissinghurst in 1931. I never met

Hilda, and yet I owe her a debt of gratitude. It was through her, by way of Vita, that in 1935 I was interviewed by Hilda's brother MacLeod Matheson, the secretary of the National Trust, and given a job at the Trust the following year. Her, therefore, I posthumously and fervently thank for a momentous landmark in my life.

My friendship with Vita was of slow growth. She won my total affection, although I cannot be sure that I won hers. This may explain why I remain her faithful fan, without reservation. For I have discovered at the end of a long life that love between a man and woman, which is the most fugitive of all emotions, will best endure if it is partially withheld by the woman. And this applies to platonic as well as physical love. In other words, I do not claim that my affection for her was returned in the same measure, fond of me though I believe her to have been. Indeed, why should it have been? I belonged to a younger generation. My intellect and creative ability did not nearly reach hers; my ignorance of plants and horticulture was lamentable. In the last respect my deficiency was in some wise later on amended by Alvilde, whose single-minded dedication to plant rearing and tending directed her into a closer bond with Vita than ever mine was. And platonic love, which is what I am referring to in both Alvilde's and my relations with Vita, must, to be completely reciprocal, be based on one mutual, over-riding shared interest, one which transcends superficial sympathies.

I am able to date the first flowering of what I term my empathy affair with Vita. To be precise, it happened on Friday 9th March 1945. In my published diary under that date I wrote: 'Eardley [Knollys] and I walked to King's Bench Walk to a party Harold and Vita gave together, a very exceptional occasion. Harold in a gay and frolicsome mood; Vita very beautiful, regal, tall and slender, wearing a wide-brimmed hat over her eyes and smoking from a long cigarette holder. She is never frolicsome.' We sat together on a window-seat, away from the multitude, and agreed that we never could feel at ease at any large gathering. We suffered from agoraphobia, a sense of not belonging, and a sense, not of superiority (far from it), but of inferiority, an inability to give what was socially required. More than two years later we passed the empathy barrier. Our empathy welled and, like the silent waters of a weir, suddenly overflowed, mingling in a cascade of happiness, joy and love. With Harold we went on a ten-day tour of the west country, visiting country houses, gardens and churches, staying in pubs and simple hotels. On parting we embraced – a thing I had often longed to do before but did not dare (an indication of how things were before the both-cheeks era in which we now wallow). We exchanged mementos, mine to her a commonplace hand-bag, bought at Woolworth's in Glastonbury and which she never parted with, hers to me a silver pencil which I have twice lost for long periods, and mysteriously recovered. It is prized among my greatest treasures.

Thereafter we met occasionally when she came on a day trip to London. Luncheon in my flat to meet Doreen Baynes, author of *The Regent and his Daughter*, Vita wearing her usual old terracotta dress instead of the customary Sissinghurst jodhpurs, riding-boots and jacket, and looking awkward like a sheep-dog endeavouring to be a borzoi – Doreen, over-sensitive and inclined to be mystical, so impressed by Vita's features and eyes that she shook with nerves. Or luncheon at Sibyl Colefax's little house in Lord North Street, James Pope-Hennessey present, Sibyl talking non-stop, accusing Vita and Harold of selfishness for not 'getting' their two sons married, and shouting Vita down whenever she opened her mouth, and Vita dissolving in laughter. Again, Vita at a concert in aid of the Keats–Shelley Committee, reciting rather haltingly two odes of Keats before the Queen, and afterwards standing composedly while the chairman Lady Crewe announced that she would pass the Queen round to the left like the port. Finally, a June visit to Sissinghurst in 1949 when far into the night she and I in her tower room discussed everything under the stars until I walked under them to my bedroom (which was Ben's) in the Priest's House just before sunrise in a gauzy haze of mist and dew heralded by a chorus of birdsong. From her I learnt that a human was capable of loving a place even more than a person – 'Knole which I love more than anything else in the world, except Hadji' (rather as though Harold were a secondary place). Vita wrote down next day that the evening had led to 'one of the most peculiar conversations I have ever had', and 'I wish I could talk with Hadji as Jim and I talked last night, but it would only bore Hadji if I tried to, and he would just roll away like a woolly ball.' I have never known any human being male or female with whom I have been able to talk more freely. Nigel was right in telling her that 'What you admire most in a person is sympathy for other people.' He was right if he meant that she had an inexhaustible fund of it herself. But was there an underlying criticism in this statement, to the effect that his mother dissipated too much of her intellectual energies on friends and hangers-on unworthy of her?

Towards the end of her life, meetings with Vita were not always like this. Slowly her health deteriorated, and she took to the sherry bottle. The first time I noticed what Harold would never acknowledge in bald terms and referred to as her 'muzziness' was when Jamesey Pope-Hennessy and I went down to Sissinghurst for dinner with her in August 1952. The visit was not a success, and she was aware of it. She told Harold that it was a dreadful failure and she felt sore and inadequate. Victoria Glendinning quotes from a poem she wrote about this date:

> There are times when I cannot endure the sight of people.
> I know they are charming, intelligent, since everyone
>   tells me so,
> But I wish they would go away.
> I cannot establish contact with anybody;
> They are all unreal to me, the charming intelligent people,
> And I daresay I seem as unreal to them.

This poem makes me dreadfully sad. Vita's reclusiveness became more and more persistent. The effort of keeping her end up with those she knew was far greater than that involved in passing the time with strangers in Sissinghurst's garden. To strangers she was always positively forthcoming, always courteous and at ease. She welcomed their enjoyment, would stop and talk, giving them hints how to grow this and that, even giving them cuttings. She knew of course that she was not beholden to them. She could turn from them the moment she was bored or tired. The languor of advancing age has a terrible relentless grip. However hard one tries, one cannot release it. Addiction to sherry does not mitigate languor, and muzziness leads to mistakes, of which Harold was too well aware and of which he sometimes bore the brunt. Addiction may even have intensified the spreading arthritis and the heart dilation of her last years.

Harold, who was blissfully gregarious, could not understand this retreat within herself. To me it is entirely understandable, and I don't see it as extraordinary. It was compatible with Vita's refusal to share those of his interests which were not hers, first his diplomatic and then his political ones. She loathed both. Yet she wished him well in both, just as she cherished and was jealous on his behalf of his literary reputation. This she understood because she had her own.

Vita and Harold came to Alvilde's and my wedding in November 1951. It was not a joyous occasion. We were not allowed to be married in church, and in a register office, without God's blessing, a permanent union has a hollow ring, at least for a man and woman who mind.

Victoria Glendinning's *Vita: The Life of V. Sackville-West* could only with difficulty be bettered. It is so fair and factual that another full-scale biography and assessment of Vita's strange personality will not be needed for a very long time. Victoria is compassionate, although the reader senses that by her very nature she cannot be in full sympathy with Vita, does not think much of her writing, and is a little contemptuous of Harold. It may be that this attitude has contributed, albeit unintentionally, to the downgrading of Vita's place both as a person and a writer to the low ebb it has now reached. Whenever Vita's name is mentioned in print today, it is with sneering and contumely. She is dismissed as snobbish, reactionary, middle-brow, shallow in thought and facile in style.

Her love life is treated as a joke. Although the last thing Nigel can have intended was a disservice to his mother's memory, it is evident that her declension from grace was immediately precipitated by his sensitively edited book, *Portrait of a Marriage*. He was right in publishing the story of her affair with Violet Trefusis: Vita had expressly directed that it should be told, if only to arouse in the sexually straight some compassion for lesbians of the future. For all his infinite tenderness and tact, nevertheless its publication in 1973 was too soon. It horrified and hurt many people who reverenced Vita, as a poet whom they found they could comprehend and as the creator of the most famous English garden of the century, a garden which they knew and loved. Many were people who had hung on every word of her weekly garden articles in the *Observer*. They had also idolised her and Harold as a dear, old, faithful married couple – which indeed they were, only in a manner people in general knew not of. When bluntly apprised of the details by *Portrait of a Marriage*, their illusions were shattered. And they took to reviling, ultimately to disparaging her. Had Nigel waited, say, twenty years, the older generation would not have been taken by surprise. Nor would they have been shocked. As it transpired, the story was then distorted by a loathsome film into a travesty of vulgarity and a misrepresentation of the true Harold and Vita known by those who loved them. Through the film the public came to visualize Vita as a sort of moustachioed female sergeant-major (a caricature of Clive Bell's grenadier), a dragoness lurking in the byways who could not keep her hands off any woman who took her fancy.

Vita was undeniably amorous and impulsive. But, if not strictly monogamous, she was not promiscuous, and always circumspect. She had a lurking dread of scandal. Not that she minded tuppence friends knowing about her unorthodox sexual tendencies. But she was damned well not going to air them in public. Above all, she was loth to cause hurt to Harold, her two sons and her friends.

As for Harold, he was presented in the film in the guise of a wet little office clerk, a twerp under the thumb of an overbearing wife, and also as an unmitigated snob. Even reputable historians have been influenced by the film to accept this misleading portrait. The twerp and snob interpretations were in fact to some extent provoked by Harold's endemic wit and humour, which always verged on the frivolous. It amused him to appear to his familiars a slightly comical figure. When he wrote to Vita that a remark of hers made him feel like the crushed hen she had run over in her motor-car, it was meant for her reception alone. On the printed page it was apparently read as an indication of his feebleness.

In-jokes between loved ones are apt to give rise to derision when read by the masses. Furthermore, Harold did not always choose his words carefully enough. For instance, when as a Labour MP he was asked by a television crew whether Albany in Piccadilly, where by that time he had rooms, was not 'a privileged sanctuary', he answered yes it was, adding that 'highly developed civilizations specialise in variety whereas lower civilizations impose uniformity'. As for his off-parade jokes made in the family circle and published from his diaries and private letters, they have been taken in deadly earnest by critics as the expressed convictions of an undemocratically-minded intellectual. When Harold failed to regain his seat in the House of Commons in 1945 he longed to be back in Parliament. The only way open for him was by means of the House of Lords. And it very nearly came about; that it didn't was due to Harold's unwise lobbying. Again, charges of snobbery greeted the diary speculations as to what title might be appropriate if he was ennobled. Lord Middlesex? Lord Cranfield? were suggested round the family dinner table. No, these were old Sackville titles which were not fitting for him, a mere Nicolson, to aspire to. Lord Sissinghurst, then? No, acquaintances would call him Lord Pansyhurst. As things were, Harold stood in line as eventual heir to his father's barony of Carnock: he was therefore quite indifferent to nobility as an end in itself, but he dearly wanted a seat in the senate. He made the mistake of loving Parliament, in which he had not excelled, more than literature, in which he had.

He did not at all care for his knighthood, although he much appreciated the fact that the KCVO he bore had been the sovereign's personal gift. As for Vita, she detested it in so far as it concerned her. To be addressed as Lady Nicolson was an affront. It was tantamount to being under an obligation to somebody else, even though that somebody was her husband. It was insufferable to share a paltry denomination which she had not earned, yet the equivalent of which she was capable of earning. She was her own person, not an adjunct of her husband. She was a poet, a horticulturist of note, a Sackville, a daughter of Knole. When she was appointed a Companion of Honour in her own right, *then* she was delighted.

This official recognition was all very well. But she was fully aware that 'the Tom Eliot and Stephen Spender–Auden school' did not esteem her poetry by which she set much store; that they ranked it middle-brow, middle-range, middle-everything but middle-class. On the contrary, it was not middle-class enough. It was upper-class and therefore aloof, out of touch, unprofessional, and non-conformist: lacking political content. The acceptable poetry of the Thirties, Forties and Fifties had to be, and was, left-wing, anti-Fascist, pro-Stalinist. (The one exception that comes to mind is the poetry of Roy Campbell, who was as extreme to the right as the rest were extreme to the left.) Vita was totally non-political as far as political parties were concerned. She claimed that her verse dealt with the everlasting values while disregarding 'temporary things'. It was none the worse for that. True, at times it verged on bathos. Yet at others it reached heights of pastoral description that take the breath away. But I wonder how many enthusiasts who have modelled their gardens on Sissinghurst, have also read *The Garden*. A pendant to *The Land* and likewise a Georgic, it is possibly the best poem she wrote. It encapsulates all the advice which readers so eagerly garnered from the weekly garden articles she contributed to the *Observer*. It took her twenty years to compose. Conceived in the mid 1920s and resumed in the last years of peace, it was not concluded before the war was over.

Much of it was written during the height of the fighting and bombing while the British and German airborne armadas screamed backwards and forwards over the Weald of Kent. It abounds in beautiful passages concerning the history and habits of plants. I take at random lines from the 'Summer' section:

> June of the iris and the rose.
> The rose not English as we fondly think.
> Anacreon and Bion sang the rose;
> And Rhodes the isle whose very name means rose
> Struck roses on her coins;
> Pliny made lists and Roman libertines
> Made wreaths to wear among the flutes and wines;
> The young Crusaders found the Syrian rose
> Springing from Saracenic quoins
> And China opened her shut gate
> To let the roses through, and Persian shrines
> Of poetry and painting gave the rose...
> Yet Albion took her name from her white rose
> Not from her cliffs, some say. So let it be.
> We know the dog-rose, flinging free
> Whip-lashes in the hedgerow, starred with pale
> Shell blossom as a Canterbury tale,
> The candid English genius, fresh and pink
> As Chaucer made us think,
> Singing of adolescent meads in May.
> That's not the rose in her true character;
> She's a voluptuary; think of her
> Wine-dark and heavy – scented of the South,
> Stuck in a cap or dangled from a mouth
> As soft as her own petals. That's the rose!

Although she was so allergic to wasps that she once nearly died from a sting, and had to carry an antidote with her, she even acknowledged the wasp's place in the garden hierarchy:

> So let me grant the hated wasp his due,
> He showed me beauty where I had not thought
> Beauty to find...
> The persecuted wasp, so neat, so fine,

That in sarcastic verse I thus enshrine.
It was a wasp that in a glass of wine
Once killed a Pope.

Which one? I do not know. And here is the tribute she pays to the old-fashioned gardener who plods the same old round, never stale and ever fresh in promise, who seldom if ever takes a holiday, and who but for her goes unrecognized, unsung:

> ... in the gloom, with his slow gesture, moves
> The leathern demiurge of this domain,
> Like an old minor god in corduroy
> Setting and picking up the things he needs,
> Deliberate as though all Time were his.
> Honour the gardener! that patient man ...

No wonder that the belittling of Vita's verse — what the prevailing 'concrete and cement, meaningless school of poets' considered her 'out of date rubbishy words' — drove her to muted anger and resentment. We are arrogant and stupid to ignore her poetry. In it she celebrated the earth which through her own bare hands as well as with her receptive mind she loved and understood. And, happily, what she conjured out of the earth is there for all of us to see, to read about, to enjoy and to ponder over.

It may be that by the time the centenary of her death is reached Vita's literary works will be esteemed as they deserve and ranked as high as Harold's — if not higher, in that they are more creative, are cries from the heart, previsions of what was to come, and elegies of what was going, a lost world of cosmic culture and manners. This is the view which I sensed, not from any intellectual deduction but from sheer youthful intuition, when I first came upon her poetry at Oxford.

Sacheverell Sitwell

1897–1988

THE HEIGHT OF the Sitwells' renown was in the 1920s and 1930s. Teasers rather than rebels (for the three siblings never let the world disregard their ancient descent and belief in traditional values), they revelled in provoking the sedate, the old-fashioned and the vulgar. I never knew Dame Edith, whose poetry I always found difficult to take seriously and whose antics became more and more histrionic as she grew old. Her flamboyant dress and affectations I found neither beautiful nor amusing. Yet she was an original, and her message had a distinct nursery appeal to aesthetes of a limited mental calibre. Her verse with its rocking-horse rhythms exhorted the pre-war teenagers among us to smite the philistines hip and thigh on every occasion that offered. And that in those days was no small achievement. Sir Osbert I knew and feared a little – he could be devastatingly rude with a mere look – while tremendously admiring his five autobiographical volumes, *Left Hand, Right Hand!*

Sacheverell (what a tongue-twister! Servants and strangers soon found themselves obliged to refer to him as Mr, later Sir, Sachie) I first met during the Second World War at Emerald Cunard's table when she was living at the Dorchester Hotel and resolutely refusing to hear the bombs fall in Hyde Park (never shall I forget her look of scorn if a guest had the bad taste to duck over his plate of caviare, and as for an exclamation of

67

fear, it was unthinkable). Sachie was then in his late forties. Instantly I was captivated, for he elicited affection as well as admiration. He had perfect manners, not natural but acquired, polished, inevitably Edwardian and yet surprisingly convincing. He was the most attentive guest and host. He did not over-awe young people, snub or overtly laugh at them. On the contrary he would gently query their more outrageous and portentous statements by feigning to see their point, and then sweetly demolish them. He was all sympathy and solicitude and fond of giving the young advice – how to have their hair cut better, how not to try too hard at their writing, how not to heed their parents' criticism or contempt, or anyone else's for that matter. Although very sensible of his status in the literary rat-race, he was never – which Osbert could be – arrogant. He did not assume that his writing was superior to that of other authors whom he respected. He merely knew its worth when others often did not, and towards the end of his life bitterly resented that his poetry, which pre-eminently he cared about, had not been adequately appreciated. In fact, however, his literary reputation was first won through his verse, which he then abandoned in 1936 from lack of sufficient appreciation. On resuming after almost forty years he would not submit it to a publisher, for fear of rebuff, but had it privately printed and distributed among his friends.

Of the bulk of his writings I am incapable of assessing the worth. I think he wrote too many books too effortlessly. Yet he once assured me that he found writing a great mental strain. What writer doesn't? But somehow I assumed Sachie not to be among the number. Perhaps, then, he wrote too disparately. *The Homing of the Winds, The Hunters and the Hunted, Monks, Nuns and Monasteries* and dozens more were about everything and nothing, often lacking sequence and cohesion. So crammed are these books with anecdote, historic allusion and poetic inflexion that they tend to give the reader indigestion, as from a surfeit of rich pudding; his themes, overladen with colourful and sparkling imagery, become repetitious. The books are hard to read at long sittings. In truth, they are prose poetry. And poetry, let us face it, is jolly difficult to take in long draughts. Who today can sit over the fire and quaff *Paradise Lost* from beginning to end? With the exception of Byron's *Don Juan*, I can think of no epic in seventeen cantos or their equivalent that would pass this test. Poetry to be taken in slow sips is confined to lyrics, sonnets, rondeaux, the ode, the elegy, the song: above all, song. And a poet is what Sachie was above all else, even if his verse is not memorable because he seldom used rhyme; and to repeat reams of fruity prose poems, however exquisite, is likewise no easy task.

Yet he left several prose masterpieces. The best known of these is *Southern Baroque Art*. It proved so popular that the semi-well-read would often assume it to be the only one he had written. This annoyed Sachie, just as Harold Nicolson, another prolific author, was annoyed when strangers had only heard of his semi-fictional sketches in that minor classic *Some People*, of which he came to hate the mere mention. Anyone picking up *Southern Baroque Art* for the first time need not suppose that it contains art-historical jargon. No professional art historian could, or would, write three essays so slight, so short or so evocative of a whole period of aesthetic history. They are totally non-factual, devoid of dates, arguments and assumptions. What the young Sachie did, with the lightest feather, was to brush the dust of prejudice off one artistic style, the baroque, while revivifying in architecture, sculpture, painting, furniture, the fine arts, music and also literature another, namely the rococo.

With this small volume Sachie reopened the eyes of art-loving people to an epoch of taste which had for a century and a half been despised and rejected. He did for the rococo (which is in effect an appendix of the baroque style in southern Europe) what Geoffrey Scott in *The Architecture of Humanism* had done years previously for the full-blown baroque itself. He put the rococo firmly and squarely on the cultural map of the Old and indeed the New World, his circumference embracing such polarities of European colonization as Mexico and Goa.

British Architects and Craftsmen, published at the very end of the Second World War, was a pioneering work which had immense success in stimulating the interest of connoisseurs, before the Courtauld Institute spewed forth waves of specializing historicism for scholars. It taught simple lovers of old buildings to realize that these islands had given birth to, apart from our much vaunted Jones, Wren and Adam, other highly worthy architects, such as Hawksmoor, Talman, Gibbs – names now to conjure by, but then awaiting conjuration, names just as venerable as the greatest hitherto recorded. Over and above that, he demonstrated that in our anonymous stonemasons, carvers of marble and wood, plasterers and stuccoists, iron- and silver-smiths, locksmiths, tapestry weavers, needleworkers, book-binders, and native masters of the decorative arts generally, our islands could boast craftsmen as skilled as those of ancient Greece and Rome, of Renaissance Italy and France. Yet Sachie was no scholar. By enthusiasm, observation, comparative study and infinite curiosity he sought out, saw for himself and described in an infectiously inspiring prose, devoid of narrow schoolmanship, the wonders which his readers had hitherto either ignored or taken for granted. It was an astonishing performance.

It was indeed the wonders that got beneath Sachie's skin. To him the great Tudor and Jacobean houses, the Knoles, the Forde Abbeys, the Chastletons and the Hardwicks were on a par with the dramas of Shakespeare and Ben Jonson, creations infinitely haphazard, infinitely English, infinitely rare. It amazed him that the academics had not seen them in this light before. The Georgians like Horace Walpole had regarded them as wretched accidents of a barbarous class of parvenus who knew no better; the Victorians, like Joseph Nash in *Mansions of the Olden Time*, as quaint old dwellings to be illustrated with figures in 'Vandyke' dress; the Edwardians as frankly vulgar Netherlandish pastiches; and his contemporaries as whimsy and folksy non-architecture, not to be considered seriously at all. Sachie was the first writer to stop patronising them. He invested them with poetry. We have only to read his description of a first view of Hardwick Hall looming out of the bleak Derbyshire landscape on an autumnal afternoon:

the bold masses which compose the house have the habit of grouping curiously, according to which angle they are seen from, sometimes spread out to great extent, with the four towers at the corners, or, from this approach, all four close together, as though the building is shaped like the diamond on a playing-card, more still, like the ace of clubs, so that the fourth tower is hidden, almost, behind the other three.

What previous architectural historian would have chosen these poetic analogies for a textbook? And he continues: 'But the towers sink back again behind a wall, till the wall itself becomes more elaborate, with a battlemented ornament like a halberd head upon it.' Through his pen the house attains a personality almost transcending the human. Inside he rhapsodizes over the *verdure* tapestries which have never left the walls for which Bess of Hardwick ordered them in the old Queen's reign, the glowing needlework, the blackened portraits, the idyllic plaster ceilings and enormous coloured friezes, depicting hunting and forest scenes, the whole betokening a link between the receding Gothic and the dawning Renaissance ages in one transitional burst of splendour peculiar to our nation and to no other in the world.

Hardwick had a niche of its own in Sachie's heart. It was not without coincidence that legend associated this marvellous house with one of his romantic heroines, Mary, Queen of Scots who, if she was never actually imprisoned in the old house, nevertheless has left her visible imprint upon much needlework and furniture. The mysterious and puzzling marquetry table, its surface inlaid with musical instruments and scores, backgammon boards, chessmen, playing-cards and love-knots, in the high great chamber, 'The most beautiful room, not in England alone, but in the whole of Europe', enthralled him. He would repeat over and over again the inlaid inscription which mystified him:

> The redolent smele of Aeglentyne
> We stagges exault to the deveyne.

'It is absolute poetry,' he once said, with finality in his voice. To which I replied rather fatuously, 'It is hauntingly beautiful.

But what exactly can it mean?' To which Sachie retorted, rather sharply for him, 'As though it matters.'

Sachie's several topographical books were wonderful introductions to foreign lands, whether or not some of the places he lovingly described still existed or had been demolished long ago. That too hardly mattered. The point was, they had existed. They had enriched world civilizations of the remote past, and accordingly merited remembrance. He captured the enduring spirit of Austria, Spain, Portugal, Romania, Belgium and South America by pointing out the unobvious but characteristic works of art and the crafts of each country with broad and deft touches.

I have never met a man whose mind so brimmed with knowledge and understanding, well- and ill-assorted. For these reasons alone he has won our reverence. His mind was like an aviary which released in rapid succession fascinating flights of information like exotic birds. Before you had, in talking to him, adjusted your concentration upon, say, Fulbert's emasculation of Abélard, he had flitted off to the habits of the Incas in the valley of Cuzco, Peru. Seconds later he was inside the Grand Duke's palace at Weimar, describing how Liszt reacted to the high notes of Paganini's violin; or in royal Queluz, where the cries of the mad Queen Maria of Portugal were echoing down empty, resounding corridors; and before you had time to follow him into a Zen monastery in Yamagata he had alighted at Renishaw, where he was picking strawberries with Edith during a June heatwave. It was practically impossible to keep pace with him. As for his understanding, let me say that his books, though too often unreadable from cover to cover, contain nuggets on practically every page. In this regard he resembles Proust – and dare I extend the resemblance to Shakespeare? – in that the reader will stumble upon a thought so profound, or so trivial, that he will gasp with pleasure or surprise, and always with gratitude, while saying to himself, 'that is the very experience I have had. Only I never had the courage, the candour or the wit to express it.' To take one simple example: in the story (and it is so diffuse a piece of writing as to be hardly a story at all, and accordingly the reader's interest is not easily held to the theme) entitled *All Summer in a Day* the narrator, travelling by train, stares shamelessly at the reflection of his beautiful neighbour in the window, thereby believing, possibly erroneously, that he will not be detected.

Sachie was partly a leprechaun, partly a precocious child who never properly grew up. Which is why it was hard to believe the love affairs of this incorporeal and extremely fastidious being were actually sexual. Whatever else they were, they were extremely romantic and intensely passionate. The image he fashioned of the women he loved seldom corresponded with the actuality. In fact he would sometimes lose his heart before he even knew the object of his desire; and would invest a mere name with attributes which he fancied she, be she ballet dancer, 'bright young thing', society flibbertigibbet, artist or musician, ought to possess. He might picture her by virtue of her circumstances as a figure familiar to him, say, in a canvas by Tintoretto or Veronese, and in that guise she had to remain. And although his wife Georgia's love affairs vexed him, he considered that she ought to condone his. He was always vastly entertained by other people's tangled affairs, and the more absurd the situations were, the more he was amused. When he laughed, in a short staccato trill, his Gothic features would break into tiny fragments like wavelets on a beach, his eyes become pinpoints and his little mouth work itself into a pursed triangle. Yet there was nothing little about him in other respects. In stature he was very tall, slender and upright, although frailly built and frangible-seeming. He was always immaculately dressed, in a way not that of the country squire which he was by right of inheritance. If encountered outside the purlieus of Weston Hall, even in the village, he would look out of place, almost anachronistic. Not exactly a dandy, he was a twentieth-century counterpart to a Georgian *milord* in a Batoni portrait, who although painted in everyday dress could not by a stretch of the imagination be related to the farmyard slush and mud of his rural acres.

He lived in dread of such impending calamities as a penal tax on capital, cancer, burial before death, and the destruction of everything he loved best — works of art, buildings, birds and flowers – by 'the bomb'. In an instant these horrors would be dispelled, temporarily at any rate, by some boyish enthusiasm, and he was ready to fly to Japan in order to look at a drawing by Hokusai which he suddenly remembered he had not seen when last in Tokyo. As he was not a millionaire, this meant persuading a publisher to commission a book on the Shinto cult which would involve an agreeable jaunt to Eastern Asia for Georgia and himself, thus avoiding the forthcoming winter months in England. I do not believe there was any country in the world he had not visited, or very many great works of art he had not closely inspected. Moreover, a prodigious memory like a magical computer enabled him vividly to create works of art in words at a minute's notice. Georgia told me that she accompanied him once to a school where he was billed to deliver a lecture to very senior boys – the most exacting of all audiences. He had prepared nothing and arrived without a single note. He asked the boys on what subject they would like him to speak. It was obvious that they were slightly nettled by what seemed to them casual treatment. To put him through his paces they chose some highly abstruse subject. For an hour and a half, quite undaunted, he addressed them fluently and amusingly. They were entranced, and when he stopped they begged for more.

It was curious, in one so preoccupied with the occult, the macabre, with saints, nuns and superstitions, liturgical rituals, not to mention churches and holy places, that Sachie had no religious faith at all. There was something tragic about this lacuna in his make-up, a lacuna which induced an ineradicable unhappiness throughout his life. It is succinctly summarized in the most despairing and certainly one of the very best of his poems, 'Agamemnon's Tomb', composed in 1925 when he was still in his twenties.

> Knock, knock, knock, these are the nails of the coffin.
> They go in easy, but must be wrenched out,
> For no strength can break them from the walled night.
> They are little shining points, they within; they are cloves
>   that have no scent,

But the dead are kept in prison by such little things,
Though little does it help them, when the guard is gone.
It is night, endless night, with not a chink of day,
And if the coffin breaks there is no hope in that,
The bones tumble out and only dogs will steal them;
There is no escape, no tunnel back to life . . .
There is nothing at the other end, no door at which to listen,
There is nothing, nothing, not a breath beyond.
Give up your hopes of it, you'll wake no more . . .
O give up every hope of it, we'll wake no more,
We are the world and it will end with us:
The heart is not a clock, it will not wind again.
The dead are but dead, there is no use for them,
They neither care, nor care not, they are only dead.

It is no exaggeration to state that Sachie was haunted, even in those moments when he was transported by a work of art in architecture, painting or music, even in the lists of love, by the realization which assails most people only between three and four o'clock of a sleepless night, before dawn fingers the bedroom curtains, that after death there is everlasting nothingness.

He intensely disliked and shunned priests and never attended services, even in his own parish church. I once listened to him deliver an address from the pulpit of a church at a friend's memorial service. He rushed through it in an inarticulate manner, as though he felt stifled within alien and hostile walls that were repugnant to him; as though he was longing to have done and get out into the fresh air of life. Yet when as a young officer in the army – it is difficult to imagine Sachie as a soldier subjected to drill and discipline – he was detailed to play in a cricket match for his regiment against another, such was his horror of games that he spent hours on his knees praying for rain. His invocation was granted, the heavens opened, the pitch was inundated and the match indefinitely postponed. Even this evidence of divine compassion did not move him from an obdurate atheism.

Georgia Doble, who came from Montreal, shared all Sachie's enthusiasms for fifty-five years. Beautiful in a full-moon sort of way, business-like, intensely practical, down to earth, yet adoring and watchful, she was his absolute complement. She has been accused of dragging Sachie into social activities from which he would otherwise have been averse, where he squandered in frivolous pursuits on other people's yachts and in night-clubs the precious time which he should have reserved for intellectual and poetic creation. This of course was nonsense. Sachie was not easily led. He was a willing participant in pleasure for its own sake. He enjoyed the company of the rich and privileged, of minor royalty and the racy, and what they had to offer, so long as they were sophisticated and stimulating. The moment he was bored he became silent or moved away. He liked beautiful women to be glamorous and well dressed according to his standards of good taste. And woe betide those who were flashy. Dowdiness was another failing, only to be overlooked if the dowdy dresser was bright in the head. Georgia regulated his daily work routine, provided his comforts, and protected him from bores.

Sachie's was a retiring disposition. He could never fall in with his siblings' brash campaigns of advertising the family wares. He found the famous performance of *Façade* in which Edith bawled nonsense from behind a mask into a megaphone frankly embarrassing, although his loyalty obliged him to play a spear-carrying role. Trumpeting abuse of the philistine and bashing the enemy while vindicating the Sitwellian virtues and overlaying their allies with praise and gifts were not in Sachie's line. Yet he was Edith and Osbert's little brother, whose genius it was their joy to exalt before the wide world; what could he do but accept it gratefully? And, at first, not altogether without pleasure and assent. Only later, after his marriage in 1925, he secretly resented it as patronage. He wanted, not shared, but his own independent renown. And he was probably right, in that posterity already ranks him higher as a writer than his sister and brother. To his credit, he never forgot that in his early and insecure manhood he depended almost entirely upon his 'darling' Osbert. They lived together in Carlyle Square, Chelsea, went to the same parties, and moved in the same intellectual and artistic circle. In fact the two brothers and sister (for Edith, the eldest partner, always hovered near) were accepted by the public as an indivisible and indissoluble entity. One may well ask, where were Sir George and Lady Ida all this time?

Sir George was too eccentric and self-concerned to be guide and counsellor to his brilliant younger son; and Lady Ida far too unreliable, dotty, and at a later stage drunken, to be in any sense a protector. As it was, she looked to Sachie to get her out of the terrible troubles in which her gambling, her consorting with fraudsters and her terror of her cold, tight-fisted husband constantly landed her. All she achieved was to wring his affectionate and sensitive heart with pity and misery over her humiliating plight and the shame it brought upon her children. Her trial and conviction at the Old Bailey for fraud, followed by three months' imprisonment in Holloway in 1915, left a wound on Sachie – but not the other two, who merely disliked her for what she had done – which he bore throughout the rest of his life. It engendered in him a need to seek out damsels in distress. He saw himself as a heroic Perseus rescuing Andromedas from rocks and dragons.

When he learned that Lady Ida had been sent to prison Sachie was a schoolboy at Eton: it was during the First World War, and Osbert was fighting overseas. On her coming out of prison, it was he who gave the wretched woman the comfort and encouragement she needed. Her case was made more poignant because she was not wicked; silly by nature, she had been utterly spoilt in upbringing, as though she were a doll which would never have to face the hardships and roguery of the wide world but only glimpse them through the gilded windows of noble mansions. His mother's fate was worse for Sachie than for Edith and Osbert (as for Sir George, his affection and pity were not even called upon) because of his susceptibility to her beauty and infantile charm – a charm which she exercised, not perhaps unconsciously, like blackmail, upon his adoration and sense of duty.

The irony of Sachie's sense of tragedy over Lady Ida's disgrace was that he too was dogged all his life by lack of money. Whereas his sister, who was unmarried, had no extravagant tastes and was content to live like a nun in a cell, Osbert, though likewise unmarried and childless, inherited as well as property a great deal of money which he was reluctant to spend on his brother and sister-in-law. Georgia brought Sachie no money to speak of, and had extremely extravagant tastes. The antipathy between brother and sister-in-law – founded on Osbert's resentment of Georgia for depriving him of Sachie's exclusive attention as well as for not being, as he thought, socially good enough, and her resentment of him for his enjoyment of great riches (which she supposed he, childless, didn't need) at the expense of Sachie (whose wife and two sons clearly did need them), added to her jealousy of his greater reputation as a writer than Sachie's – became accentuated as the years went by. Differences were magnified, misunderstandings abounded, ugly insinuations became rife, and missives of reproach and hurt feelings flew through one solicitor to another. Before Edith's death in 1964 the literary triumvirate was already extinct. By the time 'poor dear Osbert' followed 'poor dear Edith' to the grave in 1969, Sachie's once overwhelming love for both was to all intents and purposes atrophied.

With Georgia's death in 1980 Sachie lost his guiding star, and was never the same man again. He had little to cling to except memories, and they were fugitive. His mind began to wander. The stories got more and more involved, or dried up altogether. He could no longer write, not even poetry, which had been a solace after he abandoned prose and then lost Georgia. His sons were very good to their father, who had been a generous provider if not very paternal. Yet the presence of children was, like the absence of money, distracting. He was fortunate, if anyone in his late eighties and early nineties can ever be so described, in that he spent his decrepitude in the romantic old manor-house which he had inherited, looked after by one of nature's saints, Gertrude, who had been in Sitwell service for sixty years.

Rosamond Lehmann

1901–1990

THE THREE REMARKABLE Lehmann siblings were not exclusive; they did not put up a united barrier against the world, like the three Sitwells of a slightly earlier generation. They did not collectively rally against ignorance, philistinism and brutality, which as individuals each vehemently rebutted. At the same time they were perfectly conscious of their intellectual eminence. Independent they were, although the products of a shared upbringing.

The Lehmanns were actually a brood of four: three sisters and a younger brother. The eldest sister Helen, never in the public eye, would from what Rosamond told me have been accounted exceptional in an ordinary family. She married and led a retired life in Scotland. Sister Beatrix I often saw on the stage without knowing her. She was a great actress, a woman of powerful, astringent personality. One admired, even marvelled at her rendering of Miss Bordereau in *The Aspern Papers*, of Lady Macbeth, of the disturbing heroines of Ibsen plays, like Hedda Gabler. Totally uncompromising and lesbian, she was Marxist and disbelieving in God until her dying day.

John, the baby brother, was very well known in the literary field. He was immensely able and discerning. Like Beatrix he was more interpretative than creative, setting store by his poety which, though good, was not great. Yet he was a fine prose writer. His lives of Edward Lear and Rupert Brooke were first-

79

class biographies. His lasting achievement was the editorship of *New Writing* in which he promoted many young authors, several of whom, like Denton Welch, he established. In this respect he was magnanimous, though his nature was not generous. He could be cynical, snubbing, cantankerous and even cruel. Yet very charming too. Despising all sentiment, he was not always kind to Rosamond and positively mocked her later writings, especially those connected with psychical research, into which towards the end of her life she plunged heart, mind and soul. Rosamond, who at bottom remained *ingénue*, not unlike her own Rebecca Landon, did not comprehend his rancour, and felt hurt. Yet loyal as she always was to her family, she loved him in so far as she dared express tender feelings towards one so rebarbative of them.

The background of the Lehmann siblings was nineteenth-century free-thinking radicalism. Their grandfather, Frederick Lehmann, younger member of a large Jewish family of craftsmen and artists, had emigrated to England from Hamburg in the early 1850s. Determined to earn money, he worked for the English engineering firm of Naylor Vickers. But he was artistic and passionately musical. Sent by Vickers from London to Edinburgh, he soon joined a cultivated circle revolving round the brothers Robert and William Chambers, enterprising booksellers who out of nothing had founded the publishing firm of their name and launched *Chambers's Edinburgh Journal* in 1832. Robert was the more remarkable and go-ahead brother. As a youth he introduced himself to Sir Walter Scott, for whom he did minor literary services, earning the great man's respect, and commendations which stood him in good stead. He wrote local histories before tackling the work which brought him much money, namely *Vestiges of the Natural History of Creation*, and which he published anonymously in 1844. It went through many editions, was widely read and almost universally condemned for the heterodox views on evolution it revealed, views which in a broad sense anticipated Darwin's *Origin of Species* by fifteen years. When in the 1880s the true authorship of *Vestiges of Creation* was disclosed Robert, who was a profound believer in the Christian faith, desperately minded the adverse criticism he received.

Young Frederick Lehmann became a frequent visitor to Robert Chambers's Edinburgh household, where he enjoyed countless evenings with a family as musical as himself. He was in his element and would sing to Nina, one of Robert's daughters, who was a talented pianist. She was also lively, extremely well read and of an enchanting disposition. In 1852 Frederick and Nina married. In due course they moved to London where they in their turn formed a musical and literary circle, comprising such distinguished persons as Joachim, Pauline Viardot, Dickens, Wilkie Collins, Browning, Bulwer Lytton and Richard Monckton Milnes. Frederick's business interests often took him abroad, sometimes for long spells. The devoted pair corresponded at length, and wretched though the absences made Nina, they turned her into an incomparable correspondent. Her letters, a selection of which John Lehmann published in 1962 in *Ancestors and Friends*, can, as he modestly averred, be compared for wit, descriptive ability, sharpness, openness of mind, only with those of Virginia Woolf – but without the bite.

Rosamond was extremely proud of her Scottish descent, as well she might be, and of her Chambers forebears' adherence to the Jacobite cause. She gave me a contemporary portrait of Bonnie Prince Charlie, inherited from her grandfather, which she had previously lent to a great friend, Hester Chapman, the novelist and biographer, for her life. I assured Rosamond that when my lease expired, it would be returned to her descendants.

Frederick had a brother, Rosamond's great-uncle Rudolph Lehmann, who likewise migrated to England where he became a popular Victorian portrait painter. In 1861 Rudolph married Amelia, another accomplished daughter of Robert Chambers. In 1894 he published *An Artist's Reminiscences* of the celebrated people who were his friends and frequently his sitters.

Rosamond's father, Frederick's son Rudolph Chambers Lehmann, was a Liberal MP, and a contributor to *Punch*. A champion in mind and physique, journalist, barrister, oarsman, sportsman, he is described in *The Dictionary of National Biography* as 'talented but without driving ambition'. His wife Alice Marie Davis, of old New England Puritan stock, was a beautiful woman whom her children reverenced and adored. In their London house and later at Bourne End, where Rudolph Chambers Lehmann built a house on the Thames, they received, just as Frederick and Nina had done, writers, musicians, actors and actresses. I once gave Rosamond a lock of Dickens's hair with a card, certifying its authenticity, in the handwriting of the novelist's sister-in-law Georgina Hogarth, who surely loved him more than did his wife Catherine. Rosamond, with the true novelist's vivid recall of childhood impressions, gave me an exact and moving description of the stout old lady's appearance and dress when she visited Mrs Lehmann's drawing-room. Her thin white hair was parted in the middle, with corkscrew curls at the sides. Half her head was covered with lace. She was swathed in black bombazine which rustled as she talked in a faraway voice.

Rosamond loved her childhood home on the Thames, making it and the neighbourhood the background scenes of nearly all her stories, although she drew the participants from stock-broking, games-addicted families, very unlike the intellectual set which revolved around her parents.

If her childhood spanned the carefree, prosperous reign of King Edward VII her adolescence coincided – for she was thirteen in 1914 – with the Great War. When that devastating episode was over she was on the verge of emancipation from the schoolroom. Having been educated at home by the usual succession of governesses, she became a scholar at Girton College, Cambridge.

This might have been a fairly innovatory step for a girl from a rich and protective upper-middle-class background. But her parents, who were not conventional, circumscribed or over-solicitous, fully approved. On leaving Cambridge Rosamond lost little time in making the best of her fortune, which was by no means only her face, but her mind and general distinction, for she was tall and slender, with an upright figure. As for her head it was of great beauty, carried by a long, proud neck. She had classical features and wonderful slanting, hawk-like eyes, also inherited by her brother John. She had an abundance of curling hair, which quickly turned grey. (In her middle and old age this pile of curls, then rinsed pink, was her most conspicuous attribute. It led Maurice Bowra to refer to her bitchily as the meringue-outang.)

At once she was taken up by the Sitwells, Bloomsbury and the literary and art avant-garde generally, not to mention the social hostesses. The young men fell at her feet like ninepins. It was not long before she was married to Walter Runciman, brother of (Sir) Steven Runciman and rich heir to a baronetcy (later a viscountcy). This marriage, like Rosamond's second, and indeed nearly all her subsequent love affairs, ended disastrously. While her husband worked in the family shipping business the couple lived in Newcastle upon Tyne, which proved uncongenial to the young wife, whose world was already cosmopolitan. As their relations deteriorated so did the affection of his parents who, having at first welcomed the scintillating bride, turned against what they came to consider a designing minx.

In her disillusionment and wretchedness Rosamond began writing her first and most famous, but by no means best, novel, *Dusty Answer*. Published in 1927, it had instantaneous success; was translated into numerous languages and in France, as *Poussière*, was more acclaimed than in any other country. Rosamond later resented her renown for this juvenile work.

Extraordinary though it may seem today, *Dusty Answer* deeply shocked her parents' generation, because of its intimations of free love, or rather of the author's acceptance of intermarital infidelity without a qualm of conscience. Today the novel, still eminently readable, strikes us, accustomed as we are to the baldest descriptions of physical practices and anatomical details, as being correct as a tale by Charlotte M. Yonge.

Before Rosamond freed herself from her first non-marriage, as she subsequently termed it (a period of her life on which she was reluctant to dwell), she had fallen madly in love with Wogan Philipps, later the Communist peer, Lord Milford. This liaison finding no favour either with his or her parents, the errant couple were obliged to live, certainly before they were able to marry, almost entirely on Rosamond's literary earnings.

A Note in Music, inspired by her dismal life in Newcastle, followed in 1930, and *The Weather in the Streets* in 1936. Both these mature books increased her reputation among the intelligentsia, and were eventually made into a sort of composite play called *No More Music.*

Rosamond was not a prolific writer, any more than she was a promiscuous lover. Her novels took years of gestation, just as her attachments were slow to catch fire and became tenaciously monogamous. In fact, her attachments eclipsed all her other interests. Whereas mental discipline, controlling her extraordinary imagination, fashioned her books into works of art, the emotions with which her affections were charged destroyed, in a sense, her loves. She was overwhelming in her demands and proprietary in their realization. In love she played no gentle solo. She gave vent like a full orchestra to a resounding symphony of sound and fury. These performances led to chaos, terror in her partners, and their eventual escape in a way which was often covert, abrupt and unkind. The renegades would then be pursued by Rosamond with bitter recrimination and not unjustifiable grievance. Although the marriage to Wogan Philipps did not endure it brought her ineffable happiness in the birth of two children, a daughter Sally and son Hugo.

I barely knew Rosamond while these tempestuous storms were brewing, raging and reaching their inevitable climax. A diminuendo is hardly the appropriate term for what followed. Her affairs ended, not with a whimper but with a bang, rather like the shrieks of a Grecian chorus in *Electra.* The most notable were with Geronwy Rees, leader-writer and don, and the poet Cecil Day-Lewis. After the latter's sudden and greatly distressing jilt Rosamond enjoyed an interval of comparative calm in a bestowed and reciprocated love.

The experiences of her harrowing love affairs were inevitably reflected in all her novels, notably in the two masterpieces *The Ballad and the Source*, which Logan Pearsall Smith pronounced the best novel since Henry James, and *The Echoing Grove*. Certainly both must be accounted among the best mid twentieth-century novels, if it is not exaggeration to call the former the very best. The portrait of Sibyl Jardine, that injured, unscrupulous, ruthless woman of persuasive authority and sinister machinations, has none of the ingredients of the author's self. It is just a smashing creation of her fertile mind.

Although no professing feminist (she actually disliked the Women's Lib. movement), from the beginning to the end of her writings Rosamond raised the agonized cry of the woman wronged in love and a diatribe against, not the calculated wickedness of man, but his pitiable weakness allied to cowardice. Ricky in *The Echoing Grove* is for all his dalliance and feebleness an object of pity, the victim of his ill-fated charm. This novel was to be her last for several years. In the ensuing decades she kept herself busy with reviews, occasional short stories and articles, and the vice-presidency of the writers' union PEN. A domestic catastrophe, which she took extremely badly, prevented concentration on another sustained novel.

In 1958 her daughter Sally, happily married to the poet P.J. Kavanagh, died in Java. Rosamond was prostrated with grief. On to this sweet and lovable child she had projected her own personality. She made a mistake, for Sally's character entirely lacked her mother's fire and brimstone and capacity for self-immolation. Sally was placid, level-headed, and not creative. Nevertheless in her daughter's sunny disposition Rosamond somehow quenched her own fret and fury. In Sally's bright future she had anticipated a vicarious happiness for her own old age. She had built her daughter up as the cathartic means of her own salvation from the horrors of old age and loneliness. Now the whole dream-like fabric had collapsed. The focus of her powers of enduring love had gone. There was seemingly no possible substitute. After a period of intense misery and lamentation she derived some comfort, not to say a glimmer of renewed hope, from the shattering tribulation. With the help of psychical research she became convinced that her daughter survived on a preternatural plane, condescending from time to time, as Nancy Mitford cruelly put it, to slide down to Rosamond on a sunbeam. A friend in need, Cynthia Sandys, widow of a saintly landowning peer in Worcestershire, was the principal medium in establishing contact with her daughter's psyche.

Rosamond's ultimate beliefs, reached by a process of rational exegesis – for she was a profoundly intellectual woman – were expressed, if not convincingly explained, in a short book, *The Swan in the Evening*, published in 1967. At the same time she became a fervent, unwavering Christian – at least, this is what she honestly maintained – while refusing to be initiated into any Church. Instead she became a member of the College of Psychic Studies, and eventually its vice-president. These backslidings from the agnosticism of the majority of her friends and the atheism of the Bloomsbury set to which her brother John was closely linked, provoked their ridicule and even hostility. Rosamond minded their derision, but would not be deflected from her convictions.

One last novel, *A Sea-Grape Tree*, followed in 1976. It was not up to the standard of her best work. She did not write another.

The Rosamond I knew and dearly loved was a tolerant, understanding, deeply read and highly educated woman. Her memory was prodigious. She was a disciplined and professional writer. She was inward-looking and outward-giving. Upon her children, grandchildren and friends she directed her energies and affections without stint. Towards the end of her life, when immobile and practically blind, she positively lived for their welfare, supported by her unorthodox brand of Christian faith.

I recall her when we first met, in her flowering and beautiful middle age; it must have been after my marriage in 1951, through Alvilde, one of whose friends she then was. How often did I not dine in her pretty flat in Eaton Square behind windows looking down upon the flat tree-tops. Three was her favourite number, so long as the two guests were congenial to each other, for she was curiously shy, shown by the hesitations of her speech, until the company warmed up. Sometimes I sat with her and Jim Mossman, a tragically gifted man with whom Ros was platonically in love, and whom she desperately attempted, in vain, to prevent from taking his life. Talk would range over every subject under and, one might say, behind the sun. Slowly and deliberately, after much forethought, and between short gusts of rather stifled laughter as though seeking our approval, Rosamond would give rein, in clear and earnest tones remarkable for their sincerity, to her views while reclining on the sofa, enveloped in a kaftan, her noble head always in profile, gazing, seldom at her interlocutor, but into space, and pulling at a cigarette in a long, elegant holder.

William Plomer

1903–1973

WILLIAM PLOMER WAS one of the intimate friends whom I very seldom saw and (to be truthful) knew very little. If his shade could be made aware of my claims to his intimacy, he might well declare them grossly presumptuous. And I have no idea how far, if at all, I registered with him. I believe we did not meet more than a dozen times in all. The first was through an introduction by Eddie Sackville-West in the coffee room at Brooks's during the war. I was lunching by myself. They beckoned me over to their table and we drank coffee together. I recorded him then as 'a thick-set man with small moustache, age about forty'. His face was unremarkable until I had the chance of looking closely into it. It was not altogether unlike what Philip Larkin's turned out to be, only more refined. His manner was gentle but when he spoke, he spoke forcibly. He had rather a winning smile. He was by no means handsome, and resembled the sort of decent shy man you might hope, after the death of someone near to you, to encounter at the undertaker's. I went away enchanted.

Years later we were brought together through the death of his half-brilliant, half-mad cousin Richard Rumbold, who one fine day in a Taormina hotel, while (seemingly) happy in dictating part of a book to his devoted friend and minder Hilda Young, walked to the window and hurled himself through the glass roof of the lounge at the feet of people drinking *tisanes* and eating *petits fours*. William was cogitating whether to edit the diaries which, as literary executor, he had come upon among Richard's papers. Having lunched together (on the first of several occasions) we parted at half-past five, both firmly under the impression that it was only half-past two. Subsequently he stayed with Alvilde and me for a weekend in the country. Again, I recall the three of us talking far into the night. He and I corresponded, not often but fairly regularly, and anyone reading our letters might, I daresay, assume that we had been friends of a lifetime. Alas, I wish I could boast this had been the case. Nevertheless, I looked upon him as one of the dwindling band whom I held in much affection. In other words, I suppose we clicked. At any rate I clicked. There were things about him which were very engaging. He had a deep and velvety voice which caressed and made acceptable the gentle irony of all his utterances. He was not only intensely wise – he peered through owl-like spectacles with the thickest lenses imaginable – he was wrily humorous and, above all, infinitely understanding and sympathetic.

There was no subject which I could not talk or write to him about, no opinion that he brushed aside as boring or re-pugnant. If I felt like this about him, how much more those older friends who saw him constantly over long years must have so felt, I just cannot imagine. I suspect that he often aroused affections and devotions which were an embarrass-ment to him, since he was a natural recluse and did not need the society of fellow creatures unless he was in love with them. He seldom stayed away from home, in fact hated doing so. Nor, I gathered, did he often invite even the most privileged to stay with him. It was only by reading, posthumously, his autobiographies that I learnt how undomesticated he was, how indifferent to immediate environment and even to possessions, of which he had very few. Like many celebrated poets (Byron, for example, and Shelley, whose living-rooms were, accord-ing to friends, not merely chaotic but totally non-aesthetic), it may be that he was blind to everyday surroundings, as though the narrow belt between the inner eye and the eye which encompasses the distant landscape and the cerebral concepts beyond were a closed vision to a man suffering from glaucoma.

Towards the end of his life he lived in a large nondescript house, number 45 Adastra Avenue, Hassocks, Sussex (which, he remarked, sounded like three sneezes). His establishment consisted of one ailing servant-cum-companion of long standing – a gondolier? a Turk? an Arab? his fleeting mention led me at the time erroneously to wonder – who, I have since learnt, was a refugee from Nazi Germany, a shy, retiring and devoted helper, rescued by William before the Second World War from some menial and uncongenial job in Soho.

William Plomer had been born and brought up in the Transvaal in a small town called Pietersburg, the son of a South African government official of English descent. His father, Charles Campbell Plomer, the younger son of an old landed family, had decided at an early age to seek his fortune in the dominion. Not a highly educated or sensitive man, Charles nevertheless treated the native Africans under his jurisdiction with justice and, better still, unwonted kindness and sympathy. But he was by nature mercurial and spendthrift. William's mother, Edythe, also of what used to be described as gentle, and certainly of clerical stock, was an extremely pious Anglican, well read, broad-minded and infinitely tender. Accustomed to a well-run and comfortable Nottinghamshire home, surrounded by adoring relations, she did not adapt happily to the rigours and tumble of a poor white husband's domicile in a circumscribed South African community.

William's first induction to learning was at St John's Roman Catholic College in Johannesburg. He never forgot the kindliness of the simple fathers who guided his infant footsteps. At the age of nine, on the outbreak of the First World War, he was sent to a preparatory school in Kent, which he loathed. The experience inculcated in him a lasting rebelliousness against all established institutions and conformity to regulation, and also a tendency to secrecy. In the holidays he lived with a maternal aunt, Hilda, to whom he became much attached and whom he regarded as a substitute mother. And then he went to Rugby School, which he loved. Unfortunately this lasted only a year, because of serious trouble with his eyesight and a threat of complete blindness. For obscure reasons his parents thought fit, in 1917, to call him home to Pietersburg, where one might suppose oculists were no better qualified than in England. One reason may have been Charles's fear lest his son, were he to stay longer in England, might become too exquisite in his habits to readjust to the easy manners of South African people. Indeed William recounted an amusing incident that took place in a hotel at Cape Town soon after his return. At dessert the boy washed a bunch of grapes in the finger bowl provided before eating them. Suddenly Charles lost his temper, thumped the table and roundly abused his son for over-delicacy. William retorted, 'I shall do what I like', and promptly gave the grapes a second rinse. Thenceforward relations between father and son were strained.

At all events, William was sad to leave behind at Rugby the first companions of his childhood whom he had found literarily inclined and even literate. Soon the inevitable question arose: what was he to do for a living? For lack of any other opening he felt obliged to take a job as farm apprentice on the Basutoland border. With his Rugby School friendships in mind he felt like a fish out of water on an isolated prairie station owned by a rough-and-ready albeit indulgent Boer, with whom he got on fairly well. In this lonely outpost he wrote poetry which he submitted by mail to Harold Monro, the highly esteemed founder of the Poetry Bookshop in London. Monro dispensed encouragement, but little applause. Plomer felt that he belonged nowhere, a sophisticated South African who had tasted cultural life in England, with a message to convey and no one to heed it. His upbringing among and his experiences of working with black Africans as his fellows, together with his nonconformist and compassionate nature, made him vehemently opposed to the colour barrier in South Africa. He became deeply resentful of the unquestioned dominance of whites over blacks throughout the whole continent. He had to give vent to his feelings in some medium or other. The easiest path for a tyro who shunned ambition and leadership and was disinclined to stand for Parliament was writing. And yet he was fully aware that thereby he would arouse first the suspicion and then the hostility of the Dutch and Anglo-Saxon settlers, who would regard him as a traitor to kith and kin.

Somewhat incongruously, it may be thought, he linked up with a Fascist-minded countryman, the poet Roy Campbell. In the early 1920s Roy Campbell had not yet emerged in those extreme and always rather absurd political colours which made him so hated throughout the rest of the decade. For Roy Campbell was an example of that type of earnest person whose tendency to exaggerate in order to make a point turns their true inward principles, which may even be just and acceptable, into travesties, leading into cumulative folly and often inviting unmerited obloquy. The Roy Campbell connection was pre-eminently a literary one. Poets were rare in South Africa and the two men were thrown together by a mutual urge to compose verse. Together they co-edited a periodical, *Voorslag*, which, having democratic overtones, mostly supplied by Campbell, did not 'take' with Dutch- or English-speaking readers. *Voorslag* did not survive beyond three issues.

Meanwhile Plomer moved with his parents to Entumeni, an uninviting township in Zululand where, out of filial loyalty and in spite of disinclination, William helped his improvident father to keep shop in a new venture, a native trading station. There he managed to write his first novel, *Turbott Wolfe*, which through the indirect solicitation of Harold Monro was published in London by the Hogarth Press in 1926. Its anti-racist tone and the daring introduction into the story of a white and black marriage made the author even more unpopular with the white community in South Africa than he had been before. The seemingly mild and diffident poet had become a fearless warrior in the incipient conflict with apartheid. Another friend and contemporary ally of these years was Laurens van der Post. Between these two an enduring sympathy was to grow. Whereas William's friendship with

Campbell soon cooled in the face of the latter's violent right-wing views and often outrageous behaviour, that with van der Post was cemented by a mutual determination to better the lot of coloured people the world over. In an obituary appreciation sent to *The Times* on William's death van der Post recorded that no white man in South Africa had been so courageous or done so much for the black cause.

Spurned by the settlers whom he regarded as barbarians, made furious by their malevolent reception of his novel and frustrated by his powerlessness to stop racial segregation, William decided quixotically to shake the dust of South Africa from his feet. The stir made by *Turbott Wolfe* convinced Charles Plomer that his son's literary ambitions were serious; moreover, he shared his political convictions. Generously he gave consent to William quitting the hated Kaffir store at Entumeni. Within three days William and Laurens set sail together for Japan. William was not to return to South Africa for thirty years.

The way their departure came about was as strange as it was unpremeditated. Van der Post met a friendly and Anglophile Japanese naval captain of *samurai* rank about to sail from Durban to Tokyo. Captain Mori had recently learned that two Japanese tourists had been insulted as niggers by an Englishwoman in Pretoria and that van der Post had indignantly intervened on their behalf. Accordingly he offered Laurens and William free passage in his cargo boat; he became a great friend of both. While van der Post returned to South Africa with Mori in his next navigational circuit, Plomer remained in Japan for two and a half years.

William retained an immutable love for the African landscape which had first evoked in him a response to nature in poetry and song. Until his dying day he recalled it with nostalgia and much feeling, as expressed in *African Poems*, of which 'Tugela River' is often quoted in anthologies.

> The winter river, much reduced,
> Past shaped alluvial clean white sand,

Past stalks of maize upright but dead
In hillside patches poorly tilled
By dwellers under domes of reeds
Who by their poverty seemed to expiate
Their furious past.

Even in his poetry, politics were never far away. The beauties of plant, animal, bird and insect life, of light, cloud, lake and sky had always to be celebrated against a backcloth of the indigenous people's misery. Most of *African Poems* were overtly satirical at the expense of bloated imperialist white men exploiting the noble black workers, whom Plomer would never admit were savages in the raw. He consistently ignored the patent cruelty to which the tribes were prone amongst themselves, just as he gave no credit to the white man for those benefits he conferred upon the indigenous inhabitants. It was all too easy for William to relentlessly mock, revile and make fun of the explorer, the pioneer, the Boer, the big-game hunter whose insensitivity, greed, and arrogance were too often hard to stomach, as in the following alliterative stanza, which is little more than a schoolboy's outburst of indignation:

A big-game hunter opens fire once more,
Raconteur, roué, sportsman, millionaire and bore –
But only shoots his mouth off, knowing how
He's safer on a sofa than on far safari now.

Yet not all these men whom William castigated as oppressors were devoid of principle and a sense of Christian, or Judaic, justice and compassion. Some of them (poor deluded fools, anticipating posterity's gratitude) honestly believed that they were spreading the gospel of perpetual peace, goodwill and prosperity in the path of primitive peoples.

Plomer's poem 'A Transvaal Morning' (under the subordinate heading 'After Thirty Years') was to express a maturer appreciation of a landscape under 'saffron glare... sharper than a quince', yet a landscape still rendered false by the iniquities enacted daily upon it.

The strangeness plucked the stranger like a string.
They say the constant sun outstares the mind,
Here in this region of the fang, the sting,
And dulls the eye to what it most defines.

The middle-aged prodigal son never ceased to be beguiled by memories of his native land's stark and staring sun and its primeval colours, of the moss-green thrush, the shoulders of quartz on the hillside, the glitter of diamonds beneath the earth's sullen surface which had so incited the explorers' cupidity and rape. But he never allowed himself to be seduced by these memories into returning to live in Africa.

On quitting his homeland for the second time the twenty-three-year-old William, penniless, ventured to another continent and another alien culture. In Japan he subsisted on what he earned from teaching English; and he relished a new landscape and new friendships. The fruits of the Japanese mill amounted to several short stories. *Poems Written in Japan* were not so evocative, nor indeed so provocative, as those written about Africa. That they were not so provocative was because the militaristic nationalism which was to disturb Japan's well-wishers in the Thirties and terrify and disgust the Allies during the Second World War was still dormant. The Japan of the mid Twenties was a very different nation from what it became within the decade of William's sojourn: and still more different from what it is now. It was a land cut off from the west, geographically and culturally. Its people were children of a very ancient feudal and rural society. They were self-contained, contentedly divided into noblemen and artisans, lacking a middle class, unexploited and uninfluenced by distant powers. Japan was not then the highly industrialized and intensely organized country of today. There was no overt political issue for William with his Shelleyan ideals to grapple with or kick against. Instead his muse was free to dwell upon and be stirred by the harvest of Japanese nature in azaleas, chrome-yellow-leaved ginkgo trees, heraldic paulownia avenues and fat autumnal persimmons: and above all, the beauty of the

Japanese youth of both sexes, with their smooth, expansive brows, gerontophilic, far-apart eyes set aslant and evocative of the paternal instincts in western admirers, their mouths like pouting rosebuds – all features to which William was particularly susceptible. Not that this meant he frequented the geisha haunts and brothels of Tokyo. Far from it. His tastes were homoerotic and his inclinations monogamous. He fell deeply in love with a youth from whom his eventual parting was very difficult and distressing. But on this aspect of his make-up he was particularly guarded. There are the merest pointers to it in his writings, and it was not until I read his autobiographies after his death (before his sympathetic biography by Peter Alexander, published in 1989) that I had an inkling of it. One might say – or, rather, one would have said of William Plomer a quarter of a century ago – that he was the most correct and circumspect writer alive.

In 1929 he was back again in London. One of the first things he did in the process of re-Anglicizing himself, which I find rather touching, was to change the pronunciation of his surname from Plomer to Plumer, while retaining the spelling – quite a difficult feat, and one indicative of his wish to reintegrate with his English family culture.

In no time William was knocking on the doors of Bloomsbury. Leonard and Virginia Woolf (who had already published that first novel which got him into so much trouble at home) took him up, and E.M. Forster became a close friend. Virginia, having at once grasped to her heart the new young poet from faraway continents, soon characteristically began to find fault. 'A little too rigid I fear, and too much of a gentleman' was perceptive in one who knew this attribution to be the last any true Bloomsburyite wished ascribed to him, yet was strange from her at a time when she was infatuated with Vita Sackville-West largely on account of her nobility. Virginia was hard to please. And then she complained of his verbosity. 'Talk, talk, talk,' she who revelled in conversation commented tersely. 'A compressed inarticulate young man,' she confided to her diary of 15 August 1929, 'who tells a nice, dry prim story.'

At least this entry shows an understanding of his shyness and his readiness to please. Presumably unaware of her stricture upon his inability to present himself clearly, William was to write years later of their friendship, 'She was at her best with persons who like herself were not merely articulate but articulate in a new way.' How little do the young know the impression they are making upon their elders. Then Virginia was to observe ambiguously, 'but [Plomer] has the wild grey eyes which I noticed in Tom [T.S. Eliot] and take to be the true index of what goes on within.' What those grey eyes indicated she did not enlarge upon. One can only surmise. The tumultuous mind of a fellow poet behind them? Or, because to her all targets of the dart were the same, merely love gone awry?

Soon William was staying at the Woolfs' Sussex house, bringing with him a Firbankian Old Etonian painter three years his senior, Anthony Butts. Butts was the last male descendant of a family, in William's words, 'notable for its association with remarkable men, among them...Henry VIII, Holbein and Bacon' in the person of 'Dr Butts, Physician to the King', in Shakespeare's *King Henry VIII*. 'In a Bombed House', a very moving elegy in memory of Anthony, who took his own life during a London air raid, not in fear but out of boredom, contains Plomer's eloquent stanza on:

> Courage that throws the body like a glove
> At panzer Fate that crushes in its stride
> Man, concrete, harebell – Fate, the tank
> That never turns aside.

With Benjamin Britten, William struck up an alliance rather than a friendship. Their relations were mutually warm but wary, respectful and fruitful. *Gloriana*, not Britten's most successful opera and certainly not a felicitously chosen theme with which to celebrate the coronation of our young sovereign, was to Plomer's libretto, and led him to make frequent visits to Aldeburgh in spite of his hearth-binding dislike of staying away from home. It must be admitted that there was an

element of the brindled puss in William, which is said to have
struck his friend Stephen Spender so forcibly that it drove
Stephen into matrimony. At all events a full correspondence
relating to music and poetry ensued between Britten and Plomer.
It was Plomer who introduced Britten to the *Noh* plays, which
resulted in an amalgamation of Japanese theatre, as experienced
first-hand by the poet, and the composer's western music, in
three church operas ('chopperas', William called them) or
parables between 1964 and 1968, namely *Curlew River*, *The Burning
Fiery Furnace* and *The Prodigal Son*.

As a poet William is best known for his ballads – *London
Ballads*, *Country Ballads*, *Ballads Abroad* – ballads on topical
occasions; ballads kind, caustic, whimsical, tear-inducing; ballads
mocking, often very macabre, and somehow never malign.
Gruesome, certainly, like 'The Dorking Thigh', 'The Bungalows',
and 'Murder on the Downs'. And sad, like 'The Self-Made
Blonde', 'Atheling Grange', and 'Ludwig The Second' with its
haunting refrain, 'Remind me to look happier tomorrow.' And
all by the rebel satirist against authority. He became a master of
this particular medium of conveying what he absolutely thought
in deceptively facile scansion and rhythm. For unadultered wit
and humour I can think of no anecdotal ballad to beat 'The
Heart of a King: An Incident at Nuneham 1856', wherein the old
and bumbling lapidarist Dean Buckland gabbles:

> As I was going to say,
> As I was thinking just the other day,
> Memory's not as active as it was
> Since I was young (I *was* young, was I not?
> I ask because my memory's not
> As active as it was),
> Since I was young, I say,
> I've never tasted claret quite so choice,
> It warms the memory and restores the voice.

Dean Buckland, who prides himself on being able to identify,
blindfold, stones and marbles by one lick of the tongue, suffers
from an alarming hiccup:

I little thought I'd live to see the day
When I'd incorporate Le Roi Soleil,
Or even part of him.
What would he say
If he but knew an étranger
Had swallowed, like a pill, the very heart of him?

As I have already said, William among other friends got in touch with me on the untimely death of Richard Rumbold in 1961. Now, Richard was a manic-depressive with a touch of literary genius. His father had been a tyrannical brute and a bore of the first water. His mother, feeble and over-sensitive, committed suicide when her son was a schoolboy, by throwing herself into the Seine. His sister likewise took her life. Richard may have inherited insanity from either parent. He described his purgatorial youth and the effects it had upon his character as an adult in a brilliant autobiography, *My Father's Son*, which was published in 1949. Harold Nicolson praised it as 'a memorable description of the spirit of love conquering the demons of personal hatred'.

Richard's diaries were quite another matter. No less fascinating than the autobiography, they were candid, tormented, often repetitious, and more often than not quite unprintable. William nevertheless decided that they should not be ignored or destroyed, and that they must be tackled by himself, who had known and been fond of Richard and felt infinite compassion for his woes and recurrent ill health, physical and mental. Richard had been a victim of consumption, enduring with considerable valour years of agony and distress in and out of sanatoria before a cure was finally achieved. It is extraordinary to realize that even during my adulthood consumption was still the scourge which had destroyed countless generations of great-uncles and aunts in every family, not to mention geniuses like Keats, Chopin, the Brontës and Francis Thompson. It was still rampant and still being treated by a prolonged and painful process throughout the world. Now it is practically extinct in the West.

I was immensely struck by the delicacy with which William tackled the editing. There was much in the diaries – so William explained, for I never saw the manuscripts – to cause offence to the living, including those friends who had striven to help the author, and much to bring discredit upon him. An insensitive or an unscrupulous editor could have permitted the publication, to his own financial advantage, of a sensational, certainly a scandalous and an invidious, self-portrait of our friend. Not so William. On the contrary, in *A Message in Code* (1964) he produced a condensed, fair, yet truthful version of his cousin's diaries. In consequence they made so little sensation that I suppose few people read them. After all, Richard Rumbold was no public figure, having received scant notice from the literary reviewers in his lifetime. Nevertheless the book is in its way a minor classic about a gifted, tormented and pitiable soul. I cannot help suspecting that the reticent William, when wrestling with Richard Rumbold's confidences, may also have been wrestling with some similar predicaments in his own life.

In contrast, Plomer's editing and publication of the diaries of the Reverend Francis Kilvert (who was admittedly a far more remarkable figure than poor Richard Rumbold) received great acclaim. The editing of diaries, the pruning, the elimination of repetitions, the fashioning and balancing of the text without alteration or distortion, can surely be more of an art than the diarist's actual recorded words. Indeed, it is open to question whether a man's diary can ever be a work of art, any more than a photograph can; the very nature of its spontaneity, the shallowness of its impressions and their evanescence, prevent it.

Although in his own right and time a poet of the front rank – and I believe that his verses will be read in centuries to come when much of his better-known contemporaries' are forgotten – he was also endowed with the attributes of a biographer. He had the gift of entering into and sympathizing with the thoughts and feelings, however alien to him, of others. He had a humility and empathy rare in a man of his creative ability. These qualities were hugely appreciated by a whole generation of authors published by the firm of Jonathan Cape, whose literary adviser William Plomer became in 1937 in succession to that well known paragon among editors, Edward Garnett. One of the authors he was responsible for bringing to Cape's was Ian Fleming.

The last time I saw William was when he lectured on Francis Kilvert at the Royal Society of Literature in July 1972. What he had to say about his subject on this brief occasion was not of outstanding moment, for he had written and spoken about him at length many times before. But the way in which he quietly delivered the lecture was itself a work of art. In reading some funny passages from the diaries – funny because his tone of voice was in gentle mockery of the serious-minded cleric – he was obliged from time to time to stop and laugh, which greatly enhanced the amusement of the audience. Yet the amusement and fervour with which he spoke of Kilvert made me understand why Plomer loved him so much: it was because he was able to identify himself with this obscure Victorian country curate who peered so closely, almost myopically, just as William had to do through those thick lenses, into all natural things and creatures and saw deep meaning in little events. It was as though he was seeing through Kilvert's keen eyes and turning them upon the comicality of his own purblind self. There in the lecture room was a handsome and distinguished old man – which is what the dour and almost commonplace-looking young Plomer had turned into – with his white hair, sharp yet genial features, and beautiful manner, extolling the prose poet of exactly a hundred years before, the parish clergyman whom he had retrieved from oblivion for our perpetual delight and the immortality of them both.

Plomer could not be described as a religious believer, although he was certainly no atheist. Nor was he ever hostile to the Christian churches. On the contrary, he felt great sympathy for the Church of England and had always loved the Prayer Book liturgy in which he was brought up. It sometimes happens with sons of deeply religious mothers whose credulity when alive perhaps riled them, that on the mother's death they become subject to a compulsion, emotional, intellectual or gracious (in the divine sense), depending upon circumstances, to follow in the footsteps so long ignored and maybe spurned. After Edythe Plomer's death at the beginning of the Second World War William would often slip into a church for contemplation, and some indefinable solace. I once accompanied him to Clyro church in Radnorshire; it is true that he was to give an address on Kilvert from the pulpit, but he followed the service with an earnest, almost searching concentration that was very impressive. It is not improbable that his affection for Kilvert and admiration of the young clergyman's simplicity, sheer goodness, high spirits and devoutness, notwithstanding frailties which made him the more endearing, were further incitement to a return to Christianity. Kilvert had a weakness for young girls, and yet led an exemplary spiritual life. The Church of England did not cast him out, but embraced him. Who can tell in what direction William might have turned had he survived longer? As it was, his death from a heart attack happened within minutes. He went off like Hamlet's father's Ghost, 'Unhousel'd, disappointed [probably], unanel'd'. It is inconceivable to me that this courteous, gentle, brilliant man was not welcomed at the pearly gates with open arms.

Patrick Kinross

1904–1976

PATRICK BALFOUR BELONGED to that scintillating Oxford generation immediately before mine – by which I do not mean that mine was scintillating but that he went up three or four years before I did. He belonged to the group of Evelyn Waugh, Harold Acton, Peter Quennell, Cyril Connolly and Anthony Powell, eminent and revered figures in the retrospection of my age group. To their juniors in age they were a mixture of the socially sophisticated and the enviably gifted. They were notably Twentyish, and also alarming.

Whether Patrick could claim kinship – that very important issue among the Scots – with the really grand Balfour clans of Whittinghame, of Burleigh, of Inchyre, I imagine was doubtful. His branch derived from a line of worthy Lowland elders in Fife and ministers in Forfar. They were neither rich nor territorial, and Patrick was never to inherit a square inch of land. Two years before his birth in 1904 his grandfather was created a baron, modestly taking the title of Kinross, a tiny county which nestled against the border of the even tinier Clackmannan, and is nowadays smothered by Perthshire and Fife.

The grandfather had been a respected Lord Justice General and Lord President of the Court of Session in Scotland towards the end of Queen Victoria's reign, just as Patrick's father was an eminent jurist in King George V's. I never met him, but

knew Patrick's mother, a most charming and distinguished
Scottish gentlewoman with the faintest, just-perceptible timbre
in the voice which my several Scottish great-aunts shared and
which derived, I always liked to think, from the royal Stuart
court speaking amongst themselves in French. Her ambience
was as far removed from Mayfair as from the Antipodes, and
for all I know she may not have gone to England more than a
dozen times in her life. She was the most tolerant mother,
amused by the world her elder son had chosen to move in, and
relishing his stories of its goings-on. I described her in 1943 as
'silvery and radiantly good'. Patrick adored her and was devoted
to his three sisters, all of whom married scions of the Scottish
gentry. Lady Kinross was born Caroline Johnstone-Douglas
of Lockerbie, and through her Patrick was entitled by
that mysterious code of the Scotch to wear a tartan kilt which
gave him much pleasure. I remember him explaining to me
triumphantly how the right came from a Highland great-
grandmother, whereas no right came to me through my
great-grandmother who was a McFarlane. Although neither a
law lord nor a lord of territorial descent, Patrick eventually
inherited a perfectly authentic barony – notwithstanding Evelyn
Waugh's snide comparison with a mutual friend who, at the
same time, had inherited an earldom of long descent: 'Now he's
a *real* peer, unlike *you*, Patrick.'

Patrick's upbringing was not a country but an Edinburgh
one. For years his parents lived at number 17 Heriot Row, a
simple but dignified terrace house in the Adam tradition.
Heriot Row was part of Robert Reid's monumental and
residential northern extension of the city's New Town, dating
from the first decade of the nineteenth century. Number 17
had been the childhood home of Robert Louis Stevenson.
Patrick was immensely proud of his background, as he was of
his total Scotchness, and grateful to both his parents for not
having reared him in grandeur, luxury and idleness.

After Winchester, where I don't think he distinguished
himself inordinately, Patrick followed the normal course of a
bright Wykhamist to Oxford. Balliol College matriculated him.

At Oxford he at once plunged into the social and intellectual group I have already alluded to as being formidable to outsiders. There his closest friends were to be Evelyn Waugh and Cyril Connolly. Since Cyril had only just emerged from a platonic yet deeply emotional love for his Eton school-fellow Noel Blakiston and had not yet embarked upon a series of affairs with women, that with Patrick was a sort of stepping stone in his amorous career. Patrick was to claim that Cyril was the first person he had been to bed with. The somewhat gross physique and featureless face with tiny alert eyes now associated with the mature Cyril belie the merry guttersnipe charm of the youthful Cyril, a charm which survived his bodily declension through good living. In talking to me one day about Cyril's famous correspondence with Noel, Patrick said that he possessed at least forty letters written to him by Cyril. He claimed that they were even more brilliant than the published Eton ones. At Oxford Patrick was inevitably shepherded with the rest of his lot into the exclusive fold of Maurice Bowra, then Fellow and tutor at Wadham College, and only six years older than himself.

In the summer of 1927 Patrick and Cyril rented a small house off the Brompton Road, in Yeoman's Row, then comprising plain Regency artisan dwellings. Cyril dubbed it a slum street. The houses no longer exist: they were demolished soon after the last war and rebuilt along mock Georgian lines, fit for rich business executives. At number 26, which they referred to as the Yeo, the two young men, both aged twenty-three, were soon entertaining the literary lions of an older generation – Maurice Baring, Desmond and Molly McCarthy, Logan Pearsall Smith, the Sitwells, Harold Nicolson, and Rosamond Lehmann, whose 'good bad novel' *Dusty Answer* Cyril was much taken with, as well as their own contemporaries like Harold Acton and Kenneth and Jane Clark.

John Betjeman was very young when he first gained entry to this temple of nymphs and muses, androgynous playboys and bearded sages. The poem he addressed to Patrick for his seventieth birthday is not one of his most accomplished,

but it sums up in his unique and evocative manner the feel
of the Yeo towards the end of the Twenties. And it
pays tribute to the joy that Patrick then dispensed to all and
sundry, while touching upon the hero's kindness and
generosity.

> How glad I am that I was bound apprentice
> To Patrick's London of the 1920s . . .
> Kind fortune led me, how I do not know,
> To that Venetian flat-cum-studio
> Where Patrick wrought his craft in Yeoman's Row.
> For Patrick wrote *and* wrote. He wrote to live:
> What cash he had left over he would give
> To many friends and friends of friends he knew,
> So that the 'Yeo' to one great almshouse grew –
> Not a teetotal almshouse, for I hear
> The clink of glasses in my memory's ear.

Betjeman was much in Patrick's confidence during the trying
time when he was endeavouring to keep his first jobs, first
as secretary to Sir Horace Plunkett, and then as a private
schoolmaster, each of which came to a speedy and ignominious
end. Sir Horace's chief appeal to John lay, not in his justifiable
claim to have promoted agricultural development in Ireland on
a large scale (a signally un-Betjemanian interest), but in his
experience of reading, after a false report of his death in 1920,
some unflattering obituary notices of himself in the
newspapers. When John found himself jobless and moneyless
he was taken, out of the goodness of Patrick's heart, into the
Yeo almshouse for nothing. Patrick was then editor of a social
column in the *Daily Sketch*.

Cyril, who still kept up a correspondence with him, though
on a lower key, informed Noel that he got on perfectly well
with Patrick. He described him as incorrigibly social, and
evidently he was not to be bracketed with them as serious, in
that he was 'an amateur pro intellectual', which was 'a good
thing in itself', and showed a correct disposition. The diagnosis
was not entirely short of the mark.

It is true Patrick Balfour was not, strictly speaking, an intellectual, like Cyril and Noel. He was conspicuously one of the Bright Young People. He went to every party and participated in every escapade that raised eyebrows and infuriated the remnants of the pre-1914 generation. Elizabeth Pelly (the first girl to wear shingled hair), Elizabeth Ponsonby ('in leopard-skins') and Brenda Dean Paul, addicted to drink and drugs, were among his intimates. Always amused by the vagaries, quirks and conceits of the privileged among whom he moved, he cultivated an air of cynicism and mocking disillusion. Having very little money of his own, he managed to jog along on the strength of his gossip-writer's passport, his fine figure and presence. Never strictly handsome, for he had rather staring pop eyes, he was eminently personable, had charm, was an enjoyer, responsive, optimistic – and heir to a peerage, which helped, however much he played it down. He knew everyone. This is an overdone phrase, but to no other of my contemporaries is it more pertinent. Rich and poor, upper class and lower, devout and wicked, staid and raffish, highbrow and low, all accepted Patrick's invitations, all were grist to his mill. All were pleased to see him.

The life Patrick led was reflected in his first book, *Society Racket*, published in 1933. *Society Racket* was not a bad book, although some critics made out that it was mere gossip, beneath contempt, and that Patrick was biting the hands that had fed him. Its theme was that the roaring Twenties were a decade in which the children of those men and women directly involved in the hell of the First World War sought to escape from its haunting memories in an *après moi le déluge* attitude, while well aware that the unavoidable social changes wrought by the war meant their lives of licence could not endure.

Theirs 'was in every sense an age of transition...', he wrote. 'It had the best of both worlds: the remaining dignity of an aristocratic order combined with the luxuries of a cosmopolitan machine-civilization...' It was 'a turbulent epoch', he admitted somewhat melodramatically, 'but vital. We fiddled while London burned. We ate, we drank, we were merry, for we knew that today we should die. We counted not the cost.' Their hedonism was really a protest of the aesthetes against the hearties who had dominated the social world too long, of the Bright Young People against the reactionary capitalists who had brought about the horrific war in which all had suffered so much, and which had made the consciences of the next generation so uneasy.

In years to come Patrick was shy when reminded of *Society Racket*. Yet it is an interesting commentary on the social manners of the time and often very funny, especially when it recounts the mad crazes which the upper crust launched upon a bewildered, sometimes angered, but usually copy-cat world of would-be sophisticates. First of all there were the dotty refinements of jazz-dancing – the Twinkle, the Missouri Walk, the Flirtation and the Camel Walk. Everyone took to dancing like lunatics on the slightest provocation, in between courses at restaurants, by day as well as by night, in public and at home, to the gramophone, the carpets having been kicked back. There were dance halls in practically every street throughout the land, to which young and old with ten minutes to spare would resort. Men had even been known to jump from a taxi caught in a traffic queue, dash into a hall, seize a strange lady, take a whirl, and jump back into the cab. Then there was the motor-scooter mania. Women were particularly partial to it. The scooter was held to be useful for shopping but, there being no seat, you had to stand and balance, slinging carrier-bags over the handle-bars – if you were not stationary on the pavement, tinkering with the carburettor to make the engine start. And there was the pogo-stick. The mania for this idiotic and dangerous toy spread to the provinces. Even my father, who was not given to manifestations of extreme folly, imagined he was a proficient exponent of the pogo-stick art. One Christmas morning on the slippery stone path leading from my grandmother's house to the gate he demonstrated before a gathering of carol singers. Alas, he wobbled, and fell flat on his face. In ignominy and considerable anguish he was carried indoors. Since this was a period when we were all, in John

Betjeman's words, 'estranged from parents', I remember, to my shame, being not totally displeased.

The whole of Patrick's adolescence and his early adulthood fell within this stimulating decade, the zenith of which was reached while he was still at Oxford. Nostalgically he recounted the drunken orgies of John Sutro's exclusive Railway Club dinners. The young bloods would board the Penzance –Aberdeen express at Oxford station, drink themselves silly, and disembark at Leicester. There they crossed the platform to the Aberdeen–Penzance express, and climbed into a reserved dining-car. On the return journey they would eat, continue drinking, and speechify themselves even sillier still, to be ejected at Oxford station the worse for wear, but in time to be let into or to clamber into their respective colleges before midnight struck. Writing in the Thirties, Patrick deplored the decline of these patrician practices and the emergence among Oxford undergraduates (and in London society, too) of a dreary, middle-class culture. Yet while Patrick was participating in these juvenile pranks, he somehow stood aloof as the detached, amused, indifferent observer. Perhaps that is what Evelyn meant by his remark about Patrick being not a proper peer. In *Society Racket* Patrick stated that the anonymous Dragoman of the *Daily Express* was the first gossip columnist to take a Gilbertian view of the peerage. If so, then he himself was undoubtedly the second.

While *Society Racket* was in the printers' hands in September 1932 I stayed with Patrick, his mother and two of his sisters on the island of Lismore, in Loch Linnhe between Mull and Oban. Lady Kinross had rented it, not for stalking, fishing or anything of that sort, but for walks, expeditions in an ancient motor-boat, and actual bathing in the loch. The *Sketch* devoted an illustrated page to the party, which included the sisters paddling among rocks and about to dive into the icy waters. Lady Kinross was photographed, benevolent and matriarchal, in an old felt hat drawn over her brows, next to Patrick resplendent in kilt, sporran, and bonnet worn at a rakish angle somewhat incongruous for the Highlands. The guests, besides myself, were Margaret, the sculptor Clare Sheridan's nubile daughter with whom Patrick fancied he was in love, and the architect Frederick Etchells and his dear wife Hester. Etchells, as he was invariably addressed as though he possessed no first name, was one of Betjeman's beloved butts. His eccentricity was considerable, his genius acknowledged by John (and seemingly nobody else) in between teases. Etchells seldom drew breath but although undeniably long-winded and husky-voiced, was never boring to us. Concerned as he was mainly with church commissions, he had an unrivalled knowledge of ritual and theology. His *Architectural Setting of the Anglican Worship* was a classic on the subject. He was also, with Canon G.W.O. Addleshaw, the translator into English of Le Corbusier's revolutionary theories of aesthetics. In the autumnal Lismore evenings Etchells dragooned us into playing Consequences in rhymed couplets of the most hilariously non-theological sort.

One of the nastiest experiences of my life happened during this otherwise enchanting visit. It led me to a realization which, alas, has since too often been confirmed, that my inadequacy during a crisis is deeply reprehensible and shameful. It ensues from lack of all practical instruction when I was at school, undergoing probably the most expensive education in the world. Patrick and I were walking away from a picnic luncheon with the family under a cliff. We came upon an enormous stag, termed a royal, which had evidently fallen from the heights on to the shingle below, but too far from the sea at high tide to be swept away. The stag must have been lying a long time in great distress. The stertorous breathing was agonizing to watch. Two legs were hopelessly broken. There was only one thing that ought to be done, and that quickly. But how were we to put it out of its misery? We had no rifle, no implement with which to knock it on the head. Desperately we ran back to the picnic basket. There was one small blunt knife that would not have peeled a banana, far less have cut a stag's jugular vein. Meanwhile Lady Kinross and the sisters were exhorting us to be men and kill the poor, proud, and beautiful creature. In the end we managed to find an inadequate length of rope. We tied it to the hind legs and dragged the stag across the sands into the sea to drown. The effect of pulling the weight nearly broke us physically and certainly wrought in us compassion and misery because of the additional pain we were inflicting. Somehow we reached the edge of the waves, immersed the head and left it to be deprived by the rising tide of that flickering life which the two of us were otherwise unable to extinguish.

The good-timing in which Patrick had apparently been absorbed soon grew stale. *Society Racket* was in a sense a purge. He next worked on the editorial staff of several newspapers. I do not remember in which year he was enlisted by Lord Beaverbrook to the *Evening Standard*'s 'Londoner's Diary', but it was certainly not long after the rackety years. In fact, he earned his livelihood as a social columnist for quite a time. Finally his disenchantment with gossip writing led to dislike. He was meant for worthier purposes. When Beaverbrook suggested that he might cover the Abyssinian troubles after Mussolini's invasion of Ethiopia in 1935, he leapt at the opportunity. His reporting was a success. He brought me back the present of an ancient Coptic Bible. In its battered leather case with a long shoulder strap it resembled an old-fashioned camera, and may have been mistaken for one by some acquaintance, for it soon disappeared, not to be seen again.

After Abyssinia Patrick travelled extensively in Africa, the Middle East and into furthermost Asia. The bright young dilettante turned into a dauntless voyager, braving the hard way and almost masochistically revelling in discomfort and self-abnegation. The fact is, he had never been sybaritic. Nor, it can honestly be said, was he ever properly house-trained. As a guest he was always clumsy. He would spill drinks, break chairs, sofas and springs and, unawares, knock over occasional tables bearing precious *bibelots*. His penitence was minimal. He seemed neither to notice, nor to care. The older and bulkier he got, the more like a mechanical thresher of household objects he became. Nor was he exactly garden-trained. His London neighbour habitually complained of him urinating through his fence into her herbaceous border.

After each journey overseas a book would appear. Travel through Persia to Nepal, Malaya and Siam yielded *Grand Tour* in 1934. It was funny and observant. His experiences in Central Africa were followed by *Lords of the Equator* in 1937. These were precursors of a spate of books published after the war which earned him *The Times* obituarist's accolade for being 'among the outstanding travel writers of his generation'. Patrick's books, he went on, 'the product of sympathy, observation, wit and an unconventional mind, reveal unusual powers of evocation and description. They have their own flavour and can stand beside the best of their time.' They reached a crescendo of excellence with *The Orphaned Realm*, *Within the Taurus* and *Europa Minor* (a journey along the coast of Turkey) in the 1950s and 1960s. Greece, Egypt and Morocco were treated to individual volumes as a portrait of each country.

Just before the outbreak of the Second World War Patrick took the most conformist step of his life. Having fallen madly in love, he married. For someone so self-contained as Patrick, his choice of wife was unwise. Angela Culme-Seymour was extraordinarily beautiful. She had camellia-like skin of the softness of satin, large glowing dark eyes of a dreamy quality, which smiled even when her lips were solemn. Often the only overt movement of her face came from long bewitching lashes, which, while intoxicating the beholder, gave her an air of complete innocence. Indeed it was difficult to tell how innocent she was or whether, like a small child, she was amoral. She needed constant nurture. Or, like a pet animal, while demanding care, she needed keeping to heel. Commonplace codes of behaviour simply did not apply to her. Loyalty to one partner even at the start of a love affair appeared not to concern her. And yet she could not be accounted scheming, because her amours seldom brought her particular happiness and never material gain. She was indifferent to money, luxury and jewellery, and the high life, those things normally associated with adventuresses. She was like a ravishing cat with sheathed claws (though possibly she did not possess these natural instruments), a cat which happily settles on whatever cosy cushion presents itself. And, like that elusive creature, having slept and purred she would amble off into the wilderness without warning and without predictable inducement.

I knew her when she was the wife of Johnny Churchill, Randolph's cousin and nephew of Sir Winston Churchill, between 1934 and 1938. That marriage came to grief neither with a bang nor with a whimper. Angela just strolled away while changing buses at Malaga in the south of Spain, not because she was bored with Johnny or in love with anyone else, or with any particular intent. It merely happened to be easier to accept the kindly offer of protection out of the blue from a persistent admirer. It was shortly after this event and her divorce from Johnny (who suffered agonies of spurned love and injured pride from which I don't think, in spite of a handful of successive wives and non-wives, he ever properly recovered) that she hitched up with Patrick. One evidence of the depth of Johnny's distress was his extreme hostility towards Patrick, who had had nothing to do with the ending of his marriage, and towards those mutual friends who continued to associate with either Patrick or Angela. This union was doomed from the start. Patrick's essays with women had been tentative and, until Angela's dawn on his horizon, half-hearted. There had been one previous engagement, to the daughter of a very rich Glasgow industrialist who did not look with favour upon a prospective son-in-law who was a gossip columnist and, he supposed, a 'lounge lizard'. It was broken off and Patrick did not appear to mind. But the failure of his marriage was a surprise and a blow to him. He had been longing for a permanent Derby-and-Joan marriage around a cosy fireside, with plenty of children to come. Besides, war was imminent, and his father on the brink of death. It was high time to prepare the foundation of a stable and permanent home to return to when peace should eventually be restored.

Angela was never unkind. It was not in her nature. She accepted without responding. Patrick Balfour succeeded as

Lord Kinross, and war duly broke out. Angela broke (no, floated) loose. Patrick joined the Royal Air Force Voluntary Reserve. And that was that. Before their divorce came through in 1942 Angela gave birth to two sons by another man. Their births were registered under the name of Kinross, but on Patrick's protestation an order in court obliged Angela to re-register them under her own name.

His brief marriage, his accession to the title and the Second World War marked the great divide of Patrick's life. The transmutation of Patrick Balfour to Patrick Kinross was accompanied almost overnight by a change of character. The frivolous good-timer had turned into the studious academic, the society racketer into the professional historian. But before he could devote all his energies exclusively to travel and literature, the Hitler interruption had to be dealt with. He took the Allied war aims very seriously.

He was too old to be a fighter pilot, but had he been allowed, would have become one like a shot. However, on account of his extensive knowledge of the Levant and the Middle East he was soon drafted to Egypt, with the rank of squadron leader. Cairo remained his base until the end of hostilities and after. He was made press counsellor and director of the Publicity section at the British Embassy, jobs for which he was eminently suited. It hardly needs telling that despite his reformation he took like a duck to water to the cosmopolitan social rounds that went with these duties – duties which also took him on frequent forays into the front lines. From Cairo and the desert I received many letters written in his neat round hand, hardly less amusing and flippant than those of peacetime, for he could never stifle his merriment for long. He was a lively correspondent.

Patrick was no appeaser. He threw his heart into the unconditional destruction of Germany. His naturally pacific demeanour turned to that of a bellicose First World War squeeze-'em-till-the-pips-squeak officer. When he did come home on leave he adopted a faintly disapproving manner towards the rest of us who were destined to remain in London,

Kathleen Kennet

Paul and Norah Methuen

Vita Sackville-West

Sacheverell Sitwell

Rosamond Lehmann

William Plomer

Patrick Kinross with his mother
and two of his sisters,
Rosemary and Ursula

Henry Yorke

Robert Byron

John Fowler

Osbert Lancaster, self-portrait

Everard Radcliffe

Richard Stewart-Jones

James Pope-Hennessy

as though we were evaders of military service. He pined to be back in Cairo in close touch with the front lines, missing the camaraderie of the troops and airmen of the desert who were in the thick of the fighting. On reflection I can of course understand this. What amazed and displeased him was the apparent un-war-mindedness of Londoners. He was aghast to find civilians leading the same sort of Ritzy life as in the Thirties. He did not however realize that although in Egypt he often (but not always) led a semi-gypsy life with mere basic comforts, we all the time were putting a brave face on nightly pandemonium and destruction from bombing raids such as were not experienced in Cairo. When eventually he was back in England for good, he soon became again his old, jolly, cynical self, tolerant of all mankind. Nevertheless, he was also different. He had developed strong convictions, just as he had developed physical girth. He was a bigger man in every way.

He was not released from Egypt until 1947 – an expatriation of seven years. By now he was rather gross, panting and puffing and not in good trim. Once the shared excursions, exercise and company of his beloved Desert Rats were past history, the fleshpots of Cairo began to have their effect. Towards the end of November I lunched with him at the St James's club. He was about to retreat to Devon to begin a novel, *The Ruthless Innocent*, inspired by Angela. The following April Eardley Knollys and I, on a National Trust jaunt, stayed the night with him at the Easton Court hotel in Chagford. It was a favourite haunt of writers: Evelyn Waugh had frequently patronised it when immersed in a book; Christopher Hobhouse wrote his *Charles James Fox* and Peter Quennell went into retreat there. It was run by an oddly assorted couple, known conjunctly as the Cobweb – Mrs Cobb, an American lady, and her much younger partner Norman Webb. Their food was simple but very well cooked, their wine well chosen. Easton Court was off the beaten track, absolutely unpretentious, and welcoming with wood fires, smoke and shelves of books.

Patrick was one of those people who do not glide so much as tumble from youth into middle age. The transition was not graceful. The elegant, trim young dandy became careless in his dress, uncouth, portly, and not over-clean. In this physical declension what never changed were his delicate hands. The fingers were long, slender and sensitive without being in the least effeminate.

The Yeo had years ago been given up. With Angela he had moved to Little Venice. On her departure his domesticity was reduced to chaos. Although his furniture and possessions were attractive and covetable, it would have been a mistake to peer inside cupboards and drawers, and rash to move cushions from armchairs and sofas for fear of revealing dirty linen thrust there when the front door rang. This it did, never during the day, but from eve till night. Guests were invariably received in the most open-handed manner, for Patrick was an inveterate dispenser of hospitality and pleasure; plied with drinks and pressed to stay for dinner, they would stagger away hours later, replete with alcohol and warmed by the friendliness and geniality of their host, whom all and sundry referred to as 'dear old Patrick'. He was indeed the most charitable of mortals, helping and supporting with money which he hadn't got an accumulation of lame dogs and their female counterparts. He took in and gave lodging to Nappa (later Sir Brian Kenneth) Dean Paul whom he found after many years selling matches at a street corner, and Diana Selby-Lowndes after she had married a man she seemed scarcely to know and found herself pregnant and deserted within a few months. Gallantly he would plead with the irate fathers who had washed their hands of both these bright layabouts. Never censorious, Patrick accepted the follies, peccadilloes and adversities of those he loved as part of the diurnal run. He shrugged off other people's malpractices just as he turned his back upon the slings and arrows aimed at himself. And when he was reduced to penury, which was often the case, he managed just the same. He was a natural optimist.

He lived from hand to mouth. I often wondered how. Of course, he had kind and devoted relations and a multitude of friends. But I don't think he received financial support from any of them. He simply lived on his wits, which were considerable. When eventually he was demobilized, he earned no steady income from journalism. For a few years in the Fifties he wrote for *Punch*, edited by his friend Malcolm Muggeridge. Soon he gave up journalism, to live precariously and solely on his books. They included hack-work – such as *Between Two Seas*, to mark the centenary of the Suez Canal, and ghosting for the Duke of Windsor.

Again he resumed a great deal of wandering-with-a-purpose. His interest in Turkey, then shared by few travellers, became an obsession. Between 1947 and 1954 he made a series of journeys ranging from Antioch and the Syrian frontier in the south-east to Adrianople and the Greek frontier in the north-west. A first-hand knowledge of Turkey and its people was fortified by weeks of study in the British Institute of Archaeology at Ankara, and frequent visits to the British Consulates-General of places like Iskenderun, Izmir and Mersin. The travel books that emerged were exactly what both the armchair voyager and the specializing student of the Balkans and Asia Minor needed. They were trail-blazers, written in an easy, confidential vein, abounding in the history and mythology associated with each place visited. They are vividly descriptive of the landscape, and humorous, although they may not rank with the sustained and wickedly sardonic travel books of his friend and contemporary Robert Byron; nor had Patrick's adventures been quite so far-flung and pioneering. Yet his travel books are still recommendable to the educated package tourist of today, bound by motor-coach to fairly outlandish parts. And a century and more hence they will surely occupy an honourable niche on the same shelf as, say, such minor masterpieces by historians and travellers of the past as R. Chandler's *Travels in Asia Minor* (1817), Robert Curzon's *Armenia* (1854), C.T. Newton's *Travels in the Levant* (1865), Sir Mark Sykes's *The Caliph's Lost Heritage* (1915), and others, from whom Patrick liberally quoted.

Back in London at his house, number 4 Warwick Avenue, adjacent to the Lennox Berkeleys' at number 8 and two or three removed from Diana Cooper's, he would be up and about early, if research-bound to the British Museum library or the London Library, or seated at his vast writing-table in the front room on the right of the entrance, all day scribbling. He gave up luncheon parties. He became a veritable tiger for work. The late 1950s and the 1960s were devoted to compiling his best of all books, *Atatürk: The Rebirth of a Nation*. It was a remarkable achievement, for at the time nearly all the dictator's papers were inaccessible in the Ottoman Bank; in basing his text on private information, Patrick had to rely upon memoirs or correspondence that were available in public libraries. With astonishing insight and understanding he unravelled the almost mythical ethos in which Atatürk had managed to envelop himself during his lifetime. Receiving an official imprimatur, *Atatürk* was translated into Turkish and enjoyed enormous sales, and won Patrick an unique reputation in Turkey as the impartial biographer of a national hero who was regarded by his countrymen as a superman, yet whose notorious private life his compatriots had hitherto merely speculated about. Patrick's *Times* obituarist was to quote the curator of the Bodrum Museum as having said that 'Greece has her Lord Byron, but now Turkey has her Lord Kinross.' Patrick's dedicated interest in and love of Turkey and the Turks had rendered him a redoubtable authority on the Ottoman, the Levant, and Asia Minor; the Foreign Office and the Institute of International Affairs in London constantly consulted him and sought his advice.

Few people positively like being, and no one can surely like looking, old. But Patrick seemed more than indifferent to the passage of time and change: he seemed to glory in them. The world became a better place to live in year by year. Advancing age made him, he claimed, look and feel venerable. The nearest admission he made in my hearing to regret at the loss of his gilded youth was in remarking that, whereas it had been heaven to be twenty and desirable in the Twenties, it was rather less fun being sixty and undesirable in the Sixties. In his last decades he never considered whether his physique could stand up to the severe strains and stresses he would occasionally push it to. And when he was indisposed he attributed it to some accident of fortune which must be countered by plans for a strenuous journey in the immediate future.

When stuck in London few things gave him more pleasure than having old friends, one by one, to dine at Warwick Avenue. He much prided himself on his culinary expertise, which he entered in *Who's Who* as his only recreation. And when engaged in this operation he liked the invited guest to gossip with him over the stove. Certainly he presented an astonishing vision, his puce and beaming face – to quote *The Times'* obituarist again, 'like that of a splendid but benevolent Old Testament prophet' – bent over an enormous aluminium saucepan of stew, into which he hurled from time to time any ingredient within reach. It really did not seem to matter what it was. And if one had added the butt of a cigarette, the pick of a nose, or mud from a shoe, he would have considered it just another succulent contribution. The outcome, however, was always the same. The conglomerate dish tasted of very little. But the risk of catching botulism or aluminium poisoning, or any other form of olla podrida infection, was thrust aside by the enjoyment of his hospitality and talk.

Having partaken in the basement dining-room, the guest would follow his host's swaying figure to the front room on the ground floor. Patrick would slump into an armchair below a large board on which over the years he had pinned photographs, carefully selected, of his best-loved friends in their most beautiful prime. He may have been a little inclined to press his opinions on current affairs and his friends' foibles, but never in an ill-natured manner. His pronouncements and advice were delivered with much twinkling of the prominent eyes, lowering and raising of the bushy eyebrows, the rise and fall of which were accompanied by a rapid compression of the lips and the utterance of a knowing chuckle deep down in the throat. The memory of his chuckle now suggests the sound of running water over a rapid. It was unleashed as a prelude to another emphatic pronouncement.

Patrick dealt with everyone, friend or foe, high-up or low-down, Churchill or Hitler, and every subject whether cathedral or brothel, in a manner apparently flippant. This was a notable trait of the exclusive Twenties and Thirties, a sort of obligatory stamp of aristocrats when with their own kind, seemingly to treat no one and nothing, least of all themselves, seriously.

Soon after *Atatürk* was published in 1964 Patrick boldly ventured on a two-volume history of the Ottoman Empire, a task which occupied him for the rest of his days. It necessitated diligent research and study, which he relished; it involved lengthy travel and staying in low-grade Turkish hotels, which tired him, for during these years his health was failing. Moreover, between *Atatürk* and *The Ottoman Centuries*, his two major works, he produced four minor books, hardly less time-consuming and exacting.

In December 1975 I visited him after he underwent an operation in King Edward VII's Hospital for Officers. He told rather gleefully how they had cut a malignant growth from his colon. He would soon be well and was longing to resume work. He was irrepressibly cheerful and forward-looking. He made out that the few weeks of luxury in hospital, free of all expense, had come as a blessed interlude in which he could collect his thoughts while recharging his physical strength in order to carry on with renewed vigour. I was to understand he was blissfully content. He came out. A few months later I met him one dismal winter evening after dark, crossing the road by King's Cross station. He was clutching to his bosom a pile of books loosely tied together with string. His overcoat collar was turned above his chin because of the rain. He smiled broadly from a face so ravaged by suffering that I could barely recognize him. There was that ominous black brilliance in the eyes. He disclosed that he now had cancer of the intestine; that *The Ottoman Centuries* had been accepted as it was by the publishers, although there was still some tidying up to be done. It was also being translated and about to be serialized in the *Turkish Times*. Everyone was pleased. Furthermore, by a wonderful stroke of luck, not anticipated, he had been left a little money in Violet Trefusis's will. The world for him was still rosy.

I did not see him again. I was living in the country then. But I understood that he went once more to Turkey, where at the end of a day's work he took part in some wildly unsuitable orgy which practically finished him off on the spot. What precisely it amounted to, I never learned. But he managed to get home. I had a date to dine with him on the 8th of June in London – which was two days before his funeral, for on the 4th he died. So I rang up Elizabeth Cavendish and John Betjeman, who were both dreadfully upset. And I dined with them instead, joining in lamentations and recollections, tears and laughter. John was very pleased at getting a letter from Ros Fisher calling Patrick 'the best friend of our generation'. His funeral in St Mary's lovely little Paddington Green church was one of the saddest I ever attended. It was packed with friends, literally to the roof. All of them had some cherished memories of this generous-hearted, pleasure-giving man who had made good to some tune. 'Dear old Patrick.'

An author's death is always bad news for a publisher who has the author's latest book in the press awaiting release to the bookstalls. For some reason it does not catch on with the reviewers or the reading public, as though it bears a taint of the tomb. 'Oh, he's dead! Whatever he had to say must be out of date and irrelevant now,' people seem to think, even if they do not say so. Patrick did not live long enough to see *The Ottoman Centuries* in page proofs. It is a monumental work of Turkish history and, in so far as any record of an ancient empire written by a person of an alien culture can be, it is, like Patrick himself, informative, fair and true.

Henry Yorke
and
Henry Green
1905–1973

I GOT TO know Henry Yorke in the early 1930s; Henry Green
I never got to grips with as perhaps I should have done. Henry
Yorke then lived with his beautiful and gentle wife, Adelaide,
known as Dig, in a house in Rutland Gate. We had mutual
friends, one of whom, Desmond Parsons, introduced me.
Henry had been brought up at Forthampton Court, a large,
rambling, romantic, slightly spooky house which had been in
Yorke possession for more than two and a half centuries (and
still is). It lies on the boundary between Worcestershire and
Gloucestershire. I believe that the house, or the garden, actually
straddles the line that divides the two counties. To the east
some water meadows and the slow-flowing Severn separate
them from Tewkesbury Abbey, which for motors is only
accessible by a circuitous and winding route. My old home was
fifteen miles further east, in Worcestershire. We had both been
educated at Eton and Magdalen College, Oxford. These basic
factors were but a frail link. Henry was three years older than
I, and in boyhood three years makes a wide gap: we did not
know each other as children. Throughout the 1930s we met
fairly frequently in London, and I was as much a friend of Dig
as of Henry. The Yorkes were by my standards rich; they gave
delicious dinner parties, with silver candlesticks and
parlour-maids. Then came the war, and we met hardly at all.
The last time I sat at the same table with Henry was at

Boulestin's restaurant in Soho in 1943, at a small dinner party I gave on my birthday. On that occasion Henry was charming, but reserved. He had very beautiful manners. He spoke little. When the war was over he became more and more reclusive. I fell out of touch, as indeed did most of his old friends apart from a handful of close intimates with whom he (or, I should say, Henry Green) had been accustomed to discuss his writing. Among these were Nevill Coghill, Goronwy Rees, Robert Byron (who died during the war) and John Betjeman. I think I met him only once again (I guess about 1948), on the top of a bus, when I found myself sitting next to him. For twenty minutes he talked, not in his habitual mild manner, but vehemently, revealing a side of himself which I had not experienced hitherto. I shall refer to this meeting later.

During the 1930s I was not even aware that Henry was a writer. I merely knew that he was a younger son who was obliged to work in a family business and moved in a somewhat exclusive circle of friends, not by any means all literary. He was certainly very well read, articulate, but inscrutable. Inclined to be morose. I did not fathom what was going on in that dark head, beneath that sallow skin, under that sleek black hair, behind that straight, stern nose, those deep-set, wild bird eyes and that strange mobile mouth which changed shape and expression according to his thoughts even when he was not speaking.

Although Henry's first novel *Blindness* had been published when he was twenty-one, in 1926, I had not read it, nor did I read any of its successors until *Caught* came out, in 1943. I saw *Caught* in Heywood Hill's bookshop where Nancy Mitford was then working. She was amazed that I did not realize Henry Green was really Henry Yorke (indeed, it was a difficult thing to grasp). At a luncheon party Nancy remarked in her languid Mitford voice that if only Henry had spelt the title *Court* and written about royalty and the aristocracy instead of firemen the novel would, in those days of austerity when everyone pounced upon books recalling glamour and glitter, have sold like hot cakes. As it was, *Caught* only appealed to existing fans, who were few in number. Nevertheless, I bought it; and I bought all Henry's previous novels; and thereafter all his subsequent ones, as they were published. In 1974 I got rid of the lot for a pound each: now I am told that the first editions are worth their weight in gold. Why did I get rid of them (apart from the reason that I was moving from a larger to a smaller house)? Because I never really enjoyed them.

The moment I opened *Caught*, however, I realized it was out of the ordinary. I was fascinated, but not enchanted. It was one of Henry's autobiographical novels, about his wartime work in the London Fire Service. In conveying a picture of pre-Blitz, Phoney War boredom it was unsurpassed. It was a random record of working-class talk which had no beginning and no end. The episodes were disconnected, lacking sequence. The dialogue was fragmented, telescoped. There was little story in *Caught*, only symbolism, which did not the least interest me, doubtless because I too had been a victim of the Phoney War boredom, first in an Air Raids Precaution unit and then in the army. The interminable chat and feeble jokes, the interests confined to motor bikes, girls and football, the jazz music played and hummed, the boasts of sleazy, sexy adventures, so irked me at the time that I wanted only to forget the wasted hours I had been obliged to spend subjected to them, along with the fug of gaspers and dirty feet. The experience was something I never wanted to be reminded of.

Living (1929), to which I next applied myself, was likewise autobiographical, in that the principal character became by inheritance head of an iron foundry, just as Henry was heir to H. Pontifex & Sons, manufacturers of equipment for the food and drink trade, established by his father Vincent. In *Living* the sentences are compressed, the scenes more abbreviated than in the later *Caught*, and the author adopts a tiresome trick of suppressing the definite article. Evidently he had no use for plots. I for one unashamedly like a story to have a beginning and an end, just as I dislike reading about the uneducated and ineducable, be they noblemen or humble artisans, especially when they are my own countrymen, who seem, I suppose from familiarity, obtuser than nearly all foreign low-brows.

For years I persevered with Henry Green – always fascinated, but not enjoying. *Party Going* was about a lot of maddening, spoilt good-timers in a fog of indecision and fatuity; *Pack My Bag* was about a miasma of alcohol fumes. *Loving* was about an Irish country house, remote from the war, where everyone seemed to sleep with everyone else. *Back, Concluding* (a day in the life of old Mr Rock who represented Mr Nobody at All), *Nothing, Doting* were ambiguous to me, if not to clever people like Mr R.S. Ryf, who in his literary study of Henry Green* said that the title of each novel explained the story inside. To me, reading these novels was like walking, at best down a long lane shrouded with boscage on either side, at worst down a narrow slum street between derelict hovels, hoping, hoping for a turning which would reveal ultimate sunshine and sense. Now, Mr Ryf has casually observed that God is, if not dead, then absent from Green's novels. This, I think, partly explains my inability to enjoy them. I find a total lack of concession to the spirit inordinately depressing. There is no promise in Henry Green's novels. The tide forever recedes, leaving nothing but flotsam behind. Women who have nits in their hair miss the irritation when the insects are removed. Birds – they figure repeatedly through the novels – seldom fly or sing; they drop down dead from station roofs, not to be swept into dustbins and forgotten, but to be stowed by old ladies in suitcases, to be brought out and gloated over, maggots and all.

Edward Stokes, in *The Novels of Henry Green* (1959), has written that no mid twentieth-century novelist has shown such stylistic variations. But to my mind Henry Green's style seems to vary little, if at all. It is always staccato, enigmatic, and maddeningly elusive. One episode slides into another. The reader is perpetually brought up against blank walls. At the finish of every novel the story is unresolved, and the reader is

---

* R.S. Ryf, *Henry Green* (New York, Columbia University Press, 1967), p.45.

left in the air. In venturing these criticisms I do not mean to imply that Green's style is a bad one. Far from it. Quite apart from being – to employ a pedantic term – *sui generis*, it is seldom strained. It is damnably direct, colloquial and powerful. But quirky, my God! Moreover, and this is why I persevered in reading everything he wrote, the novels contain poetry of a morbid kind. They are embellished – if that is the right word – with passages that take the breath away, passages that could be extracted from the book without in the least affecting the book's theme. Let me quote one at random from *Living*:

> Smell of food pressed on her. All were eating. All was black with smoke, here even, by her, cows went soot-covered and the sheep grey. She saw milk taken out from them, grey the surface of it. Yes, and the blackbird fled across that town flying crying and made noise like noise made by ratchet. Yes and in every house was mother with her child and that was grey and that fluttered hands and then that died, in every house died those children to women. Was low wailing low in our ears.
>
> Then clocks in that town all over town struck 3 and bells in churches there ringing started rushing sound of bells like wings tearing under roof of sky, so these bells rang. But women stood, reached up children drooping to sky, sharp boned, these women wailed and their noise rose and ate the noise of bells ringing.

This is fine sentiment and reminiscent of Gerard Manley Hopkins, only without the devout confidence of the Jesuit who throughout life's terrors and dubieties certainly glimpsed light at the end of the tunnel. Henry Green saw none. Consequently, all his synonyms are grey, or soot-covered. Could any passage in English literature be more depressing, and more devoid of hope and redemption, not to mention speculation? And yet could any be more horribly arresting? It and reams more like it belong not to fiction: they are monodies in blank verse.

This does not mean that all Green's descriptive passages are horrible. *Loving*, for instance, also contains passages of sheer poetry, albeit seldom uplifting. I am not sure that this is not the best of all Green's novels. The scenario is a remote, down-at-heel Irish country house in wartime, and the book encapsulates the withered arrest over the centuries of the lost Irish landscape. Both family and staff are self-seeking, deceitful and dishonest. Yet the well known description of the two little servant girls, caught by the infamous butler dancing to the gramophone in a dust-sheeted drawing-room – supposedly the famous white and gold drawing-room of Gothick Birr Castle, County Offaly where Henry Yorke often stayed with Anne and Michael Rosse – is worthy of one of Henry James's 'English' novels, say *The Tragic Muse* or *What Maisie Knew*, or perhaps one of Robert Browning's dramatic romances like *My Last Duchess* or *Porphyria's Lover*.

The dialogue of Henry Geeen's lower-class characters is often tremendously funny without being the least bit cruel. He never high-hats or condescends, for he was wholly un-class bound, if class aware he surely was to a morbid degree. Besides, Henry Yorke preferred the company of the lower to that of the upper classes whence he derived. In his writings he never animadverts upon their behaviour, however outrageous, and he makes nearly all of them rogues. Also he never gets carried away by them. He firmly directs and controls them. Is coldly detached. Has no compassion for even the poorest and most underprivileged, not even for Lily Gates whom he found sexually desirable. As for the upper classes, they fare no better under Henry's surgical scrutiny. They receive neither mercy nor pity. Just consider the uproariously humorous pages in *Loving* where Miss Burch, the housekeeper, discloses to her reluctant listener Nanny Swift the adultery of Veronica, Nanny Swift's late charge, with a dreary neighbour on the eve of the return of Veronica's husband on leave from the war. Nor is Veronica's mother-in-law, the chatelaine, vouchsafed a word of sympathy over her abominable treatment by the servants.

No more does Henry Green have compassion for his reader, whom he has a striking capacity for thrusting immediately into a situation without any ado. Reader must take it or leave it.

So Miss Gates did not look at anything. She just followed Mr Jones.

They went by public house. Man played on instrument which was kind of xylophone, laid flat in the doorway. As the air sweats on metal so little balls of notes this man made hung on smell of stale beer which was like a slab outside the door. Man playing on this instrument was on his knees, and trunk of his body bent over it, head almost touched ground on other side of this flat instrument. Mr Jones saw position that man was in. He's never seen one like it. Feeling of uneasiness grew up in him.

Is not this empathy of a cold, clinical sort? Like that of a sadistic surgeon brandishing the sharp steel knife?

Henry for some obscure reason took against his old home, Forthampton Court – he declared the place was unhealthy – even after his brother Gerald, of whom he was fond, inherited. He never went there again. Gerald was anything but the conventional English squire. Certainly he was a conscientious landowner, but his chief absorption was the occult. This kindly and highly intellectual man was a great authority on vampires and werewolves. But a paucity of other teeth and the prominence of a single somewhat alarming canine were a fearful intimation of his speciality – and he was constantly called upon by the editor of the *Times Literary Supplement* to review books on psychical research, magic, ghosts and the supernatural generally.

Until he threw his hand in and gave up life, Henry took his writing extremely seriously. In 1950–1 he delivered a series of addresses on BBC radio's Third Programme, 'A Novelist to his Reader'. They were spoken in a suave, silken, silver-spoon voice, that of a man apparently at peace with the world and his maker. How deceptive a voice can be. Green's message was that, art being non-representational, descriptions of situations ought to be reduced to a minimum of words. He claimed that since no one wrote letters any more (not strictly true, this, considering that among his contemporaries were Nancy Mitford, Harold Nicolson, Evelyn Waugh and James Pope-Hennessy) and communication was only by telephone, the time had come for a change from traditional methods of story-telling to an emphasis upon oblique dialogue. Dialogue 'must mean different things to different readers at one and the same time', he said. 'It is only by an aggregate of words over a period followed by an action, that we obtain, in life, a glimmering of what is going on in someone, or even in our-selves.' The novelist should use tone in the way that a painter uses dabs of colour, to convey fleeting incidents. Only in Henry's case, the colour was always muted. Certainly his novels are puncuated by dabs, like those channels marked by grey wooden piles for the guidance of gondolas and motor-boats across the shallow Venetian lagoons.

Thus we get from him dialogue like the following (again from *Living*):

> 'Where are you goin'?' said Mr Dale.
> 'I'm not goin' anywhere.'
> 'Aren't you goin' out?'
> 'I'm not goin' anywhere without you go.'
> 'Don't trouble about me,' Mr Dale said. 'I'm used to that.'
> 'I didn't mean you particular, I meant all on you.'
> 'I'm stayin' in with me pipe,' Gates said half asleep.
> 'You go and get the beer.' Mr Craigan reached out and took wireless and headphones which he fitted about his head.
> 'I thought you couldn't mean me,' said Mr Dale.
> 'No, I should think I couldn't.'
> 'But don't you put yourself out for us. You go on out.'
> 'I got nowhere to go.'
> 'What, ain't 'e waitin' for you at the corner?'
> 'Who's that?'
> 'Who's that!' he said.
> 'Well, what business is it of yours if 'e is?'
> 'I wouldn't keep 'im waitin'.'
> 'I tell you I'm not going out this afternoon.'
> 'Then what's it all about? 'Ad a lover's quarrel or what?'

There is no reason why this boring conversation between an indeterminate number of uneducated individuals should not have continued for another ten pages. We have all overheard such snippets of chatter between people who lead dreary lives and are incapable of expressing themselves. In fact, it is difficult to go through a single day and avoid them. But do they really amount to a communion of ideas worth recording? And does the dismal aggregate contribute to whatever action may follow? It entirely depends upon the manner of its telling and the humour of the author. And Henry Green can often, but not always, be very funny.

I return to my last encounter with Henry Yorke, on the London bus. He was on his way home from the office. I asked him how he was. 'Bloody awful!' he answered. I said I was sorry, for he looked all right. 'I am not at all all right,' he barked, 'and I will tell you why.' There was no question whether I wished to hear the reasons or not. I had to. Henry then launched upon a diatribe of hate against his octogenarian father who, he claimed, refused to retire from the family firm, in order deliberately to retard his son's succession and ruin his prospects. I have in my time heard people rage against their parents, but never with the concentrated venom which Henry gave vent to on the bus. It was evident that he was being deeply thwarted in his middle age by a tyrannical and senile parent who would not relax his grip of the wheel, Henry's wheel by the rights of nature. Henry's position in the firm, which was his livelihood, was being made intolerable. The whole business – everything and every one – was suffering.

The bus reached Henry's destination. He jumped up and left, throwing me as he did so the words, 'It's unmitigated hell, I can tell you!'

While I continued my journey I ruminated upon this unsolicited outburst. Henry must have been in a very bad way to nourish so monstrous a grievance. I wondered whether he supposed he had not much time to enjoy a free hand in Pontifex & Sons even if his old father should retire the next day – that perhaps his own death was approaching. As it was, he lived another twenty years. Certainly Henry Yorke's business ambitions were being cruelly frustrated; above all, Henry Green's writings were being adversely affected.

By now Henry Green was recognized by the highbrow critics as one of the most interesting novelists of his generation. But he was approaching the end of his gamut of fiction writing. He just about reached it when at last Mr Yorke senior retired (by dying) in 1957. It was ironical that when Henry did inherit what was, it is true, a failing business, he went completely to pieces. There was evidently some very subtle connection between Henry Yorke's father and Henry Green's novels. Without the nits in the hair, inspiration flagged.

Most of Henry's friends were dropped. Dig kept up with hers, by whom she was much beloved. Whenever I met her she would say, after the usual enquiry from me about Henry, that he was doing fine, with a 'you must come and see him soon.' But I knew better. Patrick Kinross, who had known him infinitely longer than I, called, and was subjected to a volley of abuse, and nothing else.

In 1951 Henry told a journalist that he had ceased to believe in anything at all. He became almost a hermit, if you disregard his daily walks to the pub down the street. There he would sit in an old mackintosh, often for hours at a time, beside a glass of gin. He seldom spoke to others. But he listened, listened, and looked, until the day dawned when he stayed at home permanently with his saintly wife, devouring contemporary novels whether good or trashy, it did not seem to matter which. He did not wish to see anyone. When asked what were his reasons for not going out, he said one was because the woman at the tobacconist's shop along the road had been dragged by the hair from behind the counter and stabbed to death. She was the same age as himself. Danger threatened. It was clearly safer to remain indoors, and this he did until his death in December 1973.

His body was taken home to Forthampton, as though in defiance of his perverse determination, while he was alive, not to revisit the home he had never ceased to love. When the coffin was lowered the mourners were embarrassed to see that the sexton had not made the grave long enough. As she turned away Dig was overheard to remark, 'How Henry would have laughed!'

Robert Byron

1905–1941

I QUOTE FROM a page or two I wrote in an (unpublished) diary of August 1941; I had just opened a copy of *Country Life*.

' "Robert Byron", I see heading a leader. "Since the ship taking him..." and I know what is coming: "Byron has been missing, and now hope has to be abandoned." And out trot the tributes convention demands, tributes justly paid for all their hackneyed phrases: "incision and brilliant personality", "impish wit [more than impish]", "loss heavy to his friends". "It is no less tragic..." the epitaph continues. We know the rest. How Robert would have barked at them.

'It is correct of *Country Life* to write like this, for they are indebted to him for many learned travel articles and original photographs of hitherto unknown architecture in remote Asiatic regions. Justly they say two things of him: "Two things he hated: oppression in any form – he was a bitter critic of modern autocracies – and the vulgarity and mediocrity which pass too often today for liberty."

'Four years ago Robert composed almost identical sentiments in memory of Desmond Parsons [younger brother of Michael, 6th Earl of Rosse, of Birr Castle, Ireland]. We were dining together at Claridges the day that Desmond's body was brought to England from China. Over coffee Robert drafted an appreciation to be sent to *The Times* that evening by telephone. He was so deeply moved that I was surprised. Desmond's loathing of oppression and mediocrity: "What people valued in him was his truth." Robert's words resolved themselves into "He never compromised with the pretentious or the second-best." The coincidence makes me question whether the bereaved feel unconsciously impelled to attribute their own virtues to their dead friends.

'Now what of Robert? He would have liked to be considered a foundation stone in the vast bulwark or dam against recurring tides of the barbaric past, which he regarded with the utmost scorn. He had passionate faith in a defensive future that would safeguard mankind against the past. He did not believe that the past could be or ought to be annihilated. He believed that it ought to be controlled behind the stout bars of a cage, like a wild animal; the present to be out of its range to inflict harm.

'He held in no awe the offices of those who wielded authority, none whatever, for he would ruthlessly undress kings and presidents of republics in order to laugh like a hyena at their knock knees and the porkiness of their stomachs. His greatest friends were subject to the same rough treatment. After exhausting a vocabulary of caustic abuse at their physical and mental defects, and exhilarated by his own chortling merriment, he would sit up half the night composing letters and memoranda on their behalf. He was not a man of contradictions, nor of compromises, but of affirmations.

'At this moment I think of Robert bathing in the bay of Naples one grilling August morning when we were both staying at the Peter Rodds' villa at Posilipo [Nancy Mitford had married the Hon. Peter Rodd in 1933]. He would set forth after breakfast for the shore in his butterfly-catcher's suit – a wide-brimmed panama, a tight, striped, sailor's shirt, a pair of buff shorts, and sandals. From nine till long after midday he would swim fierce breast strokes, then overarm strokes, and finally float on his back spouting sea water like an indolent whale. The meridian waves buoyed him over their crests, under the bell of blue sky, under the blaze of the sun. In this attitude he would recline for three-quarters of an hour at a stretch while from a boat we plied him at intervals with chocolates, and cigarettes which he smoked through a holder. He had hired a small Neapolitan youth to row behind him with a large bottle of sunburn oil and the butterfly-catcher's accoutrement on board.

'The fact is I cannot yet believe Robert to be dead. He did not have doom written on his face. I can somehow take it that Christopher Hobhouse, like some other friends already lost in this war, has been blown to smithereens, that the long hands with tactile fingers and the ascetic face with an arrogant chin have enriched the guts of fish and worms.'

And here the entry stops. So I resume, after more than half a century.

Actually, I knew several months before August 1941 that the banana boat in which Robert sailed for Egypt in February had been torpedoed and that there was little chance of his survival in the cruel waters of the Atlantic. Harold Nicolson, then Parliamentary Secretary to the Ministry of Information, had warned me what to expect. Only recently have I learned that Robert had a horror of being eaten by sharks – 'appalled by the prospect of leaving my vile body, not even digested, in the stomach of a fish'. His small boat had not even got within range of sharks' habitats: it sank off the north coast of Scotland. Robert was within two days of his thirty-sixth birthday, nearly the same age as the illustrious poet whose name and lineal antecedents he proudly shared.

Who and what was Robert Byron? In his lifetime he was not well known to the public. Briefly, his recognized achievements were to have, with others, launched the Georgian Group and founded the Federal Union Club, thus envisaging the European community as a rampart against totalitarian aggression and an eventual force for world peace; and to have written a number of extremely provocative articles in the national press about conservation of historic buildings, and the political situation, thus intensely annoying men and women of his parents' generation. Among his own restricted circle of literary friends, however, he had won acclaim as an intrepid traveller, and author of some brilliant books. Robert would have been amazed to learn that by his contemporaries' children he would be venerated as a writer of immaculate prose and as an art historian who by his discoveries and revelations raised the understanding of Byzantine civilization and art to a parity with that of western Christendom. For although he had a just opinion of his views and convictions – 'I really never suspected before how stupendous must be the gulf between oneself and the ordinary man' – he was modest about his writing. Bruce Chatwin, who when Robert died was actually too young to have scribbled on the sea sand, as Tennyson had done in 1824, the immortal words, 'Byron is dead', nevertheless as a schoolboy immersed himself in Robert's books, putting him 'at least in the rank of Ruskin', and, being a forward youth, identified himself with his hero. He deliberately adopted Robert's candid and descriptive prose style, pronouncing *The Road to Oxiana* a work of genius. He rhapsodized over Robert's paean for Sheikh Lutfullah's mosque in Isfahan, that great masterpiece of the Safawid rulers of Persia. Indeed, Robert had written lyrically that in the monument colour and pattern produced 'a quality which must astonish the European... because he can previously have had no idea that abstract pattern was capable of so profound a splendour.' While admitting that Robert was no scholar, Bruce praised his remarkable power of empathy with his subjects, calling him an outstanding historian who 'treated ancient and modern people as two facets of a continuing story'. Robert would have delighted in Chatwin, whom by the laws of nature he should have survived to know. He would have been amused by his self-sufficiency, his panache and charm, and have admired his splendid presence.

Robert's character was very positive. He was a man who could never be overlooked. His craving for knowledge was purposeful and seemed immanent. He wrote that his urge to travel was compulsive, and that he must have a goal. For idle tourism and even adventure he had 'a loathing'. He would always prefer, when it presented itself, the soft way; however,

when obliged to, he would accept the hard way
uncomplainingly: for instance, the journey through Tibet in
1929 with Michael Rosse and Gavin Henderson was almost
unbelievably arduous. His poverty often permitted no
alternative if he was to achieve his goal. His parents were very
badly off, and their way of life in the small, dark house in
Savernake Forest where he was brought up was extremely
simple. Robert never had a penny of his own and was obliged,
as soon as his education was deemed complete, to fend for
himself financially.

His father Eric was an indigent gentleman, son of a
tyrannical hunting squire who somehow managed to dissipate
a fortune. Although a querulous and delicate man, Eric was
himself no tyrant. I remember him as mild, bent by pain rather
than age, well read and a little bewildered by his only son and
his two assertive daughters, whom Emerald Cunard wildly
alleged that he poked at meals with 'a sadistic fork'. Mrs Byron
was by no means mild or meek. Hers was a robust,
matter-of-fact nature. She was very clever, well educated, of an
enquiring mind in that, like Robert, she sought knowledge. She
was ever ready to listen to new opinions and adopt them,
provided they did not conflict with her deep-seated Christian
principles. Her adoration of her son, admiration of his intellect,
and determination to forward his interests whether or not they
were avant-garde to a lady of her old-fashioned upbringing,
were protective and solicitous. Her adoration was from the first
reciprocated in a way surely unique between a parent of the
pre-1914 generation and a child of the sophisticated inter-war
generation, particularly one of that group ostensibly raffish,
cynical and in revolt against the Victorian family home. But
although this was the group to which Robert was drawn while
at Eton, and of which at Eton he soon became a leading spirit,
disparagement of home and family was not at all in Robert's
line. On the contrary, while travelling he was homesick
practically all the time – so long, that is to say, as his home
remained in the depth of Savernake Forest. 'How heavenly it
will be,' he wrote from Calcutta in 1930, 'arriving home when

I do – just at the very best time of all – I hope you will meet me! Send me a snowdrop in an envelope.' When his parents felt impelled to leave Savernake in 1936 he was heart-broken.

I have said that Eric and Daisy Byron (to have referred to either in their lifetime with such familiarity would have been unthinkable) were hard up. Fortunately for them, at his prep school in 1918 Robert won a scholarship to Eton. To Eton he went the following year, but not, as did most scholars, to College. This was just as well: Robert was not of the reclusive, serious, poor-scholar type. He went to Robeson's house, where he at once made friends with the intellectual boys of well-to-do parents, like Billy (Cracky) Clonmore and Henry Yorke, both of whom became bosom friends of a lifetime. Furthermore, they became bosom friends of his mother too. Henry especially worshipped Mrs Byron, confided in her and gave her contemporary novels to read, including drafts of his own. Eton taught Robert how to work, and above all how to write. All aspects of his school work received from Mrs Byron her assiduous backing.

While still a schoolboy Robert developed a very distinctive prose style, lively, highly coloured and observantly descriptive. Of Oxford he made the very most by throwing himself into the social swim, and also by absorbing the architecture in which the university is so rich. Writing from Merton College in May 1924 he told his mother that 'Lord Beauchamp came on Saturday for an hour or two. We had lunch in the Magdalen guest room and a bottle of Tokay that the steward had bought from the cellar of the late Emperor Karl of Austria. It was the most wonderful taste – so extraordinary as to be like seeing a new primary colour.' Robert was getting his comparisons exactly right from the start.

Lord Beauchamp, a most distinguished and cultivated peer, was the father of another of Robert's great Eton friends, Hugh Lygon, and of the famous Lygon sisters who were part and parcel of the group of Bright Young People which Robert adorned. The Lygon home was Madresfield Court beneath the Malvern Hills in Worcestershire, where Robert and his contemporaries – Evelyn Waugh, Harold Acton, not forgetting Clonmore and Henry Yorke, himself Worcestershire born and bred – frequently assembled and stayed. It was all tremendous fun and highly stimulating. Yet through Madresfield and the benign caution of Lord Beauchamp, the vapidity of English social life was brought home to Robert. It was undeniably seductive, but had to be treated as secondary to his life's task, so soon to be defined.

Robert and Mrs Byron's relationship I find extremely touching. There was nothing mawkish about it. It was absolutely natural. Throughout his life they corresponded uninhibitedly, as though the generation gap were barely perceptible. He discussed with her his ambitions, his writings, his ideals, his friendships, his successes and setbacks, in a way that few such sons can have done. Only flutters of the heart may have been withheld: I do not even know that for sure. All his letters, carefully preserved, begin 'Darling Mibble', and nearly all conclude with expressions of his abiding affection for her. At the age of twenty-nine, as he is about to set off on a long and possibly dangerous journey, he writes to her that she has 'made me all the good I am ... If a course is proposed, involving a risk of some sort, it is at once to you that my mind springs. I ask myself if it would be fair to *you*. So you must ask yourself if it is fair to *me* to be upset because of a slight irregularity in communication.' On the prospect of war breaking out in 1939 he says, 'Don't worry about me. You gave me so much happiness in our early lives [Robert was almost as devoted to his two sisters] that you can't expect that level to continue.' And the very last letter to her, written as he was setting sail for his death a few days later, ends 'Well, goodbye, darling – and very best love – and think of the times we shall have when it is all over.'

Unhealthy? I do not see it in that light. And yet I do not believe Robert ever loved another human being with the same intensity. She was essential to his well-being. He demanded and usually accepted her judgement of his writing and of every step of his career. Nevertheless, he did not withhold criticism of her prejudices. He positively snubbed her when she ventured to insinuate that he was identifying himself with current sleazy, unorthodox philosophies. 'I don't think B[ertrand] Russell has a dirty mind,' he riposted – 'rather a dirty wit, which I enjoy. No, I don't know whether I agree with him particularly. I have no views on social subjects – but I like his attitude.' Again, he adopted an almost hectoring tone on the theme of matrimony. He deemed Russell's *Marriage and Morals* a very good, sincere, and witty book. 'It is a pity you don't . . . like all his books. It would explain to you the modern outlook on such things – even if you didn't agree with his arguments. I don't ask you to alter your attitude, but simply to *understand* the other and not to regard an outlook which is not based on Christo-Jewish hypocrisy as merely filthy. Otherwise my novels (if I ever write them), and I should imagine Lucy's too, will have to go to press without your corrections – which would be a disaster.'

When he was barely out of the nursery Robert would tutor her. She must broaden her outlook, and read this new book and that. She must go to London more often to exhibitions, and not mind the cost of the journey. With almost no money himself, he yet sent her a postal order to pay for a ticket to Paddington and the five-shilling entrance fee to the Italian Paintings exhibition at the Royal Academy on Connoisseurs' Day, plus 7s. 6d. for a good blow-out at the Ritz.

Mrs Byron was an august and self-possessed lady who inspired respect from Robert's friends. Shortly after his death I called on her at Great Overton near Marlborough where she and Eric were then living, in a tall gaunt house near the church. She was in black from head to foot and wearing a deep-brimmed hat. Severe and a little formidable. She spoke of Robert without a tremor of the lips, but her eyes told all she felt.

Unlike many of his contemporaries, notably the spendthrift Bullingdon Club set, Robert did not waste his time at Oxford. It is extraordinary how at so early an age his passion for travel developed. At just eighteen he was taken by Lord Beauchamp as companion to the earl's second son Hughie on a lightning introduction to Italy and Greece. Lord Beauchamp was an indefatigable sightseer who would map out every moment of every day, and good company to boot. The boys, who were of the same age, could not have been launched upon a continental grand tour in more auspicious conditions. Two years later Robert went on a more concentrated tour to Italy and Greece in Gavin Henderson's open touring car, which developed every sort of mechanical fault in addition to recurrent punctures. By way of Salzburg and Mozart they reached Rome. Somewhat indifferent to the Holy City, Robert was enraptured by Naples and the south Italian cities and landscape, the Roman remains in open country, the women in peasant dress, 'that our grandmothers delighted to sketch, the men on donkeys with huge panniers'. From Brindisi they crossed the Adriatic to Patras.

Italy may have been wonderful; Greece was more wonderful still. It was magical. 'It is entirely unspoilt,' he told his mother. In fact he was intoxicated, and completely lost his heart. How much the thunder-bolt of love was augmented by the discovery that his name worked miracles with the Hellenes it is idle to speculate. Through a very distant ancestor he was related to the poet, and indeed bore the same arms, crest, and motto, *Crede Biron*. He certainly gloried in the connection, and sensibly made the most of the veneration his name, coupled with his youth, evoked in the Balkans and the Near East. To a prominent Greek patriot Robert 'explained that I had my living to make and should he want a King . . . he said he would keep it in mind . . . How will you enjoy being the new Napoleon's mother?' he asked Mrs Byron. All the Byronic wit bubbled up in the vision of a reincarnated Madame Mère.

The only fly in the ointment was his appearance. He could not by a stretch of the imagination be termed handsome, or romantic. His oval face with long, disdainful nose recalled that of Queen Victoria in her middle-aged widowhood, a resemblance from which Robert profited at fancy-dress parties. Like the Queen, too, he had rather protuberant fish-like eyes and a mouth permanently half-open, disclosing teeth of a rabbity cut. His fair hair was sparse and smarmed back from a copious forehead. His figure was naturally thickset and from the least over-indulgence in food or drink ran, or rather galloped, to fat. Indeed, when he was not travelling and taking exercise he soon became puffy, yellow and unhealthy. By effort of will he as quickly reverted to fairly slim again, but for a time only. His physical disadvantages were however mitigated – except when he was in one of his rages – by an ironic humour and boisterous merriment. No one had a more infectious sense of the ludicrous; and his deep-throated, slightly strangulated laugh was very engaging. However – again, like Queen Victoria – he was not a person to be trifled with. And the sneer in his voice was not always neutralized by a hesitant smile in the eyes.

Before he was even twenty-one Robert knew exactly what the mission of his life was to be: historian of the Byzantine civilization interpreted through the media of painting and architecture. It was not to be achieved through academic research in dry-as-dust manuscripts, but through travel and first-hand observations *in situ*. Moreover, his specialized study, to which architecture was perhaps secondary, was to be the icons of the eastern churches and monasteries which to date had been almost totally ignored by art historians of the western world.

I have stressed that Robert was a man of firmly entrenched convictions, or prejudices. They were often so vehemently expressed as to take control over his judgement. He was incapable of feeling calmly about a subject that had engaged his interest or advocacy. His hates were as tempestuous as his loves; they drove him into ungovernable frenzies. A loathing of Shakespeare and Rembrandt amused and sometimes irritated his friends. When one of them expostulated that Shakespeare's plays could not possibly have been written by a grocer he snarled, 'They are precisely what I would expect from a grocer.' He did not, that I am aware, explain the reason for his Shakespeare-hate, beyond a jibe that his mother had made him recite from the works at the age of three. It was probably motivated by a compulsion to demolish the sheep-like acceptance by the illiterate majority that the Bard of Avon (and the Burgher of Amsterdam, for that matter) were beyond criticism. With his unyielding aesthetic standards he may have been genuinely riled by the rough-and-tumble of Shakespeare's archaic syntax, in which not every seam was laden with ore. It may be that he was revolted by the commonplace and bourgeois sitters to Rembrandt's paintbrush. In any case, his insular contempt for abroad, allied to his professed contempt for abroad's vindicators, that bugbear Bloomsbury, was a permanent tease on the part of this much-travelled man whose avowed amusement was to put a finger on the rift within every lute.

It was this affectation, shared with others of his group, which so shocked his friend from Oxford days, the cosmopolitan Harold Acton. 'Evelyn Waugh', Harold was to complain, 'winced at the sound of a French word, and Robert Byron rolled a consorious Victorian eye when I spoke of Cocteau.' Yet Harold added, astutely, that without being aware of it, and without having read him, both Evelyn and Robert had marked points of contact with Cocteau. 'They, too, preferred certain circuses or music-hall turns – what I called "the illegitimate stage" – to the "legitimate stage".' 'Come to Paddington!' was Robert's cry. 'Paddington is the symbol of all that Bloomsbury is not.'

Inversely, Robert's obsession with Byzantine painting begot one serious and vehement prejudice. His genuine admiration of the two-dimensional icon had to be counterbalanced by a depreciation of many-faceted western Renaissance painting. His respect for the Orthodox faith in communion with the four eastern Patriarchs had to be countered by a loathing of the Roman Catholic Church which was in communion with the papacy alone. His artistic sympathies and antipathies were largely dictated by civil or political inclinations. He favoured the oligarchy of the Greek creed while rejecting the absolutism of the Latin. In his eyes, all roads led to Constantinople. Christopher Sykes, who surely knew him better than anyone else, records how at their first meeting, when they felt drawn to one another and he remarked that he was a Papist, Robert instantly turned on him with 'Oh God! I thought we were going to become friends.'

Robert was an avowed atheist as regards creeds, whether Christian, Muslim, Confucian, Hindu, or Buddhist. And yet his entrenched aesthetic principles responded to the mystical abracadabra of the Orthodox Church's ritual.

Much has already been written in praise of Robert's travel books; and much more will be forthcoming. *The Road to Oxiana* is generally considered his masterpiece. Sykes and Chatwin are sure of it. As a mature work of literature, this may be so. Yet to my mind *The Station* is more remarkable. Admittedly a very young man's book, begun when he was twenty-one and published when he was twenty-three, it is full of rash judgements, lapses of style, and those rodomontades habitual to unfledged genius. On the other hand, how it evinces the lightning strokes of a prodigious mind! There is no uncertainty, no hesitancy in this first debt of honour (as Sykes described it) or homage to Byzantine Greece. Throughout it is laced with wit, at the expense of his contemporary native Greeks as well as his own incompetence (in all practical matters he was a congenital butter-fingers). Maddening though he often found the modern Greeks, they were to him the God-touched descendants of their ancient forebears. He saw them as the protagonists of democratic freedom from serfdom, the apostolic inheritors of the early Christian message (which he professed to despise), the rejectors of Renaissance Rome's strangulation of classical *laissez-faire* and nauseous bondage of papal tyranny and cant. Robert Byron would have it that they were of the same flesh and blood as the Ancient Greeks, discounting the Slav, Albanian and Vlach interfusions throughout the centuries. In his eyes, modern Greeks retained the Hellenic strain unpolluted.

If at times Robert found his beloved Hellenes exasperating, they must often have found him and his young companions no less so. It is extraordinary how insensitive Robert could be, he who ceaselessly reviled the ill-bred arrogance of his compatriots overseas. He would rail angrily against Greek officials who thwarted him, practically coming to blows. He resented being asked by the Athonic Fathers of Chilandari to extinguish his cigarette within the monastic precincts. He rudely disregarded his muleteer's shocked request not to ride past the sacred icon of the Mother of God in the Protaton church at Karyes (it was the accepted tradition for all riders to dismount and respectfully pass by on foot). The behaviour of his companion, eminent professor of archaeology David Talbot-Rice, was even more reprehensible. Determined to photograph the holy icon in the Protaton, he battered down the padlocked door. The muleteer was appalled. But Robert, instead of restraining, encouraged Talbot-Rice in this act of blasphemy. Their behaviour may have been aggravated by tiredness at the end of a rather gruelling trek across the Holy Mountain; it was certainly inexcusable, and largely brought about by drink. The offence did not seem to arouse in Robert one whit of remorse, and he regarded the incident as rather amusing.

Although Robert was no exception to the rest of his gilded group, whose manners could be off-hand and their pranks loutish – for example, in setting fire with petrol to harmless country-house owners' moats, digging up Piccadilly after midnight while still in fancy-dress, playing hide-and-seek in Selfridges by day, pranks deemed funny by the young upper classes of the Twenties, and unfunny by the middle – he had his own censorious side, which was almost Victorian and quite uncompromising. His standards of 'freedom, justice and truth' were dogmatic. They were rammed down the throats of his readers over and over again.

That Robert candidly recorded in writing his occasional boorishness is one of his endearing traits. Absolute truth was his holiest maxim: truth about others, and himself. *The Station* bristles with truth. The book also pullulates with provocative aphorisms and descriptive passages which for wit and vividness are beyond compare. In the pursuit of icons and their photography Robert's congenital humour in dealing with the obfuscation, denseness and sheer silliness of their guardians seldom (between his bouts of temper) lapses.

> Let him who still conceives of Byzantine painting as a hieratic degradation, imagine a Giotto un-sweetened, as Giotto already was, by Italianate naturalism, painting in the luminous colours of El Greco – those cold blues and clarets, olive-shadowed yellows, and pure, clear greens of under the sea; lit with angry brilliance; geometric in form, yet in austerity sympathetic, in power gentle. It is these, the very flower of the Byzantine Renaissance – not only the link between European art and the East, final explication of El Greco, but in themselves divorced from history, masterpieces for the world – that are threatened ... by ... neglect.

This involved sentence sums up Robert's estimate of the rare, under-appreciated treasures of art and the urgent need for their preservation, not in American or continental museums, but where they still belonged, namely the monasteries of Mount Athos. Yet in these monasteries icons which, largely as a result of Robert's enthusiasm and study, threw new light upon the derivation of the medieval and Renaissance art of Christendom and even upon the limited secular art of his own day were being allowed to rot through lack of interest, funds and expertise in caring for them.

Robert's dissertation on that familiar adjunct to an English building, the balcony – so frowned upon at home as vulgar, 'protruding its banistered platforms to the tune of dormered roof and Rhenish tower' and commonly associated by readers with the suburban villa 'when Ruskin held the torch of taste', and where 'there is no domestic function that [it] does not fill' – is exceedingly comical as well as just. 'For the individual monk it is, above all, his home and his castle.' No less entertaining is the brief sketch of the viands provided in the Athonic monasteries. At the Grand Lavra, for example,

> the grime of cloth and napkins; spoons, knives and forks slimed with grease; the inevitable hors d'oeuvre; soup of haricot beans; those unmentionable vegetables resembling large cut nails and

filled with pips tasting of stale pharmaceutical peppermint; and an omelet of whipped oil

do not arouse the salivary glands to jocund expectation. Dinner with the Abbot of Gregoriou, entailing the most exotic menu known to Athonic monks, was described as follows:

cod salted after it had rotted in the summer sun; the macaroni embalmed in the juice of goats' udders curdled to a shrill sourness; water melon, ghastly pink like some spongy segment of a body delved from the intestines of a dog-fish; and accompanying all like a rasping bassoon in a band of village oboes, thick resinated wine tasting of pine-needles and reducing the human mouth to the texture of a cat's. The Abbot continued to heap my plate ...

Half-starved as they were from their physical inability to swallow such delicacies, it is hardly surprising that Robert and his party were for the most of their sojourn on the Holy Mountain famished, weak and often irritable. On the other hand, no amount of deprivation of the basic sustenance and comfort to which students from the western world were accustomed deterred them from the pursuit of their game. They slogged on with their research work. Disappointments were many. Although they carried letters of recommendation from the Ecumenical Patriarch, the Greek government's Foreign Secretary and the Metropolitan of Athens, the great treasure of Dionysiou, namely the fourteenth-century roll containing portraits of the Emperor Alexius III and the Empress Theodora, called the Imperial Chrysobul, was denied them. Nevertheless the fantastic reliquary of St Niphon, a miniature cathedral of gables and cupolas in silver gilt encrusted with gems, was duly laid before them, and photographed. And at Xenophontos they were rewarded with the two panels in mosaic of St George and St Demetrius dating from the eleventh and twelfth centuries, works of utmost rarity in the annals of Christian art. From his study of these exquisite little panels Robert submitted (whether his deduction has been proved valid by subsequent experts on the Byzantine who now abound, I am not competent to pronounce) that El Greco, his arch-hero, was a Byzantine born and bred.

In this regard Robert's actual words need to be transcribed.

Here [by which he referred to the old church of the Xenophontos monastery] is vouchsafed the ultimate corroboration of our thesis that El Greco was a Byzantine artist of the strongest conviction, who, having dispensed with the iconographic formulae of his native Church, spent his whole life in reverting to its spirit, technique and colour; and who alone of all his nation [Greece] and of all the Slavs, Russians, Serbs, Bulgars and Rumanians over whom its influence extended, brought Byzantine art to its logical fruition. Nowhere exists a link one half, one quarter so strong with this great painter of all time, and direct forebear of modern art, as in this small church decorated by an unknown hand in 1544, three years after El Greco was born.

Robert was by no means the first traveller in modern times to gain access to Mount Athos, although many had been refused it by suspicious monks, jealous guardians of their treasures against prying eyes. But, with Talbot-Rice, he can claim to be the first connoisseur to have opened the eyes of his compatriots to the great significance of the icon painting and fine arts of the Eastern Empire. No doubt his fervent and radiant descriptions of these artefacts sometimes exaggerated their merits, just as in his excitement he depreciated the artefacts of western Christendom. In any case his was a remarkable achievement for a young man just down from Oxford, aged twenty-one, no accredited scholar, with only a third-class degree – and that not even in art history.

Robert's later travels probably had more effect upon his career, and certainly on his reputation as author, than the early ones; their importance has been confirmed by his frequent companion on the road, Christopher Sykes, and by subsequent writers. His short career still awaits the definitive telling. It included journeys to India and Tibet, Russia, Persia, the United States, Russia again, and China. The journey to India in 1929 gave rise to one of the most remarkable and percipient commentaries on that huge country ever undertaken by an Englishman. Little longer than an extended pamphlet, Robert's *An Essay on India* (1931) was a brilliant summary of the love–hate relationship between the two nations, the one still an imperialist power, the other still in subjugation to it. Robert was unsparing in his contempt for the average Anglo-Indian's patronising attitude towards the natives, and in his respect for the latter's natural courtesy towards their overlords. His conclusion was that it was high time for the British to clear out of India. Naturally the book was condemned by the majority of his compatriots at home. Nevertheless, by a few it was considered worthy of attention, if not wholehearted approval. Among those in the first category was the Liberal Viceroy, Lord Willingdon, and in the second the Conservative ex-Governor of Bombay, Lord Lloyd of Dolobran. Another outcome of Robert's three months' visit to India was his unqualified admiration for Lutyens' viceregal palace in New Delhi, which he was to celebrate in several highly laudatory articles in *Country Life*. They did much to enhance the stature of the architect in his countrymen's esteem, and cemented a warm friendship between the two men. Robert's detailed study of Lutyens' masterpiece, 'a mirage of European genius set down in the forbidding country,' as he described it to his mother, turned his own attitude of grudging acknowledgement into an enthusiastic appreciation of the classical architecture of his own land. Hence the rousing campaign he was to mount in its defence against the prevailing vandalism in London and the county towns during the mid Thirties.

The journey to Persia in 1933–4 was ostensibly in quest of those high, cylindrical, early Seljuk mausolea of brick dating from the tenth to the eleventh century. To be found in the region of Meshed, they were known to Robert only from some inadequate photographs. They had greatly taken his fancy. In them he felt sure that he would capture the spirit of Persia before the age of Omar Khayyám with its over-romanticized evocations – of 'a Jug of Wine, a Loaf of Bread, and Thou' – which was about all western historians knew of the country's culture; that in them he would capture the spirit of Persia in the age of her greatest epic poet, Firdausi; and that they would prove to be the prototypes of all subsequent Islamic architecture throughout the Middle East; furthermore, that he might see in them an affinity with and an influence for good upon modern architecture in the west, like the skyscrapers of the New York seaboard which he so immensely admired, and from which he envisaged the emanation of a global style for the future.

The Road to Oxiana was, as we know, the outcome of his successful quest. In Christopher Sykes's company throughout, and under the initial guidance of some Persian enthusiasts attached to the British Legations in Baghdad and Tehran, he made the hazardous expedition across Persia into Afghanistan. Robert took some excellent photographs and made detailed drawings of the Seljuk monuments as he went. Their charismatic beauty surpassed his expectations. He deemed the brickwork of the great vertical towers more exquisite than that of Dutch and English houses of the seventeenth century.

My friendship with Robert Byron dated from the mid Thirties. I had, without getting to know him at all well, met him several times socially, once at one of John Sutro's famous fancy dress parties, practically naked, but bearded and hirsute, representing God. Owing to the three years between us, I did not coincide with him at Eton, or at Oxford when the missionary zeal of his early adulthood burgeoned and took him overseas for the greater part of each year. Would that I had, for my architectural interests might have widened accordingly. As it happened, we shared a friendship with Desmond Parsons, whose illness brought us together. Desmond, Michael Rosse's young brother, was utterly unlike him in character. Whereas Michael was conforming, reliable, conventional, good, correct, Desmond was the opposite. He was non-conforming, unreliable, unconventional, not particularly good (without being bad), and incorrect. But for the esoteric few he had charm. He had acute perceptions. He comprehended everything and concentrated on nothing for long. He was lethargic, complaining, not readily amused, and quickly bored. When in conversation he laughed, however, the interlocutor went up in flames.

From the first Desmond was responsive to Robert's travel mania, his love of Byzantine and Asiatic art, and his caustic brand of humour. Being fairly well off he had no need to travel the hard way. On the contrary, he would always do so the soft way; and consequently would not have been acceptable as a companion to Robert on his explorations. Robert was devoted to him, and on each return from abroad looked forward to seeing him more than anyone outside his family. In some mysterious and seemingly contradictory fashion Desmond's deep wells of understanding established him, younger though he was, as Robert's guru. The relationship was almost topsy-turvy. Theirs was the love of opposites. Desmond was the stationary idol and seer, certainly the luminary to whom Robert the voyager was drawn, if not for intellectual stimulus then for perceptual sympathy and encouragement: I dare to say, from so seemingly inert a young man, a recharge of zeal for the elder's enthusiasms.

Desmond and I had been in the same boarding house at Eton, where we were inclined to huddle together in silent defence against the games-addicted hearties contemptuous of what we supposed was literature, art, and a dedication to the sublimer life. On leaving school Desmond did not go to the university. With no need to work and for lack of anything better to do, he took a house near Harold Acton's in Peking, where he learnt Chinese and translated fairy stories into English. Robert, having completed his second journey to Russia with Sykes in 1935 and desirous of finishing *The Road to Oxiana* in peace and quiet, decided to stay with Desmond in Peking before returning to England. Worn out by his travels, in poor health and glad of an excuse to avoid the packing-up of the Byron home in Savernake Forest, he was immensely looking forward to the luxury and welcome which he knew lay in store in Peking. To his great distress, he found Desmond in a far worse state than his own. Desmond was suffering from swollen glands which reduced him at times to total inertia.

One afternoon Desmond came back from the American hospital where he was being treated. He told Robert the doctor had with a grave face proclaimed him a victim of Hodgkin's Disease. He had never heard of it before. Robert watched him cross the library, fetch from a shelf *Black's Medical Dictionary*, open it, and read the entry under HODGKIN's: 'a condition in which the lymphatic glands undergo a gradual progressive enlargement . . . the glands affected may reach a great size, and also glandular tissue forms in various organs all over the body . . . the affected person becomes gradually weaker . . . very little influenced by treatment.' In other words, there was no known cure for this fatal affliction. Desmond slammed the book on the table and said not a word.

His mother, Lady de Vesci, and brother, with Anne, Michael's wife, were staying with him. They decided that Desmond must immediately be taken to England by way of the Trans-Siberian Railway. Desmond begged Robert to stay behind, work at his book, look after the beloved house – a congeries of pavilions, courtyards, bamboos and fountains, which he was never to see again – and the servants in his absence. Robert gladly consented. Then he contracted 'flu, became very ill and collapsed into bed. Overcome with a deep depression, he just avoided a serious breakdown. He was probably saved from total disaster by the ministrations and companionship of Harold, and the comicalities of his Chinese teacher Mr Jo. By the end of May 1936, having concluded an intensive study of the Timurid culture and finished his book, he set sail across the Pacific for home.

Although he did not know it, but may have guessed, because of the grave international situation, Robert's long-distance travels were to be suspended. Henceforth he made only short trips abroad – not travels – for lectures and for business purposes: he got a job advertising the Shell-Mex Petroleum Company, whose offices were in St James's Street. Robert became transformed overnight into a man with a bowler hat, topcoat and furled umbrella, pacing the pavements when not dictating to stenographers and giving instructions down the telephone. I saw a good deal of him and Desmond in London when Desmond was well enough to come up, and also in the black and white house in Long Itchington village in Northamptonshire which Desmond rented from the Sachie Sitwells.

When Shell-Mex could spare him Robert devoted his energies to promoting the interests of the Georgian Group and the Federal Union Club. In both these ventures, particularly the first, I too was involved, having recently joined the staff of the National Trust. I often acted as his unofficial amanuensis, and was with him when he wrote the famously vibrant and vituperative pamphlet for the Georgians, *How We Celebrate the Coronation*. In it he lambasted unscrupulous property developers, greedy landlords and the Church Commissioners for their cynical demolition of the nation's classical streets and Wren churches, even referring to the Bishop of London as 'this mitred serpent'. He would read out to me the most corrosive passages amid deep gurgles of throaty laughter, only occasionally deigning to accept a contributory word of venom – or a restraining alternative, for we were terrified of being sued for libel.

I was then lodging in a Chelsea embankment bed-sitting room in a house owned by my great friends the Stewart-Jones family. We were a group of young people of both sexes at the dawn of our careers, most of us very poor. Robert in his bombastic manner, and with a snarl which I vividly remember, suggested that I leave 'that refined brothel' as he termed the innocuous household and rent a more commodious spare room from him at number 1 Swan Walk. Indeed it was an improvement of my living standards. In the charming white-fronted house, approached by a short garden path, Robert on his return from dinner engagements and balls would endlessly type, with one finger, articles for *The Times* and other magisterial periodicals, to the accompaniment of late-night classical music or jazz, no matter which, from a screechy wireless set.

These last years before the outbreak of the war were bitter for him. The rise and triumph of the dictators were an agony. They provoked him to thunderous denunciations in the national press. His endeavours to persuade politicians in high places to listen to his first-hand experiences of Nazi Germany and Fascist Italy and to what he learned from his contacts with Berlin and Rome went unheeded. The lonely part he played then is appreciated now by his admirers. In the Federal Union Club, of which the honorary secretary was a son of Jack Squire, the poet, man of letters and editor of *The London Mercury*, he played the leading role as president. The Club's purpose was a last desperate bid to encourage the democratic countries of Europe to unite in some sort of loose federation and so halt a landslide into European tyranny. The Club did not have the time or prestige to formulate a precise programme for such a federation's structure before Hitler walked into Poland. Notwithstanding this tragedy, Robert's vision of a European future and means of salvation against international brigandage was clear and forthright.

The wretchedness of his life as a businessman and as an impotent witness of the Nazi menace in the last few years of peace was exacerbated by the steady decline of Desmond's health. That decline affected Robert grievously. Whenever he did not spend weekends with his parents at Overton House, which he detested, he would go to Long Itchington. Occasionally he would accompany Desmond, when Desmond felt well enough, on summer excursions. They would drive in a large hired Daimler limousine, of which the boot and roof would be groaning with delicacies – often provided by John Sutro, another close friend of the Parsons family, from Fortnum & Mason's – caviare, smoked salmon, pâté de foie gras being considered the staple diet for picnics. Country houses not then open to the general public and remote churches not then kept under lock and key by day and night were the ostensible objectives of these sybaritic jaunts. But on 4th July 1937 Desmond succumbed at the age of twenty-six to his terrible disease. Robert was shattered. Together he and I crossed the Irish Sea for the funeral at Birr Castle, the Rosse family seat and Desmond's childhood home. The gloomy Parsons vault had been adorned with flowers by Anne, who shared her brother Oliver Messel's theatrical skill in decoration. The vault might have been the entrance scene to Hades as contrived by Zeffirelli for Gluck's opera *Orpheus and Eurydice* at Covent Garden.

It was while staying either at Long Itchington or at nearby Weston Hall, where Sachie and Georgia lived, that Robert first came upon the Menagerie at Horton Park near Northampton. This lovely landscape feature built on a slight mound within view of a great house already demolished was then a near ruin. But in the central chamber enough was left of an exquisite rococo ceiling and walls to intoxicate Robert's love of the audacious in architectural composition. He took me to see it in 1938. I photographed the Menagerie with a cow leaning its head out of a window. It became for Robert his Eldorado, the golden citadel, the dream which would be realized only when the loathed dictators were vanquished, the war was over and sanity had returned to the world. He would then acquire, reinstate and live in it. It would be his rural retreat for ever and ever. I wondered at the time – were he to survive, would he have the money to rebuild this magical castle in the air?

When war did break out Robert was not depressed. He had known that it must come and I truly believe that, if it had not, he would have done away with himself for shame. What immediately irked him was that his country did not seem to have a war job to offer that might tax his best efforts towards victory. In his view, he was obliged to fritter his talents in fatuous work in the BBC Foreign Department. Then suddenly he was offered and accepted the job of war correspondent for the *Sunday Times* in Egypt.

In 1939 I did not see the issue between Great Britain and Germany in his clear-cut terms. I was hesitant about the rightness, even the long-term sense, of the Churchillian warmongers with whom Robert had so unequivocally allied himself. To my mind war never brought any country any good and usually brought indelible harm. I wrote asking for his opinion, whether he thought I ought to join the army, or a Quaker ambulance service, which was my preference. I knew there were no other choices for me. I quote not for the first time from a long lucid letter he sent me when he was up to his eyes in his own war concerns. I do so because it testifies to his positive and absolute conviction that he was always right. It also testifies to his positive and powerful intellect. At any rate, the letter made up my mind for me. To this day I do not know whether in fact I was then right in accepting his advice.

Regarding my pacifist inclinations Robert wrote as follows:

> If you say you refuse to kill your fellow men; if you maintain that the evil caused by war outweighs any good that war can preserve; if you are prepared to envisage the conditions of life that would result from our not fighting, and to accept such a prospect as preferable to war; and if you believe that by your personal pacifism you are contributing all you can to the avoidance of war in the future, then I will receive your opinions with respect and ask you to explain them further.
>
> Whether one is a pacifist or not, one must admit that pacifism isn't going to get us out of the mess now we are in it. Therefore it seems to me that the only thing to do and the only way to comport oneself is to determine to clear up the mess afterwards and to carry the techniques of preventing war perhaps one, perhaps the whole stage further.

In February 1941 I was in the army – in fact, on the verge of being discharged as unfit. Robert was staying at the Great Western Hotel, Paddington, awaiting orders to embark for Egypt. Passing through London, I called on him to say goodbye. Although it was fairly late in the morning he was still upstairs in his dressing-gown, writing. Descending in the lift together we had a row. He was being agressively critical of something my late boss Lord Lloyd had said or done – I forget precisely what – and in my loyalty to Lloyd I defended him hotly.

Christopher Sykes has borne out what an extremely exacting friend Robert was; that his friendships were never relaxing; that with him they were a perpetual challenge, an exercise in controversy; and that being a man of passionate convictions, he would not take disagreement in his stride. He would without warning take to violence. Harold Acton lamented that his friendship with Robert 'was based on argument rather than the calm exchange of sentiments and ideas, for either he had some axe to grind or sought to foist some new-found theory upon me ... he would prowl about the floor with carnivorous tread or stand fuming at me like an angry uncle.' Like me, Harold once took a room in a flat of Robert's for a brief spell, on the strict understanding that he was never to have a first bath. And when Harold ventured to help him into his overcoat Robert said 'Don't do that!', wrenched the coat off, and 'danced a war dance over it.'

Indeed, in Robert's company one had always to be prepared for squalls, and hope that sleep – for he fell into deep snores at the touch of an invisible button – would put an end to them. His boredom level was so low that without preliminary warning he might bellow, as he once did at the drawing-room raconteur Harry Melvill, 'Can't you shut up, you hideous old relic of the Victorian age?' The next moment his great glazed eyes would be twinkling with laughter, by which the offended stranger might not be mollified. But on the Paddington hotel occasion, neither slumber nor merriment intervened. Robert struck me – a rather smug officer in the Brigade of Guards, and in uniform – knocking off my cap. I was incensed, and also humiliated. As the lift gate clanged behind us I shouted, 'I shall never see you again, Robert. Never! This is the end.' And before my temper had cooled, it was.

That last encounter may have been the only one when I did not laugh with him. For, all said and done, he was more amusing and witty than anyone I have ever known. And on this count alone his friends forgave him his brutish behaviour. Some years after his death Nancy Mitford wrote, 'Impossible to convey to others what utter heaven he was. So complex.' Which was something of an understatement. And again, 'Perhaps the dead person I miss the most.'

In his very last letter, on the brink of departure, he wrote to Mrs Byron from Liverpool: 'Don't worry. We are all in the war together...I regard this as a glorious war and am glad to be taking a more active part in it.'

John Fowler

1906–1977

SOMETIMES IN THE watches of the night I try to induce sleep by counting the virtues of my friends. It is remarkable how few vices they seem to have. I truly believe that John Fowler had fewer than most people I have known, and to his intimates his shortcomings were rather endearing. His virtues and accomplishments seemed almost legion. Of the former he had courage, humility, industry, candour, kindness, generosity, discretion, humour; and of the latter the gifts of craftsmanship, painting, gardening, cooking, music – he learnt to play early music on the harpsichords in Major Benton Fletcher's collection at Old Devonshire House, Holborn – and friendship in very full measure. I could go on and on.

I first met him in 1942 during the height of the Blitz on London. The following year he and I happened to be Chelsea neighbours. I lived in a flimsy little house on the river embankment, he in a flimsy little house in a Regency terrace along the King's Road. John somehow had managed to rig up in his back garden an Anderson shelter. It consisted of a not very deep hole in the ground, covered with a few sheets of tin, and he had implicit faith in its resistance to parachute mines. There were bunks in the shelter, into which John liked to invite his friends, and indeed any neighbours who, he decided, needed a respite from fear and a night's comparative peace. Nervous dogs and cats were not excluded. I sometimes enjoyed the hospitality and cosiness which his shelter afforded, whether he was there or not. On several nights of the week he was absent on duty at Guy's Hospital, where he attended operations and dressed the wounds of badly mutilated victims of air raids, without apparently turning a hair. Moreover, on every day of the week bar one, when he attended to his own civilian work, then practically dormant, he was on Red Cross duty.

It did not take me long to appreciate and admire the sheer goodness, the almost restless desire to help others, and the fun of this most lovable man. His sense of the ludicrous was very highly developed, and he was one of the few people I have known who would laugh until he literally cried.

I never discovered much about John Fowler's childhood beyond the fact that he had had impoverished parents living in or near Newmarket. He had Irish ancestry, of which he was proud, notably blood of the Beresford family (Beresford being his second Christian name) in his veins. The name of Lord John de la Poer Beresford, a munificent Primate of Ireland and a bachelor, figured prominently in John's reminiscences. On the other hand, the Archbishop's father, the 1st Marquess of Waterford, who had numerous illegitimate children, John never mentioned. At an early age he lost his father, who had been connected with horse-racing and addicted to the bottle. His mother, whom he adored, was left extremely hard up. She underwent great sacrifices to have him educated, and her privations weighed heavily upon him ever after. This explains perhaps why he glossed over his early years. On her death he was obliged to leave school, at the age of fourteen, for work on a chicken farm in Suffolk. At sixteen he managed to get a humble job in London, in an estate agency in St James's Street, at a pitifully low salary. He once told me he knew what it felt like to go hungry. He hated the estate agency as much as the chicken farm.

A kindly cousin, taking pity, introduced him to a well known antique dealer, Thornton Smith. John remained eternally grateful to his cousin Una. Until the end of her life he would endure interminable telephone conversations with her every

Sunday morning, at great cost to his patience for she was a very dull old lady.

For the first time John had congenial work to do. At Thornton Smith's his primary training was in painting wallpapers, which John Cornforth affirms was to affect his whole approach to decoration in the future. He also learnt the arts of gilding, marbling, and repairing and resuscitating old fabrics. In fact he learnt the various tricks of the craftsmanship at which he was to become so adept and gained the background knowledge which was to make him one of the foremost authorities on textiles. It is no exaggeration to say that nearly every spare hour from Thornton Smith's he spent in the Victoria and Albert Museum, poring over furniture and costumes. He had no university or Courtauld Institute training in the arts and crafts, but was largely self-taught.

Then for a time in the late Twenties he worked on his own, but that was not a commercial success. In the early Thirties he worked for Peter Jones in Sloane Square, to become head of the antiques and restoration department. From there in 1938 he joined the society hostess Sibyl Colefax's decorating firm, taking some of the best Peter Jones staff with him. His innovative painted furniture gained him a reputation. Although he became fond of Sibyl, to whom he owed his introduction to numerous clients among the rich and fashionable, he was often maddened by her monopoly of the firm's secretaries and telephones in pursuit of her endless social engagements and parties. In no time he was her right-hand man, and eventually her partner, making Colefax & Fowler Ltd a firm of world renown. From comparatively modest beginnings he rose to achieve, in John Cornforth's words, 'a legendary name and influence in interior decoration'. Innumerable indeed are the houses of England, in private hands and those of the National Trust, which have been retrieved from decay and given new life by his magic touch. Of his country house work that remains (for a decorator's work is ephemeral), Radburne Hall in Derbyshire for the Chandos Poles, and for the National Trust Clandon, Surrey and Sudbury, Derbyshire are among the best surviving exercises of his extraordinary colour sense on ceilings, walls and fabrics. At Claydon in Buckinghamshire his idiosyncratic application of different shades of white (twelve in all in the saloon, I think) is an object lesson to younger decorators in how to bring about apparent happy contrasts in tone where no colour in fact exists.

John's early life had been a struggle. And the fruits of that struggle were enhanced by remarkable industry and power of observation. Because he worked so hard himself, he expected his assistants to do likewise. He would go to endless trouble teaching those who were willing to learn. I have often watched local builders visibly exhilarated by John's deft and lightning movements, as he mixed paints for them, climbed ladders and demonstrated how to wield the paint-brush in order to achieve some special effect he had in mind. He could be called a hard taskmaster. Yet I do not suppose that many of his pupils, on reflection, resented his severity. For one thing, they learnt so much. For another, there was no task he might demand of them which he could not do rather better than they. But John was extremely autocratic in the office. One of his assistants, who today is the leading light of the Colefax & Fowler shop, has told me how he terrified the young typists. They were obliged to knock at the door before entering his room, and expected to stand while he dictated letters. He would not suffer them to sit in his presence. When irritated he would shout at them, calling them ugly names. I do remember being amazed by his rudeness towards his tiny daily woman, Dot (Mrs Roach), who during the war braved the bombs all the way from the Mile End Road to the King's Road, wearing the same flat hat like a burnt pancake. 'Dot, you dreadful old cow, how often have I told you not to dust my precious clock with the ends of your filthy old skirt?' At first I thought he was being jocular in a rather unfunny way. But not at all. Dot may have been tiny, but she was a stalwart cockney, and gave back as good as she got. 'Mr Fowler, you old sod. You're worse than 'Itler,' she would retort in a cacophony of self-satisfaction. Perhaps this dialogue was a sort of sparring match from which they both derived a macabre enjoyment. Most of his staff, including Dot eventually, became intimate friends whom he would treat in a funny paternal manner as though they were his children. 'Now then, childie' – or 'girlie', or 'dear boy', as they might be – 'I know you won't refuse to do this, or that,' and they always did it, joyfully, or feignedly joyfully. He delighted in sharing with them whatever he possessed. The little Gothic hunting lodge at Odiham which he bought in 1947, with the exquisite garden he created out of nothing, with pleached hornbeam hedges, statues and pavilions, in the French style, was just as much dedicated to his friends' pleasure as to his own. And they all stayed with him for long weekends.

His relationship with his most faithful client, 'Wissy' Ancaster, who was Nancy, Lady Astor's daughter and chatelaine of that most glorious Vanbrugh house, Grimsthorpe Castle in Lincolnshire, was certainly a deep love–hate, more love than hate. Each depended on the other's uncanny eye for what was *right* in decoration. Yet each annoyed the other. They argued, contradicted, shouted at one another, and flounced out. 'Folly', she called him, on account of his suddenly acquired *folie de grandeur*. As Hugh Massingberd puts it, Wissy and Folly 'sparked each other off', to transform a rather dreary Edwardian interior into 'one of the most stylish, cheerful and under-stated great houses of the late twentieth century.'

As for Nancy Tree, Wissy's cousin and John's boss-to-be, no one could get the better of her. When Sibyl Colefax was obliged to give up the shop it was acquired from her by Nancy. And with it went John Fowler, to whom Nancy was overheard saying, 'Now, John, I'm replanting you from a smaller pot into a slightly bigger one.' Their relationship was similar to his and Wissy's.

John was obliged by the nature of his work to submit to the dictates of rich, often spoilt society women, whose company he might enjoy but whose wilfulness and know-allness intensely irked him. Nancy Lancaster, as Nancy Tree soon became on marrying a third husband, Colonel Claude Lancaster of Kelmarsh Hall, Northamptonshire, was on the periphery of this category. Because her first husband of only a few weeks (Henry Field of Chicago), and her second (Ronald Tree) had been immensely rich, the ci-devant chatelaine of Ditchley Park was inevitably associated with American money, of which she had been left very little by both. She was highly sophisticated, witty, mercurial, charming, and her taste in decorating old houses was no less uncanny than Wissy's. Not only did she make her own look as though they had been inhabited by her ancestors for hundreds of years, but she fashioned their gardens on classical lines as though they were extensions of the house, thus contriving an imaginative unity between them, florescent and abundant.

Nancy kept friends on their toes and in permanent fits of amusement. Her sayings were bandied from mouth to ear. John revelled in her company and in the high standards of good living she inculcated. Yet he cavilled at the privileged status which her connections had blessed her with. He remained the poor boy, resentful at being patronised, bossed around and obliged to conform to her womanly whims. Although he soon learned on which side of the loaf his bread was buttered, at heart he despised the affluent aristocracy, voted Labour at every general election, and was ready to join any protest march against the Establishment.

Nevertheless, even in his impecunious days, and long before he became a member of that Establishment which he so derided, John never compromised with clients over matters of taste and what he termed *correctness* in the decoration of historic buildings, or in modern ones for that matter. No art scholar whose learning had been instilled into him by professors, but one of nature's enthusiasts whose immense knowledge had been picked up by the wayside, John was the least academic of men. Yet nothing was allowed to stand in the way of getting a thing right. He was conservative in his treatment of old buildings. Rather than imposing his own foibles, he endeavoured, whenever possible, to reinstate what had existed originally. This was not easy to accomplish, and sometimes he did not succeed. The conundrum which seldom failed to arise was, what was original? And when was it original? And was a later alteration not sometimes an improvement on the original? John was always reluctant to redecorate the walls and ceilings of historic rooms unless it was absolutely essential. If in doubt, he would always clean paint, even paper, with water and rag. If need be he would scrape and scrape through layers of later coats of paint and wallpaper, until he satisfied himself that he had come upon what the Caroline or Georgian builder or owner had intended. Thereupon he reproduced the original colours or paper patterns as closely as he could. He was a master of related tones; his use of contrasting shades of white amounted, as I have already observed, almost to genius.

Old craftsmanship was sacred to John Fowler. Ancient artefacts were venerated by him. Even a simple Georgian nail was a thing to be cherished. Lifting off his nose-spectacles (they had immensely thick lenses, for he was blind as a bat) he would hold the nail within a few inches of his small myopic eyes and scrutinize it with a tender devotion. A craggy nose, veined cheeks and a deeply grooved upper lip made him look like Tenniel's illustration of the Duchess in *Alice in Wonderland*. Whereas in his youth his clothes were rather flamboyant, in middle age they were invariably a subfusc matching suit of light-weight tweed, tight-waisted and somewhat prim. His manner might strike strangers as tutorial. He appeared to lay down the law on the subject of the architectural orders and terminology. He was a stickler over the correct use of moulds, *cyma recta* and *cyma reversa*, and a stern observer of the Vitruvian rules relating to the spatial relationship between, say, skirting and dado, frieze and cornice; and the exact size of a chimneypiece to suit the proportions of a given room. Debo Devonshire [the current Duchess; Nancy Mitford's sister] would tease him about these niceties, and call him Simon Erecta to his face. He relished it.

Latterly, a stranger would require a good deal of courage to engage John's personal attention for work on a new house or flat, even to dare to penetrate the shop doorway. And if John guessed that the prospective task was the decoration of a hideously pretentious dwelling in the suburbs, say, of Newcastle upon Tyne or Stoke-on-Trent, he might well decline with a rather patronising dismissal.

He enjoyed telling a story against himself from the days before his fame. The formidable Mrs James de Rothschild, owner with her husband of Waddesdon Manor and of works of art no less rare and priceless than those in the Wallace Collection, demanded one day to see John, and without a by-your-leave brushed past – I feel sure, with exquisite politeness – a timorous assistant, straight into his office. It seems to me doubtful that even in his rawest years John would not have known who she was; perhaps he was busy with other matters, and did not hear her name. Unlike the typists, Mrs de Rothschild sat herself firmly down on the chair facing him. John, looking up, asked, 'Do you have … er … pretty things?' Without hesitation Mrs de Rothschild snapped, 'The best, Mr Fowler, the best.' Needless to say, they ended great friends.

Later on, he dealt ruthlessly with anyone, from royalty downwards, whose ideas he considered lacked taste. He would simply rise from his chair and, without saying a word, head in air, walk out of the room in his peculiar stiff gait, with both arms stretched against his thighs, his hands palms downward and fingers fanned upwards, the picture of disdain – leaving an indignant Saudi princess or American multi-millionaire to be pacified by an embarrassed secretary. On the other hand, if approached by the shabbiest young or old woman whom he sensed to be hard up, ready to take his advice, and absolutely unpretentious, he would be as sweet as sugar.

The eighteenth century was alive to John. By its standards of beauty he measured the achievements of the twentieth, usually to the twentieth's detriment. If ever there was a con- servationist, he was one. He made it *his* duty to protect Georgian buildings, sometimes even from his own clients. He would threaten an offending owner about to commit an architectural solecism with public obliquity, with letters to *The Times*, and with questions raised in both Houses of Parliament. Any other decorator, adopting such tactics, would have lost both job and client. But not John Fowler. His authority and charm were too compelling, and his services were too much in demand.

It cannot be claimed that he was a good business man. He cared not a hoot for big money. In fact he was wholly unmercenary, and instead of earning riches like most popular decorators – and good luck to them – he was often extremely hard up. He seldom bothered to charge the firm with his out-of-pocket expenses and entertainments, and often neglected to send accounts to his clients. Rich people like Mrs Paul Mellon were positively displeased when not charged for days of work on their behalf and the supply of the choicest curtains and carpets. This does not mean that he – or rather the firm – was not very expensive when the day of reckoning came, for Colefax & Fowler's fabrics were always of the finest quality, and often specially woven. John himself was also very extravagant. He was profligate in wanting the best, albeit the best of a narrow range of things: no yachts, no motor cars – he had none of either – but he always had to have delicious food, and wines of the very best vintage, and every comfort, for himself and his friends.

If asked to state the reason why John Fowler became such a success as a decorator I would answer tersely: because he observed. I don't mean he merely looked at things. He looked into them. Nothing escaped his curiosity, notice and judgement. Things made by human hands out of natural materials, whether spun cotton and wool, or stone and mineral, had to be dissected by him. He had to find out, often by taking them to pieces, what they were made of and how they had been made. He was also infinitely curious about people of the past, both patrons and artisans. Particularly artisans. He held history in great veneration. He had a prodigious memory for dates, into which he would at once classify works of art and craftsmanship. Then he would relate them to the kind of people who needed them and the conditions in which they lived. A rough-and-ready door latch would be examined and attributed by him to a blacksmith in the Midlands during the

Wars of the Roses; an emerald and diamond ring as having come from a Hatton Garden goldsmith patronised by the court of Charles II. Admittedly, the finer the object, the more he admired it: to him, a silver teapot by Paul de Lamerie or Paul Storr meant more than a crude slipware effigy of Adam and Eve by Thomas Toft of the Staffordshire pottery group. But if he did not wholeheartedly admire the latter, he respected it and regarded it with wonder.

As he aged so he became more recondite, more pernickety, more cautious and more precise in his definitions and his appraisal of his colleagues' workmanship. His standards intensified. In a sense he shifted from being an artist to a conservationist. Most of his work towards the end of his life was indeed done for the National Trust, the work of a restorer rather than an originator. He had to put back what went before. Clients recognized that he was the most historically knowledgable and reliable of decorators. Owners and guardians of great houses knew that their treasures would be safe in his hands. Before the Second World War, this had not necessarily been the case. One could, in the 1930s, justifiably criticize the too-easily identifiable hallmark of the John Fowler style – a surfeit of draped and flounced curtains and pelmets and tightly buttoned chair and sofa covers, which spelt fashion. These over-feminine and even camp artifices were repressed in later years.

John seemingly had the ability to recapture time. His understanding of the past was so acute that he could conjure it up, at will, like the proverbial rabbit out of a hat. His retrospective interiors could simulate suspended attrition. This mastery over wear, tear and change was no doubt partly a gift – not a legacy, because she outlived him, although she gave up working for the shop long before he did – from Nancy Lancaster. For he had studied every detail of her paradigm of conservation, that dream palace of the decorator's be-all and end-all, *taste*, namely Ditchley Park in Oxfordshire.

So John Fowler found his fulfilment in being an expert, an artist, and a fighter. All his life he fought – first, extreme poverty and loneliness, and then philistinism. To these foes yet another, crueller one was to be added. His last ten or twelve years were shadowed by an inexorable cancer. He fought it, as he fought all the other evils, valiantly to the end.

Osbert Lancaster

1908–1986

OSBERT WAS BORN two days before me, on 4th August 1908. On this account, and only this, we used to call ourselves twins – separated by, as it were, a rather extended and painful delivery. Indeed both of us saw the light in the reign of King Edward VII, a factor which I think distinguished Osbert pre-eminently, although I am not quite sure about myself. In many respects he epitomized the Edwardian age, to which he looked back as one of quality and individualism. He observed the Edwardian mores and proprieties. Even the topical cartoons for which he is justly famous seem Edwardian in their telling detail, now that one can compare them with those of his successors which are composed of suggestively minimal strokes of the pencil. Although by no means imitative, Osbert's cartoons were strongly influenced by the style of that distinctively Edwardian artist whom he intensely venerated, Sir Max Beerbohm.

Whether by design or accident, Sir Osbert Lancaster grew to look very much like his hero. He made the most of similar though robuster physical features which he shared with Max, namely a round head on a stocky body, a cleft chin, huge round eyes, thick expressive eyebrows, and a bristling moustache which he was forever twiddling, like the blimpish major he wasn't. Like Max Beerbohm he was immaculately and urbanely (as opposed to rurally) dressed, in natty suits, highly polished shoes, prominent handkerchief in breast pocket, an inch of cuff below the coat-sleeve, and habitual carnation in button-hole. When in his Sunday best, so to speak – in fact he was always in it – he had a nervous habit of twitching his shoulders and jerking an arm, as though his shirt collars were a little too tight or the sleeves of his coat were not integrating with the shirt cuffs to his satisfaction. This nervous tic suggested a slight lack of ease or self-confidence not otherwise noticeable in his bold demeanour.

Yes, Osbert was every inch the urban man. That his very correct dress was contrived is manifested by the frequent caricatures he drew of himself. By no means a vain man, he deliberately accentuated his singular appearance, not pompously but semi-self-mockingly. I fancy he was well aware of his undeniable ugliness and vainly endeavoured to temper it in the beholder's eyes by accentuation, a characteristic ploy often to be observed in those whom nature has not favoured physically at birth, and one to be regarded as poignant rather than pathetic. Not that Osbert was in any sense the traditional clown who wears alternatively the masks of comicality and poignancy. There was nothing tragic about Osbert, any more than there was in the principal characters of his cartoons. As the years went by he became no more or less real than the characters he had invented.

Although Osbert delighted in pouncing upon the sins and follies of others, which he neither condemned nor condoned but merely held up to ridicule, he was extremely reticent – again like Max Beerbohm – about himself. He had of course nothing to conceal; behind the mockery was primness and circumspection. In fine, Osbert was evocative of an earlier and more stylish age, not remarkable for austerity, than the one he was delineating. What made him stand head and shoulders above all previous caricaturists was the movement of his figures. In his reminiscences he revealed tellingly that the most authentic give-away of a person's generation, background and upbringing was not so much his voice, accent and mannerisms, as his gestures. These endemic qualities were irrepressible, and stamped him for all eternity.

Osbert was the only child of a decent middle-aged, middle-class and middle-brow father (killed in the First World War) and a mother to whom he was devoted. In describing her as 'very capable' he presumably meant dominant, if not domineering before he was able to escape from her possessive protection. Clare (Mrs Lancaster) was the last surviving pupil of G.F. Watts and as a young woman painted very commendably in the manner of the Pre-Raphaelites. She also had leanings to spiritualism, and supported the suffragette movement. She considered women a downtrodden and abused sex, domestically as well as politically. Her advice to Osbert's bride on the eve of their wedding, 'Promise me that you will not let Osbert be tiresome. I know what those Lancasters are like when given half a chance', may indicate one reason for her sentiments. But the First World War and her work in a Red Cross Unit did little to mitigate them. While remaining a prey to dotty enthusiasms and a sucker for the proselytism of cranky religious sects, she never allowed any interest to lessen her determination that whatever her ewe lamb's bent should be, he must get to the top. One of Osbert's most delightful cartoons shows Mrs Lancaster, a dumpy, square figure, handbag at the ready, striding aggressively into church with her reluctant son, spotty and rather cowed, trailing in the rear.

He was brought up in a substantial West Kensington house and educated at a well-known public school, Charterhouse – another experience which he shared with Max Beerbohm. Until adulthood he was also kept under the patriarchal eye of his grandfather, whose heir he was; Sir William Lancaster, having made a fortune in the City, lived in Wimbledon. However, Mrs Lancaster's house, number 79 Elgin Terrace, Notting Hill was, if not luxurious, then comfortable. Servants were not lacking and abundant aunts and great-aunts in the neighbourhood were attentive to the young fatherless scion. As a child among grown-ups he was rather perky, quick to air opinions, and precocious. At Clare's tea parties he was a little too eager to press the cucumber sandwiches upon the prettier lady guests.

Throughout his life Osbert was well endowed with care, and money.

I first met him at Oxford, where we were undergraduates together. I think he had been at the University a year before I arrived. At any rate he was already an established star in the aesthetic firmament. He was a prominent member of the OUDS (Oxford University Dramatic Society), a friend of John Betjeman, Stephen Spender, Alan Pryce-Jones, Randolph Churchill, and the intellectual and social élite, with a tendency towards the raffish. He had much to offer as jester and commentator. He was a regular contributor to *The Cherwell* magazine of irreverent caricatures and witty articles at foes' and friends' expense. The set he belonged to sat at the feet of the Warden of Wadham College, Maurice Bowra, a highly intelligent don, eminent Greek scholar and socialite combined. Bowra's influence over Osbert was marked, to the extent that the impressionable neophyte adopted the guru's booming voice, explosive emphasis of certain words and phrases, and a habit in conversation of regaling his audiences with rehearsed witticisms and gossip (in Osbert's case merely mischievous, unlike Bowra's, which were often downright malicious and offensive). In fact I sometimes found Osbert's verbal witticisms too staged an act to be wholeheartedly applauded and his jokes often too contrived to merit the uproarious response they clearly demanded. Osbert's conversation and raconteuring never seemed to me quite so incisive or amusing as his drawings and writings; and that is saying a great deal for the two last talents.

In the long summer vacations those of us who were privileged with the friendship of our contemporary under-graduate Harry d'Avigdor-Goldsmid often stayed at Somerhill, a large and finely appointed country house outside Tonbridge belonging to his hospitable and long-suffering parents. There in the cool of the day we played tennis until the shadows crept across the asphalt court. Osbert's prowess was not Wimbledonish, and he and I were a match in long rallies of pat-ball amidst guffaws of laughter as we mimicked Suzanne

Lenglen and the teenage wonder kid Betty Nuthall. I can look back upon no greater happiness than set after set of tennis against an opponent of one's own age, not too good and certainly not too bad, both trying hard to win and nevertheless treating the game as fun and not as a profession upon which our future depended. On our tennis nothing depended. Moreover a delicious drink, bath and dinner awaited us.

On leaving Oxford Osbert led a dandyish sort of life, visiting art exhibitions, going to the opera and ballet, travelling on the continent and learning languages. He studied at the Slade School of Art and worked under Vladimir Polunin, who had been Diaghilev's stage designer. This stood him in good stead when later he came to design scenery for Covent Garden, Sadler's Wells and Glyndebourne. Through Polunin he met and married in 1933 Karen, the younger daughter of Sir Austen Harris, a cultivated banker, and his wildly eccentric wife Cara. I daresay Osbert was as much attracted by Lady Harris as by her daughter. At any rate Karen's rich background was exactly right and her parents just what appealed to him. While Sir Austen kept discreetly out of the limelight, spinning necessary money in the City and rarely making his presence felt in the home beyond enunciating very occasionally in a dead-pan yet tolerant voice a memorable comment on the goings-on, his wife was the initiator of ceaseless theatricals, pranks and follies. She had an unconventional mind, and invented devices such as a tree-sex-detector, which might consist of a barrage of tangled wires round the chestnuts and copper beeches in the garden, or an outrageously extending pair of lazy tongs with which at parties she could command the attention of her children or her enchanting secretary, Fluff, gripping them by the hair or the hem of a skirt or, if the victim was her son-in-law, by the seat of his trousers. The amateur films she staged with Osbert's co-operation – I recall one enacted on the Isle of Wight (where the Harrises had a house), of an Edwardian party of big-game hunters in Africa – were so funny that the actors were in a permanent state of hysteria.

Karen was no mean artist in her own right, very intelligent and amusing, but loathed parties and the social round as much as Osbert relished them. In the family context, Karen's elder sister Honey should never be overlooked. Likewise a painter, she was very well educated, well read, deep and whimsical. She had a gentle but ironical and slightly deprecating laugh, which invited complicity in mischief. I believe that to some extent she took over Karen's role as admonitor and even instigator of some of Osbert's extravagant public utterances. Outwardly she was immensely tactful and after Karen's death remained as close to Osbert as he was to her. Osbert subsequently married the well-known journalist and gardening writer, Anne Scott-James. Although devoted to one another they made a somewhat incongruous pair strolling arm in arm as they were wont to do, she tall, slender, extremely pretty and naturally elegant, he up to her shoulder, stocky, pock-marked, and by now the living and visible symbol of his own cartoons.

During the Thirties Osbert contributed articles and cartoons to numerous journals on a free-lance basis. He quickly built up a reputation as a first-rate political and social satirist. Of the books he published and illustrated, *Progress at Pelvis Bay*, *Pillar to Post* and *Homes, Sweet Homes* were brilliant commentaries on the accelerating destruction of the British towns and landscape at the hands of unprincipled speculative developers and apathetic and ignorant local authorities, thanks to the philistine indifference of the public. Really the Twenties and Thirties were ghastly decades of cynicism as regards the arts, and it passes my comprehension why certain enthusiasts think fit to preserve their beastly architecture. Osbert formulated new terms for the more flagrantly imitative styles; Pont Street Dutch, Wimbledon Transitional, Stockbroker's Tudor and Banker's Georgian are now currently accepted in every guidebook and gazetteer as descriptive of the inter-war phases, all of which, though deplorably derivative, were nevertheless better than what came immediately after.

In 1938 Osbert was appointed cartoonist to the *Daily Express*. Almost daily for forty years, with only brief interruptions, he produced a pocket cartoon (a term he also invented) – ten thousand in all – for which he became world renowned. Although ostensibly non party-political, his sympathies were emphatically traditional, yet Liberal in the old Whig sense. As he abhorred violence, pretension and vulgarity in public men and women, so he detested his boss Lord Beaverbrook, the unscrupulous proprietor of the *Daily Express*. For the expanding sales of this newspaper Osbert was, to Beaverbrook's chagrin (and delight), largely responsible. As for Osbert's feelings, they were presumably pleasurable and no more, for he totally lacked greed and was incorruptible.

The cast characters of his *Daily Express* cartoons quickly took their place among the great comedians in English fiction. Maudie Lady Littlehampton, fashionable, low-brow, absurd and lovable, her husband Willie chinless, hard-drinking, womanizing, bemused, fatuous and forever treading on toes, yet occasionally shrewd; and Canon Fontwater, the trendy and yet conventional cleric – these became the acknowledged social commentators of the immediate pre- to post-war era. As the years went by, so they and the other recurrent figures of Lancaster's invention aged and their responses to topical events became more and more predictable and funny. Osbert's captions were as adept as his cartoons: at the height of the spy period Maudie, in an opera box, watching Nureyev cavorting on stage, asked, 'Is that the one we swopped for Burgess?', while Mrs Everywoman at the flower show warned her husband, sniffing a gloxinia, 'Take care what you say, Wilbur, they may well be bugged.' He was no castigator. Even when dealing with Mussolini or Hitler, he was making fun of them. Ridicule is in the long run a far more merciless weapon than invective. And Osbert used it to the knife. The British public took the Lancaster figures to their hearts as warmly as they did Winston Churchill, King George VI and the singer Gracie Fields. From the Forties to the Eighties Osbert Lancaster was a household name.

On the outbreak of war in 1939 he worked for a time in the Ministry of Information News Department, then for the Foreign Office. In 1944 he was sent by the Foreign Office as press attaché to Athens. There he developed a passion for the Greek landscape and the vagaries of the Greek people. He became a besotted Graecophil. Not for him, architecturally, the rules of the Roman, Vitruvius. He went to the fountain-head of classical architecture: he admired the cold, undiluted lines of the Doric and Ionic orders to be found only on the mainland and the islands of Hellas. But what he completely lost his heart to in Greece were the haphazard, searching, often mystical buildings of the undatable Orthodox churches in the old Eastern Empire. It was the Byzantine style of architecture which gripped the Anglo-Catholic devotee in him. As he expressed it, he 'could be knocked for six by an iconostasis'. During his short sojourn towards the end of the war at the British Embassy in Athens – a mere eighteen months – he became no mean scholar of Byzantine building.

In Greece, Osbert maintained, 'the inhabitants are part of the landscape and were they omitted the picture would take on an unreal lunar bareness carrying no conviction to those acquainted with the reality'. The people, in his view, inexplicably defined the landscape, which without them would be dull. This was a slight hyperbole (Osbert was prone to exaggerate). Nevertheless it is true that all his drawings and water-colours, whether of architecture or landscape, are enlivened by figures, usually unshaven peasants, bent at the knees, carrying a gnarled stick, leading a donkey, or drinking or smoking outside a bar, always individuals, solemn, tipsy or portentous, and rather appealing. Animals too are prominent and given wistful, resigned or vengeful expressions. Women are less in evidence.

Back in England after the peace he wrote *Classical Landscape with Figures* (1947), illustrated with his beautiful line drawings and water-colours. It was followed twenty-two years later by *Sailing to Byzantium*, a plain-sailing architectural companion to its predecessor. Numerous books intervened. *Drayneflete Revealed* and *The Littlehampton Bequest* exhibited Osbert's astonishing grasp of the social history of the past while proving him to be a highly sophisticated and humorous illustrator. But he was infinitely more than that. He was a very accomplished artist, with a sure and professional touch. His paintings are powerful and absolutely his own. They have been called poster-like, as though that denoted an inferior artistic field. Certainly they are theatrical, for Osbert was, among other things, a superb stage-set and costume designer. The flat surfaces of his architectural and landscape paintings, devoid of shade and tone and lacking dimension, hint that he was influenced by Matisse, and even Jean Hugo. His skies are perpetually blue with an occasional white fluff of handkerchief cloud, suggesting a stitched afterthought in a tapestry panel. The uncompromising surfaces are sewn as it were in slabs of bright palette colours, wherein the bold juxtaposition of mustard, custard, heliotrope mauve, olive green and pillar-box red is surprisingly happy. Osbert had the deftest knack with colours. Considering the lack of depth and shadowing in his paintings, and making allowances for their heavily marked contours, it is astonishing how much which is not there is sensed, and after all how much detail is conspicuous. Altogether they are infused with liveliness. Each human being introduced has a definite purpose and personality; and each animal, the homely cow, sheep, horse and even bird, has a jokey albeit wholly un-Disneyesque quality.

Osbert's paintings are the clearest evidence of the profound impression made upon him by the sun-staring landscape of Greece. Insofar as his art is influenced by a past culture, he might never have seen the varying subtleties of the Italian landscape, or Italian post-Renaissance paintings. And even when he depicts the most riotous rococo decorations of eighteenth-century palaces, his style remains stubbornly Hellenic rather than Roman.

Yet when we come to Osbert's prose, there is nothing Hellenic about that. It is deep-dyed Augustan. I believe he never learned Greek at school; his vocabulary is essentially Latin. With rolling echoes of the measured periods of Gibbon and Macaulay, his syntax is academic and rhythmic. It is unashamedly mandarin. It is to be revered, and not reviled. His writing is just as professional as his painting; and never more conspicuously so than in his two autobiographical volumes, *All Done from Memory* (1953) and *With an Eye to the Future* (1967). Both these books are pre-eminently descriptive and evocative. The prevailing scenario is the Notting Hill of Osbert's childhood before 1914, a microcosm peopled by self-satisfied fathers in frock coats and toppers, tightly-waisted mothers in feather boas and cartwheel hats, Sunday-processing to Morning and Evening Prayer with, in tow, the ubiquitous goggle-eyed boy (himself), as much fascinated by a peripheral world of organ-grinders, muffin sellers, hansom-cab drivers and mountebanks as by the idiosyncracies of his portentous elders.

There is one attribute which I have perhaps underplayed in these recollections of Osbert. I have said that his conversation at parties and even among a few friends never struck me as being quite as funny as it evidently struck others. To me his jokes were too high-lit, too inclusive, too clannish, too strained to seem absolutely spontaneous. Humour anyway is a difficult and dangerous thing to argue about. It takes two people to make one sense of humour; besides, jokes are topical abstracts which quickly get out of date. What does suffuse every sentence Osbert wrote, and every drawing, cartoon and painting he executed, whether landscape, architectural sketch or portrait, in pen and ink, water-colour, oil or fresco, is wit. Wit is that indefinable quality which can be appreciated only by learned people of every generation, and all time; it is not intended to make men laugh – but gasp. It was in evidence among the Greeks and Romans. The Elizabethans, the Cavaliers exercised it. So did Dryden, Alexander Pope, Horace Walpole and Lord Byron. And so have countless writers and artists since. It is a perdurable quality, unlike humour. And wit, wit, wit is Osbert Lancaster's hallmark.

Everard Radcliffe

1910–1975

I DO NOT claim to have been an intimate friend of Everard but I got to know him fairly well, and to like him much. We were near contemporaries and that fact alone was a sort of bond, strengthened when we were a good deal thrown together in protracted negotiations over the future preservation of his ancestral estate, country house and the exquisite works of art it contained. The discussions, alas, came to nothing.

We first met in the early 1950s in, I am almost sure, the car park at Venice, and I am quite sure through a mutual friend, Claud Phillimore the architect, who motored us on a day's expedition to some Palladian villas on the Brenta. Claud had a very close interest in the Villa Malcontenta – indeed, even before he inherited it in a romantic way (which is another story in itself) from his friend Bertie Landsberg's widow – where he and his family had the use whenever they wanted it of a detached dependency converted into a delightful *villino*. At all events I remember a long drive in an open car, which suggests that we drove further than Malcontena just across the lagoon from Venice, in fact hemmed in by the satanic and belching factories of industrial Mestre. We must surely have gone beyond Mestre, to Maser perhaps, even to Asolo. For some reason I sat in the front with Claud, and I have a vivid picture of turning round to see Everard sitting rather hunched up next to Alvilde in the back seat and clutching to his thinning hair an ungainly cloth hat, the sort of hat worn at my preparatory school by little boys and called a 'flopper'. There was something slightly irritating about Everard's hat, the way he ostentatiously held it very close as though it contained a sort of precious prophylactic to keep the rest of us at bay; and about his taciturnity, in fact his whole air of distance, indifference, and inconsequence, as the French say, *de la manière décousue*. I now realize that I had got him wrong. I no longer suppose he felt superior to us at all. He was just an unhappy fellow. All the years I knew him he remained profoundly unhappy. I have, however, reason to understand that for a brief spell towards the very end of his life he found relief from the slings and arrows with which in his middle years outrageous fortune had molested him.

The Captain, as in those years he was known to his friends, was heir to a Yorkshire baronetcy and landed estates in Lancashire and Yorkshire. The Radcliffes had since pre-Reformation times remained fairly staunch Roman Catholics. I say 'fairly' because I suspect that in the late Georgian age of enlightenment and almost universal cynicism regarding religion, they may have lapsed for a generation or two. Their faith certainly blossomed in no uncertain terms with the Catholic Emancipation Act of 1829. From the sixteenth century down to the eighteenth they contributed handsomely to a Common Purse for the maintenance of itinerant Papist priests. The famous James Radcliffe, 3rd Earl of Derwentwater, executed for his part in the 1715 rebellion, was one of the clan though not a direct ancestor of Everard.

Continuously the Radcliffes had married into other landed families, for the most part also Catholic. Everard, like his father, was educated at Downside Abbey. An uncle had been Gentleman-in-Waiting to the Pope, and unmarried aunts and great-aunts had been nuns. Everard by conviction was profoundly Papist, although he wore his religion lightly, just as he seemed to meet all serious matters with that casual, uninhibited, take-it-as-you-like attitude so habitual to the old English gentry. Before the Second World War he was married *to*, as his friends were apt to put it, an American, Betty Butler from New York, who was likewise a Catholic, and well-off. I remember her as dignified, exclusive and withdrawn; otherwise rather negative. It has been said that she had a strong temper. When I first stayed with Everard she would preside at meals and then immediately disappear upstairs, as though her husband's friends were not for her, which I daresay was sometimes the case. However devoted Everard and Betty might have been when first united, the way they addressed one another (at least in my presence) with scrupulous, icy politeness suggested that the marriage was no longer a congenial one. Relations soon deteriorated into positive dislike on both sides. But there were two children, of whom the boy was to become the apple of his father's eye. For over thirty years the marriage endured, finally to end in divorce – always a traumatic and painful dissolution for Roman Catholics who, however lax in fulfilling their religious obligations, regard marriage as sacramental. Everard undoubtedly suffered wretchedly until this matrimonial tie was finally severed.

After Downside Abbey under the Benedictine fathers Everard finished his education at the Royal Military College, Sandhurst, to become a professional soldier attached to the Yorkshire Yeomanry. He served for several years in the Thirties as ADC to the Commander-in-Chief of Bermuda. Then came the war. He enlisted in the 60th Rifles, only to be captured at Calais in 1940. For five years he was a prisoner-of-war in Germany. On his release in 1945 he was awarded the Military Cross for outstanding gallantry, according to a tribute published at the time of his death, 'after a spectacular resistance never forgotten by the few survivors who witnessed it'. He seldom spoke of these harrowing experiences, which scarred him both physically and mentally.

Shortly after his return to England Everard found himself the possessor of Rudding Park, an estate with a large country house in the West Riding, close to Harrogate. With his father's consent it was handed over to him by his grandfather (who was to die a few years later). His father had already inherited other family properties in Lancashire. Everard's three younger brothers were likewise provided for; a fourth had been killed in the war the same year that he was taken prisoner. What was Everard to do with a run-down estate and large house, much neglected and with few contents? His trustees advised him to get rid of the lot. But that was not Everard's way. He had a strong sense of family piety, and of pride in his Catholic inheritance. His branch of the Radcliffe clan could trace its descent from a certain Sir Nicholas de Radclyffe (previously Nicholas Fitz-Gilbert de Tailbois), one of the Norman knights in William the Conqueror's retinue who was given the manor of Radeclive (or Red Cliff) in south Lancashire. In the Middle Ages the Radcliffes had been among the largest and most powerful landowners in south Lancashire and west Yorkshire. Everard's forebears were principally established at Milnesbridge outside Huddersfield. But finding that the industrial spread had reached his gates, Sir Joseph the second baronet bought and moved to the Rudding estate in 1824.

The vendor of Rudding to Sir Joseph was William Gordon, an uncle of the 4th Earl of Aberdeen, unhappy Prime Minister of the Crimean war. William Gordon had not owned the property very long and had not got far in building a country house on it. In fact the house was in a very elementary state; no more than a few outline walls had been raised, if that, yet enough to determine the final shape of the building. The name of the architect whom Mr Gordon employed is unknown. Whoever he was he chose, no doubt at his patron's command, a good site on a plateau facing eastwards across a sloping deer park, once part of the medieval Forest of Knaresborough. From the site a splendid view is had to this day over the Vale of York; and the Minster towers twenty miles away are sometimes glimpsed in clear weather. Surviving clumps of trees in front of the house had been laid out by Humphry Repton before the Gordon ownership and actually feature in one of the famous landscapist's Red Books of 1794.

The plan of William Gordon's house is a simple rectangle broken only by five projecting ellipses, two balancing on the main east front, one on each side elevation and yet another single one on the rear or west elevation. The finished house is unadorned to a degree meriting the adjective stark. It has been described as looking like a lump of cheese with bulges. Each ellipse contains three windows apiece on ground and bedroom floor. There is no second floor and no attic. The whole is surmounted by a plain projecting cornice in place of a parapet. The plainest of plain string courses marks the division of ground and upper floor. All the windows are without surrounds, and those of the lower floor descend to ground level. The entrance front is embellished, if that is not too exotic a word for the finished effect, with an extremely restrained portico of four slender Doric columns. This essentially geometric and oddly satisfying composition is of honey-tinctured ashlar, finely cut and minutely bonded. It is a pity that no documents survive to tell precisely how far Mr Gordon's original architect had proceeded; Sir Joseph Radcliffe engaged a local architect to build upon what he found. Robert Dennis Chantrell had been a pupil of Sir John Soane, and was no amateur. His best known domestic buildings were in the Greek Revival style, but Rudding, which is astylar, does not demonstrate any of Soane's idiosyncratic exuberance and quirkiness. Rather it is typical of that post-Regency phase of architectural simplicity, a reaction if you like from the ostentation of the Prince Regent's Carlton House and Brighton Pavilion influences, in being mathematically uncompromising, almost puritanical. This stark interlude endured throughout the short reigns of the old Kings George IV and William IV and the early years of the young Queen Victoria, until the Prince Consort's romantic Italianate revival (*vide* Osborne House) did away with it by harking back to the idyllic architecture demonstrated in Claude Lorrain's paintings.

To quote from an article by Arthur Oswald on Rudding in *Country Life*, the designer of the Rudding we know, who was either Mr Gordon's anonymous man or Sir Joseph Radcliffe's Chantrell, relied 'entirely on proportion and rhythm, sharp profiles, clean surfaces and the consistent scale of the windows

...above all on the contrast of curve and straight line.'
Nothing further. In any case, Sir Joseph must have had a say
in the accomplished scheme.

I know nothing of Sir Joseph's character, but assume that he
was a rational, ordered, somewhat austere man who did not
care for excess in behaviour or any form of trumpet-blowing;
he may even have disrelished some of the more elaborate
furniture he inherited from his splendour-loving forebears, and
banished it upstairs. It stands to reason that the architecture of
a country house reflects more than the style and discipline of
its architect and the general spirit of the age; it will above
everything else reflect the whim and personality of the owner
who is paying for it. Contrariwisely, houses can and do help
mould the character of those who live in and love them.
Without the love their influence would be nought. Owners
have been known on coming into their inheritance so positively
to loathe the style of their ancestor's choice as to pull the
house down and build anew, or to sell the inheritance lock,
stock and barrel. Such owners in past centuries were fairly rare,
because acceptance of what went before was part of the
stock-in-trade of the landed gentry's birthright. Reactive
dissidents usually laboured under a particular grudge against
their parents or the relation from whom they inherited, on the
grounds of alleged maltreatment in childhood or youth. Theirs
was a terrible act of defiance or revenge. Unlike them Everard
deeply loved Rudding, and nourished a nice pride in the
memory of his Radcliffe ancestors. Having a shrewd idea of his
grandfather's plan to make over Rudding to him, he solaced
himself during his years as a prisoner-of-war with dreams and
plans for improvements to the estate.

Virtually nothing further happened to the actual house of
Rudding Park after Sir Joseph's day, until Everard came into
possession – nothing, that is to say, if we except the building
of the private chapel which, although detached, forms a
prominent part of the conglomerate whole. This strident
edifice, the size of a substantial parish church, was built by
A.E. Purdie for Sir Percival Radcliffe, third baronet, Everard's

great-grandfather. The 'wealth' of carved stone, Aberdeen granite and alabaster, magnificent in its way, just manages, rather from luck than pious intention, to avoid dominating the house, because it is recessed from the main block. Nevertheless, it is a formidable affirmation of Catholic Emancipation under Cardinals Newman and Manning. Everard, to his credit, was immensely proud of the Victorian chapel and the treasures it contained. Among them was a sixteenth-century embroidered cope, a 1350 hymnal and a lapis-lazuli crucifix that had belonged to Pope Pius VII, who was praying before it when by Napoleon's order French soldiers broke into his room in the Vatican Palace to take him prisoner in 1809. One may suppose that these treasures were collected by Sir Percival. Everard was forever popping in and out of the chapel, treating it as a supplementary music room, to do a turn on the organ.

Black-and-white photographs of the Rudding rooms taken towards the end of his grandfather the fourth baronet's reign record that meagreness of decoration and paucity of contents common to the living rooms of English squires in the 1920s. They also suggest walls of, one may safely guess, pale pastel tones. Pictures were then few and furniture was unostentatious, following the revolt of the upper classes of King George V's reign from the Edwardian forests of palm and fern, the clutter of occasional tables on spindly legs, silver photograph frames of Rajahs on elephants and presentation trowels with ivory handles. For fabrics the inter-war gentry were hipped to a man and woman on beige, or eau de Nil, with jolly chintz patterns to relieve the monotony. As for superfluous objects, by which is meant *bibelots* and bric-à-brac housed in vitrines, they were taboo, although allowance was made for such essential evidences of loyalty as, say, Queen Mary's signed likeness, or a silver-cyphered cigarette box presented by the Duke and Duchess of York. Otherwise, comfort and ease were prerequisites. Cosiness was a main objective, not always easy of attainment if you possessed an Adam house and virtually out of the question if you owned one so relentlessly mathematical as Rudding. But at least you could keep the rooms subdued and unflamboyant. Everard instantly set out to reverse this state of affairs.

In his considerable improvements Everard did no tampering with the exterior architecture of Rudding (beyond demolishing part of a redundant service wing) and little to the interior disposition of the rooms. What he did do was to redecorate, refurnish and refurbish in the style of sumptuous opulence which we associate with the Prince Regent's apartments at Windsor Castle and Carlton House as depicted in the plates of Pyne's *Royal Residences*. He was all for density, baroque lusciousness and show. And in selecting from the first-rate in works of art, he favoured the most gorgeous. He was a forerunner of Alec Cobbe, who has lately done for the National Trust's Hatchlands what Everard, anticipating him, did at Rudding.

I can detect in the face which Everard presented to the world a reflection of the correct, logical, prim, rather cold façade of Rudding Park. The flicker of a smile would, like the fractional opening of a window, disclose a tantalizing glimpse of the delights within. The apartments carefully shuttered against too much officious daylight had a counterpart in the concealed warmth of Everard's nature, the refinement of his mind and the splendid élitism of his tastes and mode of living. He was a great enjoyer, with a whimsical turn of phrase. His jokes and pranks were notably esoteric and had to be perceived: they were never explained, and not always expressed. Friends had to look for them in his eyes and, often, to resolve riddles imperfectly communicated through his lips. Within a carapace of aloofness and behind those mischievous orbs was a friendliness ready to be imparted, but not to be taken for granted. So it was that warmth and opulence were imposed upon the interior of Rudding by Everard for his own and the glorious benefit of discerning companions.

It was an experience and an eye-opener to stay at Rudding in the late 1950s and early 1960s. Every painting, every object had quality. As for the library in which he basked, wrote letters to his friends, read voraciously, drank Falernianly, and slept soundly before a roaring fire, it was the noblest of apartments, the walls covered with faded maroon flock paper, a background to enormously high fitted bookcases made for the room, or rather for the highly polished and gilded leather bindings of books from the twelfth to the twentieth century, some superbly illuminated, others hinged and buckled in silver or exquisitely embroidered on cover and spine in velvets and golden braid. Over the neo-Greek chimneypiece hung in a riotously carved frame a portrait, by the Antwerp-born and Tuscany-adopted baroque Susterman, of Cardinal Capponi, seated, in full canonicals.

Most of the portraits, however, were of ancestors. There was the Radcliffe who won the St Leger, by Reynolds; there were Radcliffes by John Singleton Copley, William Owen, Wright of Derby, Raeburn, and other artists who immortalized members of county families. There were Radcliffe children by Francis Wheatley. There were also some paintings it was surprising to find in a Yorkshire country house not describable as 'stately' – the *Madonna Adoring* by Verocchio, a young Bacchus tentatively attributed to Caravaggio, the *Madonna and Child* with angels and saints by Marco Basaiti; *Street Musicians* by Theodore Ribot; religious paintings by Guercino, Rombouts, Bassano, Guido Reni and Ribera. In practically every room were relics that had belonged to Marie Antoinette, Bonny Prince Charlie and other romantic figures of history.

Everard was rather cagey in disclosing the provenance of his possessions. His friends, without meaning to be nosey, would exclaim in admiration and awe when some little thing was indicated by a backward snap of the fingers. 'Oh Everard,' they would say, 'how did you come by this wonderful pair of bluejohn urns? These Louis XVI bronze and ormolu torchères? by Gouthière no less! This superbly preserved Savonnerie carpet? This unbelievably fine Boule cabinet?' 'Well!' he would answer in a drawl, 'that came from the Dukes of Newcastle... that through my great-great-grandfather Major What's-his-name who was ADC and bosom friend of General Wolfe... that through the Tichbornes...' Or, very often, 'I found that in the attic before my grandfather's death. I kept it dark till he died. I imagine the probate people overlooked it.' He had of course a marvellously discerning eye, and must have bought a lot, although he always pretended to have no money at all. He clearly adored his possessions, while appearing to take them for granted. And he expected his guests to appreciate their worth and interest. He would never press them upon friends. They should know, and recognize. If they didn't, they were philistines on whom he was not going to waste his breath. Such people were not invited a second time. He was extraordinarily shy with men; with women always at ease; extremely sensitive, genuinely art-loving; very musical, and a fine pianist, an accomplishment which again he was loth to display before strangers or the unmusical. An upward twist of the mouth, a flicking shadow from the eye would reveal what he was thinking about his visitors. There was never need to raise the voice. *Virtus propter se* is the Radcliffe motto – Virtue for its own sake.

And then the garden. I have no idea what it was like before the war, but I imagine just a conventional hotch-potch of herbaceous borders and perhaps a rockery and the inevitable walled or kitchen garden, quite a long distance from the house and of very little interest when one got there. Within a short period Everard had transformed twenty-five acres of it. He linked the garden proper to the house with a narrow herb-bordered walk punctuated by a huge cedar tree and the long back regions of the house, the walk stretching from the elliptical window bow of the library to a garden portico closing the vista towards the west. Sensibly he left the great sweeping lawns below the east entrance front of the house untouched, so the house could be said to stand flowerless with its feet plumb in parkscape, in the true eighteenth-century tradition. However, beyond the garden portico on the west a belt of trees, also attributed to Repton, gave (and let us hope still gives) entry to what is virtually a wood, cut into glades and enlivened by streams and pools. Straight rides radiated from a marble vase on a plinth. The longest ride, at an oblique angle from the centre of the *patte d'oie* thus formed, led through an iron gate to the walled garden and a terminal orangery. But these works were not all. Everard became a first-rate horticulturist, filling both wood and walled garden with flowering shrubs carefully selected and judiciously planted. The description he gave of them in a scholarly guidebook bore witness to his knowledge of every range of species, to his skill in making them grow and to his faultless taste. In this pleasance each bench was carefully placed: each garden ornament carefully sited. Peacocks strutted on the turf; budgerigars flitted overhead; and wild geese congregated in gaggles.

There is little doubt that after his return from imprisonment in Germany Rudding held first place in his affections. He simply loved the estate, and learnt there to readjust himself to the rural ways of an English squire. He knew every acre like the back of his hand. He was an exceptionally good shot. He led neither a social life, although he had close friends to stay, nor a public life. He consented to become an honorary representative of the National Trust, and because he was familiar with practically every historic building within a hundred miles of his own front door his advice to the Trust was invaluable. Everard admitted to a friend that his relations with Rudding were so close that they could almost be described as incestuous. And neighbours when they did meet him complained that this uncommunicative young man's only topic of conversation was Rudding.

He had a daughter born at the beginning of the war, and a son soon after. Charlie was charming, clever, sensitive and bright. Everard adored and was immensely proud of him. And Charlie reciprocated his affection. In an otherwise difficult domestic situation his son was Everard's comfort and joy. In him lay Everard's hopes for the future of his beloved Rudding. And so his thoughts veered to the National Trust for the ultimate salvation of the place. He might hand Rudding over to the Trust on the strict understanding that Charlie should be allowed to live there after his own death. It must always remain Charlie's home (mother and daughter were less and less at

Rudding). Everard's health, never robust since his imprisonment, became a worry. When he came to London he walked with a stick. There were whispers of heart failure.

I went to stay at Rudding in May 1959 for an initial discussion relating to the National Trust; then my colleague Robin Fedden took over on the Trust's behalf. He became a great friend of Everard, shared his enthusiasms and completely won his confidence. They were birds of a feather – heroes and aesthetes, with a mutual passion for good wine. For a long time no decisions were come to. Everard was feeling his way.

In 1967 Robin wrote to me from the National Trust that Everard wanted us both to go down to Rudding instantly. He also referred to a tragic situation that was confronting Everard: this concerned Everard's divorce proceedings, which he never mentioned in my hearing, and Charlie's serious illness, a form of leukaemia which attacks very young males. In November we both stayed at Rudding, where Everard confided in us that Charlie was doomed to die, and that he wanted to transfer the house, the collections and the 2,000-acre estate to the Trust as soon as possible.

The following February Everard wrote to Robin from hospital, announcing that he had been a patient for fifteen weeks and had four or five more to go before he could be released. He explained that very soon after our visit he had had a very bad accident, breaking legs and pelvis. The bone marrow was rejecting the artificial ball and wedge inserted by the surgeons in the pelvis. We learned later, though I think not from him, that one evening after dinner he had fallen from the top of the stairs at Rudding to the bottom, indeed on to the freestone paving below. The butler had found him the following morning, in a coma. The settlement of Rudding's future was now more urgent than ever.

After desperate heart-searchings of the sort which beset Roman Catholics when they have failed to get from the Church an annulment of their marriage, he and his wife settled for a civil divorce, which was obtained in 1968. Within a matter of months Everard was married a second time, to a girl of an old

Catholic family like his own. She was young enough to be his daughter and happened to be among the very best friends of his son Charlie. They went on living at Rudding. Negotiations with the National Trust dallied between his solicitor and the National Trust's, in time-honoured forensic fashion.

Less than a year later the worst but inevitable calamity befell Everard: in July 1969 Charlie died, aged twenty-three. Everard was crushed by grief. For a time he saw none of his friends. Four months later, as though to emphasize the bitter irony of losing his beloved son, he inherited the Radcliffe baronetcy on the death of his father.

Negotiations with the National Trust were temporarily suspended. Then towards the end of 1970 Everard lunched with Robin in London, telling him that he had finally decided to leave Rudding and 275 acres of land to the Trust by will, on the proviso that his wife might retain a right to live in the house after his death. He was still determined that Rudding should never become a museum, but must always be treated as a living residence. Would Robin and I please come to Rudding as soon as we could fix a date. We went. We thrashed out, not for the first time, provisional conditions and the amount of endowment fund necessary to maintain the place in perpetuity. Subsequently to these matters being settled the chairmen of the Trust's various committees visited, were duly impressed by the merits of Rudding, and recommended acceptance. A solemn Memorandum of the benefactor's wishes was drawn up by the lawyers; in it Everard expressed his indebtedness to his young wife for her care of him – in so formal a document, a rather touching acknowledgement that she had brought him immense strength and support at a time of great tribulation and un-happiness. At last everything seemed settled, and everyone appeared satisfied. A beautiful West Riding estate, a house of distinct architectural merit with a fabulous art collection much augmented by the present descendant of an ancient family, a spectacular garden and an authentic Repton park were to be saved for the nation's recreation in perpetuity. Moreover the widow, it was hoped, would remain in residence. Whereupon the lawyers once again dragged out their delaying tactics and procrastinations, so that in September 1971 a worried Everard wrote to Robin hoping that no snags had arisen to prevent the acceptance of his terms. Robin replied that there were no snags that he knew of; that on the contrary the precise endowment required had been agreed and a formal acceptance had been passed by the Council of the National Trust. Also Everard's Memorandum of wishes had been endorsed and sealed at a recent meeting. Everything was safely tied up, and the only thing left to be done was Everard's completion of his will and signature thereto.

In these propitious circumstances, what was Robin's dismay on 2nd March 1972 to learn that Everard had put Rudding on the market? He had been sent a cutting from a local Yorkshire newspaper, *The Evening Post*, concerning a meeting the previous month between Everard and his tenants. Everard was reported to have been emotionally very upset. 'It is a dream house, but we are having to sell because of ever-increasing charges, maintenance costs and taxation,' he had announced. He told his tenants that he was parting with the whole estate, the house and principal contents, to raise funds. He was retaining only small pieces of furniture. The tenants were greatly distressed by the break-up of the Rudding estate and the end of the Radcliffe tenure of 150 years. The contents for sale were valued at an estimated £200,000, a derisorily low figure even nearly a quarter of a century ago, before inflation had galloped to unprecedented heights.

When the sale took place the National Trust managed to scrape together enough money to buy two garden seats.

Why and how Everard suddenly realized, not only that he could no longer go on living at Rudding in his accustomed fashion (admittedly a fairly hedonistic one), but that he must even sell the better part of his beloved treasures because of crippling taxation, was not explained. Possibly large sums in arrears of unpaid taxes were claimed by the Inland Revenue. Undoubtedly he had all along gravely overspent on works of art. Perhaps in his quixotic way he decided that the struggle for survival as a country landowner, which had been made tolerable by partnership with Charlie, had since his death lost all savour and point, and was no longer worth the candle without a direct heir in view. Perhaps all along, in his slightly mischievous way, he had been playing a game with the National Trust. Certainly the decision was as sad as it was instantaneous. Everard may have told Robin the real reason; he certainly did not tell me. Robin merely reported to the Trust committees that Everard had been at his wits' end with worry and misery. He was a highly strung and vulnerable man. Nevertheless for one so apparently well provided, so accustomed to responsibility, so lavish in his spending, and so courageous, his action seemed strangely unpremeditated and despairing.

Everard and his young wife went to Switzerland to live as expatriates. He bought a beautiful house, Le Château de Cheseaux, in the canton of Vaud, where he reassembled what remained of his possessions. Before he actually quitted Rudding his wife, to his joy, produced for him another son. For two and a half years he was blissfully happy. In 1975 he suddenly died.

Richard Stewart-Jones

1914–1957

IT WAS ON 1st March 1938 – St David's Day – that I met him. For some reason the date and the feast day have stuck firmly in my memory, so that on each anniversary I recall the occasion as though it were yesterday. It retains all the vividness of early springtime, like, say, the appearance of the first windflower which prematurely blooms on a sunny bank before the winter is properly over. In recalling old friendships one must of course beware of becoming sentimental. Richard Stewart-Jones no more resembled a delicate wood anemone than he resembled St David, the fifth-century patron saint of Wales, whom his nonconformist countrymen call 'The Waterman' because he spurned all intoxicating liquor. On the other hand, Richard's Celtic character was compounded of some extraordinary contradictory ingredients to which St David's monastic discipline and abstinence were not total strangers. But before I touch upon some of these, I want to explain where and how I met him.

The scene of the encounter was a large, derelict, cold and totally empty house overlooking St James's Park in Queen Anne's Gate. The house's sad plight had been brought to the attention of the National Trust, on the staff of which I was then a junior member. I was detailed to meet a committee member of the Society for the Protection of Ancient Buildings, which was also interested in the house, at 5 p.m. Being of a fairly punctual disposition I arrived on the dot of five: besides, I felt it was incumbent upon me – I was twenty-nine at the time – not to keep waiting what I assumed would be some venerable, archaeological greybeard. I think I must have been given the front door key because, it being too raw an evening to loiter on the pavement, I went inside, locking the door behind me. I walked all round the house from basement to attics, assessing its architectural merits. They did not strike me as outstanding. In fact, after three-quarters of an hour's assessment I reached the conclusion that, tragic though it would be for this house, one of an unbroken terrace of early eighteenth-century architecture, to be demolished, it should not be accepted by the National Trust. No endowment was offered with it. Its structural condition was deplorable, and it was far too large for our office needs. There were doubtless other objections now forgotten which struck me as insuperable. By a quarter to six it seemed that the SPAB representative had forgotten the appointment. The poor old man, I imagined with the callousness of youth, probably had no memory, if he wasn't already gaga. Anyway, I was in no need of a second person's confirmation of my unfavourable opinions. My mind was quite made up. I decided to leave. I descended from the attics to the hall, preparatory to letting myself out of the front door. Suddenly, while turning the key in the lock I heard from upstairs a sinister tinkle of broken glass, followed by the screech of wrenched woodwork, followed by an oath.

This was an unexpected and eerie business. A burglar, presumably, in an empty house. Remember, there were no squatters in 1938. I was sorely tempted to make off, since there was absolutely nothing in the house to steal or injure, and I did not relish a disagreeable encounter. However, before I had time to make up my mind, a figure nonchalantly trotted down the stone staircase. From the twilight a voice said, 'Are you the National Trust man?' 'Yes,' I faltered, 'and who on earth are you?' – for in the half light from the fan window above the door I discerned a very youthful intruder indeed. He looked eighteen – I discovered later that he was not quite twenty-four – slender, with a slight stoop, and nimble as quicksilver. He was wearing a brown corduroy jacket. It and his brown hair were covered in grey dust. Altogether he presented a rather scruffy appearance. But his face was fresh and clean, and he had darting, inquisitive, searching brown eyes. I think, but cannot swear to it, that a cigarette was dangling, not from both lips, but from the lower lip, in a way the proletarians used to affect. It was a trick of his which I grew to dislike intensely and would rather prudishly deprecate. My disapproval would be met by him with the charge that I was pernickety and exclusive. However, discounting the cigarette, the impression made on me that particular evening in Queen Anne's Gate through the dust and smoke was of the face and form of a young Shelley.

'Why the hell', the SPAB representative fired at me rather aggressively, 'did you lock the front door and oblige me to scale a drainpipe, overlooked by public and police in Birdcage Walk, and force my way through a bedroom window on the second floor? I shall now have to mend what you are responsible for my having broken.'

I was rather nettled. 'Why the hell couldn't you have rung the bell or banged the knocker like any self-respecting person,' I retorted coldly. 'What an extraordinary way to behave, just like a cat burglar.' 'It was rather,' he said. Whereupon indignation dissolved into a discord of coughs and laughter, which was thoroughly disarming.

Well, the immediate sequel was that the young Shelley, he whom I had envisaged as a venerable greybeard, made me spend the next two or three hours going over that dismal house again by torchlight. (Where the torch came from I have no idea. But things needed by Rick always appeared from nowhere as though by magic.) I was submitted to a non-stop eulogy of the architectural and decorative merits of each room and passage, which in my ignorance, or haste, I had previously overlooked. My convictions that the house was unworthy of preservation by the Trust, incapable of adaptation, and financially unviable, were swept aside by this dynamo of enthusiasm before which each of my feeble hesitations and objections was flattened into pulp. (Incidentally, this particular Queen Anne's Gate house was not acquired by the Trust, yet happily stands to this day.)

By half-past eight I was longing for a respite, and managed to drag the SPAB representative to a pub, where I learned more about him. He had at an extraordinarily tender age been 'adopted', so to speak, by A.R. Powys, who was for many years secretary of the SPAB and a very remarkable intellectual-cum-craftsman. Powys was a brother of the essayists, poets and novelists John Cowper, Theodore Francis and Llewellyn Powys. He had known many of the SPAB's founders, including Ruskin and William Morris; he himself was the author of a book about the care of old buildings, which became a gospel of the preservation society he served so long and so authoritatively. It has lately been republished by the SPAB and is still regarded by the Society as essential reading for its members. Richard in his teens had introduced himself to Powys, sat at his feet, made himself useful, and motored him in his little open Morris all round the country. In their quest for ancient buildings he imbibed many of the secrets of Powys's specialized knowledge. I think that before Powys's death in 1937 Richard had been made a member of the SPAB Committee. For several years he was by far the youngest member. When I joined the committee table in Buckingham Street towards the end of 1938 he, with his alert, quizzical and very boyish face, appeared like some male Susanna among the Elders.

After a drink or two at the pub he and I dined together; and after dinner we talked, and talked, and talked. Our friendship did not slowly develop. It exploded like a rocket, instantly, there and then, in a way that can only happen with young people when a shared passion (in those days I was dedicated, literally married, to the National Trust, as he was to the SPAB) reveals itself. Our mutual sympathies induced a sort of *coup de foudre*. Until the war broke out eighteen months later, scarcely a day passed when we were not together, either in Cheyne

Walk, where I soon became enrolled among that close-knit circle of family and friends, or in the country, often on the strangest escapades and craziest errands of (architectural) mercy.

Now the phrase 'errands of mercy' is usually applied to human beings exclusively. And this is where a reference to Rick's sense of duty to the infirm, the indigent, the unhappy, or merely the aged, is timely. I, being a rather self-centred, self-indulgent young man, did not understand how someone of my own sex and actually younger than myself could be so stirred by compassion for the unfortunate. I should mention that he was already a Chelsea borough councillor. I am ashamed to confess that I did not share Rick's willingness, rather his eagerness, to chuck an attractive engagement in order to minister to a total stranger whose plight had been brought to his notice by an anonymous appeal over the telephone. For just when it was time to leave Cheyne Walk where he lived to go to the theatre, or deliver a lecture, Richard might be called upon to extricate old Mrs Featherhead, who had been cast like a sheep in her bath, or old Mr Simpleton, who had locked himself into the lavatory somewhere at The World's End, and couldn't get out. No matter what the urgency of Rick's engagement, or how many people were depending upon his keeping the engagement, he would allow himself to be diverted by one of these maddening errands of mercy. The simple truth is that he was genuinely and deeply grieved by the discomforture of human beings, whether known or unknown to him. He could never say no to requests to sit on committees for rehousing, rehabilitating, reconditioning, reconstructing ancient people or ancient things. He allowed himself to be put upon by the exigent to a degree that bordered on masochism. Their often unreasonable and certainly excessive demands meant that he was late for every appointment that he did not miss altogether. And I sometimes suspect that the accumulation of voluntary duties (he was not a rich man) largely contributed to the illness which killed him prematurely.

After the war and his marriage Richard worked in a voluntary capacity for the National Trust as a regional representative in the Midlands and West Country. He was tireless, disorganized and ultimately victorious in all he undertook. He would decorate, furnish and arrange the show rooms of historical houses, seldom from dawn to dusk but nearly always from dusk to dawn. And the wonderful thing was that the tenants, custodians and caretakers of these houses not only did not mind, they positively *loved* him for keeping them up all night, making them fetch and carry, do, undo, and re-do the tasks he mercilessly allotted to them.

One of the interests of old age is dwelling upon those dead friends whose qualities have influenced, or at least affected, one's own life. What has one learned from them? What has one gained? Alas, I seem to have gained precious little from the example of other people's virtues, for I don't believe I am any better today than I was half a century ago. But at least I have learned to appreciate them, and wish that some of them had rubbed off upon myself. When I look back at Rick across the years I see him in a clearer focus than I did at the time. He was not like ordinary, sublunary people. He was singularly selfless and immaterial. Almost a contradiction of those of his generation and friends, his whole life was motivated by a sense of duty towards others. It sounds horribly pious, but was in fact nothing of the kind. For although Richard could be censorious of his friends, he was invariably amused by their shortcomings. It surprised him that they could be so mundane, so snobbish or so indifferent to the things which mattered desperately – the preservation of beautiful buildings and scenery, and the happiness and well being of his fellow men. So when he found his friends comical, he might mock them. He could be caustic, he could be mischieviously witty at their expense. His sense of the ludicrous was so irrepressible that it would sometimes hurt, when one was the victim. But the moment he sensed that he had gone too far he was profligate with amends, and unsparing in kindnesses. Indeed, his generosity was boundless. Yes – Richard Stewart-Jones was, all things considered, the most virtuous person I have known. And was he, I ask myself, ever tempted (like most of us) to be anything else? In his case, I never found out.

James Pope-Hennessy
1916–1974

JAMES POPE-HENNESSY WAS a first-rate writer of prose. No philosopher, for he did not analyse causes or judge effects, he was nevertheless extremely intelligent. He was quick to grasp facts, which he shook like a dog a rabbit, digesting what he wanted and sometimes expectorating what might have been good for him. His brother John, who was an impartial but severe critic, conceded that 'in dealing with the past his understanding of the human personality was next door to infallible.'

James came of highly literate parents, not rich yet comfortable, not noble yet gentry, and very Roman Catholic. He was educated at Downside Abbey school (which he hated), and always looked at life from a Catholic angle. Although he might scoff at the Church's ritual and sneer at the peripheral superstitions and absurdities of priests, he accepted the inmost core of the Church's teaching. He was blessed with a very exclusive and self-defensive family who in those respects resembled their near contemporaries the Sitwells and Lehmanns. His mother Dame Una had had a college education and his brother (subsequently Sir John) became a universally respected art historian, director of the Victoria & Albert Museum and of the British Museum. The father, Major-General Richard Pope-Hennessy, was in the course of time left in the cold by the other three, undeservedly I considered. I found him a very charming man. Admittedly, in spite of a distinguished military career he was somewhat feckless, and one of nature's pessimists. In truth he was terrified of his two sons and his wife, all of whom were distinctly high-brow writers. I often met him skulking in Brooks's club, where we would eat together. He knew that I was a friend of the trio's, and I think looked upon me as a fellow reject who had not quite come up to scratch. Together we let our hair down, so to speak, in referring to them, like schoolboys out of hearing. Yet he was far from stupid. On the contrary, when at the beginning of the war in 1940 things were going very badly for the Allies, he wrote a series of brilliant articles on military concerns for the *Evening News*. They were by no means comforting, and for that reason were unpopular with the uncompromising come-what-might believers in victory.

John, who regarded his father with ill-concealed disdain, declared that James and the General loathed each other. If loathing really came into the picture, then I guess that it was unilateral, and only upon occasion. I cannot imagine the General to have loathed anyone, even a German, in his life, and James, who was given to impulsive likes and dislikes, was undoubtedly irritated at times by his father's old-fashioned good manners, steadfast sense of right and wrong, and intuitive knowledge of how to behave. It is true that the General, who sometimes disapproved of James's conduct and the company he kept, was much disturbed when he learnt in 1941 that his younger son, whose indiscretions and irresponsible comments on the conduct of the war were notorious, had been commissioned straight from the ranks in an anti-aircraft battery into military intelligence at the War Office. The mildest expression of his apprehension was enough to excite James's ire, at least temporarily. At all events, one morning in 1942 the two had a stand-up row in which James roundly abused his father; that evening the General had a stroke and died. On hearing of this Cecil Beaton exclaimed the words which in those days were blazoned in every public place, 'Careless talk costs lives'. Dame Una and John arranged an appropriate

Requiem Mass in Hampstead, which I attended. The Most Reverend Archbishop David Mathew of Apamea, Assistant at the Pontifical throne, presided and gave the address. And Dame Una went into deepest mourning.

Dame Una was the bluestocking incarnate, dedicated to literature and hard work. She never left the track, and expected those she was fond of to follow suit. There is no question of her and the feckless Richard Pope-Hennessy not having been, in their youth, very much in love. Indeed, Una incurred the disapproval of her father, Sir Arthur Birch, KCMG and late Governor of Cyprus, by insisting upon marriage to a penniless Irish soldier from County Cork, and a Roman Catholic to boot. In no time at all she was converted to her husband's faith, which she tenaciously adhered to. But as time went on and her two sons grew up she had less and less use for Richard, shrugged him off, and came to regard him as a liability. He was not serious enough for her; and for him, low be it spoken, she was not endowed with sufficient fun or humour. I suspect she had come to blame her husband for imparting his irresponsible genes to the beloved of her two sons, James, the apple of her eye, while discounting the good looks and the artistic proclivities of his attractive father, or rather attributing them to the staid Birch blood. While Richard was still alive she enforced order, managed the household, paid with what capital she had – he had none – and exercised discipline. She made it plain to both boys while they were in the nursery that they were to be writers, and that to write they must work. They accepted the injunction as other children accept the inclination to play. For a period after the General's death she had both boys, already in their twenties, living with her in an austere house, number 28 Lansdowne Road, Notting Hill. Whereas James soon broke away, John remained. It seemed that he studied and learnt, learnt and studied art history day and night at home, had no recreations, and seldom went out of an evening with friends.

I saw a lot of Dame Una in the mid Thirties through the Georgian Group, of which we were both founder-members, and I think I introduced her to the Committee of the Society for the Protection of Ancient Buildings, which she likewise joined. We would lunch together in between meetings and go for strolls in Regent's Park and Kensington Gardens. Although so serious, she was far from dull. Her conversation was always profound and her forceful views were based on much forethought and deliberation. I always kept up with her socially (if not cerebrally) and I think she liked me, although she had a low opinion of my learning. She had no small talk whatever. I remember one winter's day during the war arriving at Lansdowne Road for luncheon. I had had a gruelling journey to her house from Chelsea. The buses were not running, the tube trains were either frozen up or dislocated, there were no taxis because there was no petrol, the streets were deep in snow, and a wind from the Arctic raged. Dripping, perished and nigh to hypothermia I was ushered into her bleak drawing-room. The stately figure in black rose from a high, stiff chair, and advanced. There was not a word of greeting, exclamation about the weather, the conditions of the streets, my condition, not even a 'Will you have a glass of sherry?' – a thimbleful it would have been, if proffered. With outstretched hand she said, 'Do you surmise that while he was composing *Les Méditations Poétiques* Lamartine had in mind the doctor's wife Elvire, or was he already in love with my great-aunt Anne Elizabeth Birch?' The interrogation was followed by a characteristic little dry cough which indicated that, if I did have an opinion, it would not be of much use. The notion that one day I might write a book clearly struck her as derisory. Only Pope-Hennessys did that sort of thing. On one occasion I rashly remarked that my diary would not be read until fifty years after my death. At which Jamesey, who liked to fancy that he and his intimates were immortal, observed, 'Since *we* cannot possibly die, that means never. Just as well.' From Dame Una came a clearance of the throat and *sotto voce* a repetition of the words 'Just as well'. Yet I was fond of her, and her forbidding sternness was mitigated by rare and unexpected twinklings of the eyes, which had to be looked for. While the war continued, as it seemed, interminably she became as depressed as her husband had been at the outbreak, and feared the people would soon lose faith in their leaders. She was terrified of the bombing yet endured it without a break, resolutely refusing to leave London. When the V1 rockets came over the Channel we would telephone each other in the long evenings to find out whether they had dropped nearby. 'No,' the Dame would say, 'I prayed fervently and waved the last one on to Highgate or Hounslow' – the moment the engine stopped one knew the rocket was about to fall somewhere with its lethal cargo.

On Christmas Day of 1942 I lunched at Lansdowne Road. We exchanged humble little presents, a bar of soap, a bag of peppermints (the Dame was always sucking something for her throat), or half a dozen eggs acquired by one of us in the country. John and James were there, but left early for their respective offices, work in the services and in the factories over Christmas then being usual. They venerated and worshipped their mother, and dared not be overtly amused by her intense seriousness. During the war she was engaged on a rather dry biography of Dickens, and they did all they could to help her with her researches. One Saturday in August 1944 James and I accompanied her by bus to Peckham, to look for the house in which Dickens's mistress Ellen Ternan had lived and in which the novelist began work on *Edwin Drood*. Needless to say, none of the inhabitants had heard of Miss Ternan, even if a few had faint inklings of the name Dickens; and the Dame's anxious enquiries of these wretched people on the doorsteps of their half-bombed houses made James and me weep and giggle by turns. The Dame was not amused by the giggling. We did not identify the house, and returned to Lansdowne Road un-rewarded.

Endued with a good background, good health, good looks, good brain, good address and superabundant charm, James certainly did not have a deprived start in life. He did not waste his assets, and achieved an early reputation with some extremely good books of topography, travel and biography. Because the craftsmanship of his prose was so sure, his grasp of men's motives so cunning and his powers of description so vivid, it stood to reason that as he advanced into middle age he should produce more and even better books. This was the general prognostication of his admirers, in spite of John's doubts (and few knew James better than his brother), on the grounds that he 'was unintellectual, not in the sense of being unintelligent...but of being uninterested in ideas.' On the other hand, first-rate authors are not always intellectuals, just as intellectuals do not necessarily (as was perhaps the case with John) make major writers.

James's first book, *London Fabric*, about walks and explorations in the City of London, was written in the last years of peace, after he left Balliol College, Oxford, which was not congenial to him as it had been to the scholarly John. At the time he was working in the editorial section of Sheed & Ward, the Catholic publishers, a job which Dame Una's influence had procured for him. The offices were in Paternoster Row, which enabled James to spend his spare hours – and not a few of those office hours when he should have been at his desk – rambling in the Dickensian precincts of St Paul's Cathedral, which he grew to love. In those days the narrow streets and alleys of the City, the jutting house gables, the bow-fronted shops, the churches and graveyards, the underground caverns in which artisan craftsmen hammered like Nibelungs, remained still very much as the great novelist had known them. Within the next five years they were to be swept away by successive Hitler blitzes. *London Fabric* is a young man's book, a topographical elegy, enthusiastic and brimming with fanciful reminiscences and descriptions of his favourite haunts in the company of his friend Clarissa Churchill, Winston Churchill's niece, and later wife of Anthony Eden, then a mere girl, whom in the text he addresses as Perdita and to whom it is dedicated. It won him the coveted Hawthornden Prize, at the age of twenty-three.

Of James's sixteen books the most successful in Peter Quennell's opinion was *Verandah* (1964), in essence a vignette of his eccentric grandfather, Sir John Pope-Hennessy, sometime Governor of Hong Kong and Mauritius, an intemperate

Irishman, Radical in opinion, but volatile, emotional, autocratic, unreliable, and a thorn in the flesh of a succession of Colonial Office ministers in Whitehall. This fascinating but maddening representative of the British imperial government was immortalised by Anthony Trollope as Phineas Finn in the novel of that name. *Verandah*, the preparation of which necessitated James making prolonged journeys through the Far East, served as an exposition of his criticism of British colonialism. But already *London Fabric*'s successor, the life of Richard Monckton Milnes, Lord Houghton, in two volumes, *The Years of Promise* (1950) and *The Flight of Youth* (1952), had established his reputation as a biographer without an equal. These volumes were in fact as much a history of and commentary on literary, political and high society in post-Regency Britain as the biography of a delightfully eccentric landowner who knew and entertained every statesman, man of letters and artist of note of his time. James was as articulate in his speech as he was in his writing. I was present at a lecture he gave on Monckton Milnes to the Poetry Society in 1943, when he was twenty-seven. The talk was beautifully delivered in a sonorous and confident voice. His grasp of what made disciplined prose was a real asset when he was literary editor of the *Spectator* between 1947 and 1949.

As for *Queen Mary* (1959), mostly written at great speed in Germany, it was immediately hailed as the best royal biography ever published, a sympathetic and gripping character study of an individual who had she not been born a princess and married as she did, would have been a rather ordinary woman. He apotheosized his subject into a figure of immense eminence and dignity, while at the same time hinting, tongue in cheek, at what was ridiculous about her. The book also amounted to a social history in narrative dress of the late Victorian and Edwardian culture. Harold Nicolson in a letter to James praised it as 'a *pointilliste* portrait built up of a thousand significant details . . .' and remarked upon 'the skill with which you catch the sparkle of every ripple. You had before you a large bowl of jumbled pins which most people would have re-arranged as a pincushion, but which in some manner you have fitted into a pattern as smooth as lacquer.'

James's descriptive writing on whatever subject – a person, a place, an event, a landscape or a work of art – was exact, often poetic and invariably arresting. As an example of the last adjective in my list I take at random the following reflections on a visit to Mantua in 1950. James was no art student and his approach to all art was romantic, idiosyncratic and enthusiastic. 'We', he wrote of himself and a companion,

> are still under the influence or impact of the Ducal Palace, which we saw for two hours yesterday morning. It seems to me not only of incredible and varied beauty, but also the most *human* and *civilized* large building I have ever seen. The little rooms of Tasso and of Isabella d'Este are the epitome of civilization and elegance and gaiety: the great rooms are not pompous or formal, and the whole series of them, room after room, ceiling after ceiling, floor after shining floor, make an effect on one that is merely magical. The little hanging gardens, too, and the apartments of the dwarfs, the chapel, the long gallery with the grottoes, the blue Cimabue, and the large [Domenico] Feti heads are all wonderful. But when one gets to the Mantegna room, one feels like never leaving it again: I thought it without doubt the most marvellous single room I have ever seen or am likely to see: the placing of the figures over the mantelpiece, the young man looking straight out of the window at the lake, the horse, the extraordinary simple, noble, affectionate grouping of the family, and their strange high-minded, liberal eyes are all astounding...

Admittedly these words are not analytical, or didactic, not polished for effect, but the spontaneous reaction of a keenly observant connoisseur to a monument of architecture, tossed off no doubt in a hurry, in a letter to his brother. Indeed the letters of James's youth have a crispness, sprightliness and transparent honesty which are sometimes blurred by cynicism in those of his middle age. I am glad that as long ago as 1938 I told him, scarcely with exaggeration, that his must be among the very best letters of our time. 'Is there anything else in life', he asked his American friend Bill Vinson one Christmas Day, 'than writing and love?'

Love – can it always be called that in James's case? Lust unbuttoned is nearer the mark – if the phrase does not sound rather out of date these days, as well as pompous in the mouths of the holier than thou. In short, a surfeit of debauchery in sex, tobacco, drink, and drugs became James's undoing. In him they generated a lunacy, a suicidal impulse that could not be resisted. The sad thing is that James's debauchery was deliberately cultivated. It didn't just happen. He sought it out for the benefit of his understanding of humanity, his writing. And it took hold inevitably. The wide-eyed youth's assault on the tree of the knowledge of good and evil proved to be more devastatingly fruitful than he ever imagined.

John saw him as two characters in one. He wrote that 'a person might easily have known only one half of him and not had a clue to the other half.' I certainly had a clue from a fairly early stage, and came to regard the two halves as straightforward Dr Jekyll and Mr Hyde, the latter not at first perceptible. I was wrong, as I shall eventually try to point out, for there was nothing positively aggressive in James's transmogrification of his character, as there was in Dr Jekyll's.

John saw him throughout as a romantic in the French, not the English tradition. I think he was right there. Actually, James saw John and himself in the rôles of those nineteenth-century apostles of realism and naturalism, the Goncourt brothers, he being the younger Jules, and the more brilliant, and John serving well enough, to start with, as the elder, staider Edmond. Together they would be forceful men of letters, dilettanti, critics of society and collectors of antique bric-à-brac. James resented John's gradual back-sliding from the Edmond rôle, his declining to express himself outrageously, concentrating too much on conventional scholarship, and veering towards academe rather than frivolity. Nevertheless the Pope-Hennessy brothers shared several characteristics of the Goncourt brothers, namely a prolific output, a brittle and acerbic style, and the fact that in both cases the elder had a protective and restraining influence over the younger, whom he outlived.

I think I must have first met James in 1937 through Dame Una, when she and I sat on the Georgian Group committee. This was in his Sheed & Ward days. He was then twenty-one, active as a bird, slight, handsome, with a pallid complexion, and thick raven hair. He belonged to what is termed the nervous type. He bit his nasty little nails to the quick. In early summer he was a martyr to hayfever. Neither his mouth nor his hooded eyes kept still for an instant. The whites with their large brown pupils were a very distinctive feature, and his eyes were for ever roving. He had a way of looking out of the corners of them as well as straight ahead, so that he missed nothing. With slightly high cheekbones, his face had a perceptibly oriental cast which it pleased him to think he had inherited from his grandmother Lady Pope-Hennessy, Sir John's wife – she was said to have had Malay blood. Altogether, with his alertness, enthusiasm, curiosity and humour, he was beguiling. His comments were always amusing and worth listening to. There seemed no bitterness in his composition and we became tremendous friends. He took rather a shine to me (it did not last long), and I could not reciprocate although I was devoted to him then and remained so for many years to come. No doubt I was a bit callous and insensitive, as was borne in upon me on one occasion. In August of the year of our meeting I was commuting into London while staying as a guest of the d'Avigdor-Goldsmids at Somerhill near Sevenoaks. I had not seen James for a day or two. When the platform had been left behind I saw to my immense surprise, as I sat in a corner seat of the evening train that drew out from Charing Cross station, a forlorn figure squatting between a concatenation of railway lines. He was searching wistfully the windows of my train. I mention this incident merely to stress the intensity of James's emotions when aroused. I have often suspected that his treatment of me subsequently may have been motivated, if unconsciously, by the hurt pride of a distant past, for he seldom forgot a slight to his self-esteem.

A less poignant memory is of the two of us standing one summer evening at the entrance of the open air theatre in

Regent's Park with Gerry Wellesley and an elderly woman friend of Gerry's. We had assumed that we were being taken as Gerry's guests. To the ticket office Gerry advanced, saying, 'We will all pay for ourselves.' James and I, who were chronically impoverished, simply hadn't got the money. While Gerry, waving his ticket, strode off to the stalls, the three of us left at the *guichet* were at first dumbfounded and then so amused that we collapsed with laughter. James's and my predicament was solved by our generous companion paying for us as well as herself. (It is only fair to state that Gerry gave us a delicious supper in his Hanover Terrace house, crammed with exquisite Regency furniture and memorabilia of the Great Duke.)

Working for a pittance at Sheed & Ward's and not the least interested in theology, James was bored stiff with editing the holy manuscripts proffered to the firm by aspiring authors. Whereas to him the City meant Victorian fiction I at the time was particularly concerned with Wren churches, so many of which in the mid and late Thirties were being bulldozed by the London Diocese, to be replaced by high-rise office blocks which would yield a greater return to the ecclesiastical coffers. Before and again towards the end of the war, when we were both back in London, we spent innumerable summer evenings on City rambles. As well as knowing every identifiable Dickensian haunt, James was familiar with the City pubs and pub life, which I never took to, not from prudish reasons but out of shyness. One of my father's strict injunctions to my brother and me as boys was that we must not drink in pubs, and never on any occasion whatever enter the pub in our village at home. This outdated and squirearchic prohibition may explain why pushing through a pub door is uncomfortable for me to this day. However, James had no sympathy with such nonsense, and I would follow him reluctantly into beer-swilled and sweat-stinking shrines where he felt perfectly at ease. In these resorts were frequently to be encountered, mingling with the proletarian throng, the boozy faces of Bohemian acquaintances like Philip Toynbee, Adrian Pryce-Jones, Michael Arthur Stratton Dugdale, Sandy Baird and Guy Burgess. It was from The Prospect of Whitby in 1944, all other pubs having closed, that during a severe air raid James and I beheld our first German robot bomb, scuttling at a low altitude over the rooftops of Greenwich Palace, like a magnified wasp evacuating livid flames from its tail and making a prodigious buzz.

After his job at Sheed & Ward came to an inglorious end James was more or less obliged by his anxious parents to accept a six months' job they found for him as ADC to the Governor of Trinidad, Sir Hubert Young. James simply loathed and despised the formality of Government House, which he described as 'a Victorian conservatory, steaming hot, filled with vulgar flowers and clattering palms.' He deemed tropical nature garish and oversize. The governor and his wife, he wrote, were kind in their way, but slaves to a ridiculous and antiquated ceremonial, and of course regarded the natives as untouchables. On his return to England on the outbreak of war James declared that the only friends he had liked and respected in Trinidad had been the dark-skinned ones.

Trinidad undoubtedly opened his eyes to the *de haut en bas* attitude of the colonizing British (for the most part middle-class people of narrow, limited minds), an attitude which he interpreted as social injustice towards the natives which they deliberately practised, whereas in fact the majority of them did so unthinkingly. In due course it led him to detest the British Empire and all it stood for, to the extent of refusing to acknowledge the considerable benefits which it had, at least in the past, brought to the peoples under its sway. Nothing in James's eyes could condone the present, petty superiority of the Raj, which he dubbed 'criminal and ghastly'. This early antipathy was fortified by later experiences in Sierra Leone, where he went in 1965 in search of material for his anti-slavery book, *The Sins of the Fathers*.

Disapproval of the treatment he witnessed there of the Africans drove him to be horribly offensive to the British High Commissioner, D.J.C. Crawley, a distinguished diplomat who was faithfully fulfilling the requirements of his office. On learning that James, a guest lecturer at the University in

Freetown, had joined a demonstration march against him and all his works, the High Commissioner, not surprisingly, cancelled an invitation to a luncheon party at the Residency. This drove James to turn his personal resentment into a public issue by adopting a strong racist attitude, an anti-white issue forsooth. He sent an indignant letter to *The Times* on his Sierra Leone grievance by way of stoking up fuel for the forthcoming *Sins.* Although sincere the book was an hysterical expression of James's feelings about apartheid in the world generally; moreover he was too inclined to bore his friends on the subject. One of them, Cecil Beaton, told James that he refused to harbour guilt for what his forefathers might or might not have done when blacks were slaves, and so forfeited the author's company for several months.

James's anti-Englishness led him to make some silly pronouncements. One was that English villages looked forbidding and even sinister, whereas French villages looked so welcoming as to excite a stranger to speculate what was going on within. It depended upon the point of view of course, but a stranger wandering around a French village of an afternoon could be excused for assuming that it was totally deserted: when the shutters are put up, French villagers withdraw indoors as though barricading themselves against incursions from Huns and Vandals. Their cottages appear eyeless and rebarbative, the very antithesis of those in, say, the Cotswolds, the Home Counties or the Midlands, with their front gardens cascading with roses, doors ajar and curtains fluttering in the breeze through open windows.

During the Second World War James was often rendered furious by the Allies' retaliatory Baedeker raids on German cities. So too was I. The destruction of historic Lübeck in April 1942 struck us as philistine and uncivilized. We tried to enlist action from Harold Nicolson, who had been Parliamentary Secretary to the Ministry of Information and was still an MP and a governor of the BBC, to get a stop put to future strategy of this kind. At first Harold complained that James had the effect of a magnifying glass held over a pile of shavings on a sunny day, and then, I fancy, agreed with us, although it was difficult for him to come absolutely clean. As it turned out, all three of us were wrong about Lübeck, which had been a legitimate military target.

I fear that James and I, fond as we were of Harold, felt impelled at times to needle him over politics, constantly finding ourselves in disagreement with his professed bellicose views. We were irritated by his inability, as we saw it, when he was in office and an unswerving supporter of Winston Churchill, to dissociate political correctness from truth. Even Harold, the most liberal-minded of men and normally ready to see two sides of a question, was unable to tolerate unorthodox opinions on the aims and conduct of the war. For example, he felt obliged to excuse the lamentable escape of the German battle-ships in February 1943, claiming that it was to the Allies' advantage when it was clearly to the Germans'; and never would he (or indeed could he, in the circumstances, even among friends) listen to discussion of a conditional surrender or negotiated peace. Knowing Harold as we did, we considered this stance unprincipled. Our view distressed Harold much because he was absolutely devoted to Jamesey, regarding him like a son, admiring his fastidious and agile mind and his writings, and rejoicing in his company. James, who was a contemporary of Nigel at Balliol, had been immediately accepted within the Sissinghurst circle. He is first mentioned in Harold's published diaries in August 1936, when he lunched with Harold at the Travellers' Club: 'A charming young man. He may succeed in rendering Niggs a little more human and elegant.' Nigel, today the most genial of men if not the best dressed, had not perhaps in those days completely shaken off the provocative adolescent's faroucheness and shagginess. James was much flattered by his friend's father's interest in him. His affection for Harold grew with the years, never to wane. He was allowed free access to Harold's London lodgings, first in King's Bench Walk, the Temple, and after the war at his house in Neville Terrace, South Kensington. He would arrive with little presents which delighted Harold, an engraving of Byron reclining against a tombstone in Harrow churchyard, or a holograph manuscript of a lyric by Thomas Moore, things which could then be picked up in old bookshops for a song. He relied upon Harold's advice on all literary matters and in the direction of his own prose style. He was very caring of Harold in his misery over Vita's terminal illness in 1962, taking him out to dinner, being cheerful and supplying literary gossip. After Vita's death he also joined with John Sparrow in taking Harold for a change of scene to Bergamo. The good intention was slightly marred by a blazing row between him and John, his incredible rudeness, and Harold's senile bewilderment. Jamesey was in fact over the years thoroughly spoilt by Harold, whom he knew full well he could twist round his little finger. He had the cheek to read Harold's private letters and diaries in Harold's absence, pronouncing the diaries too discreet for words. He criticized Harold's abandonment of literature for politics, calling him to his face a middle-aged failure, and of course accepted loans of money which Harold could ill afford and never got back. (Nor was James the only young friend whom Harold indulged in this way. Harold's devoted secretary Elvira Niggeman was once provoked to say to him, 'It will be a great economy for us when all your friends are in prison.') James's extravagance and chronic lack of money was, he liked to claim, congenital, passed on by his Pope-Hennessy grandfather, as though it were a hereditary disease of which he was the innocent victim. The greater part of his life was spent endeavouring to evade debts and overdue taxes by living abroad in Germany and Ireland, and on advances from publishers for travel books. Harold seldom scolded him. As he wrote to Vita, 'How various and *vivace* and *verde* is the life he leads.'

Before the devil got a firm grip of James, that is to say when he was still in his twenties and early thirties, he was the most stimulating companion imaginable. He had no inhibitions. His candour was endearing. His curiosity was insatiable, his enthusiasms were brimming and his observations acute and on target. I recall his darting walk, like a wagtail's across a lawn, ceaselessly talking, his eyes active with that sidelong flash of the whites, concentrating on what he wanted to impart and bumping into one as his imagination took rein over his logic. His merriment was infectious, his charm insidious. If intent upon an objective, James could wheedle anything out of anyone. Strangers fell to his persuasions like ninepins. During an interview James had with Archbishop Fisher of Canterbury when he was writing his *Queen Mary* book, the Archbishop disclosed matters of deepest confidence, and ended by revealing that his dearest wish was to set up a small and exclusive group of Protestant and Catholic laymen to heal the rift between the two Churches, saying that James must be one of the Catholic laymen. And while he was writing the same book, a distinguished member of the Royal Household fell head over heels in love with him. Even James was slightly embarrassed by a situation which, if he had not positively provoked it, he had certainly stirred up.

Jamesey's face was always quivering on the brink of uncontrollable mischief and laughter over what was clannish and pompous. A scene comes to my mind of an extremely grand musical party given by Gerry Wellington at Apsley House. The Duke in tail coat and the Garter ribbon round his torso was seated in the front row with Queen Elizabeth the Queen Mother in tiara and diamonds on his right. James happened to be perching on, I think, a window seat at the rear of the room, next to Joan Moore and me. The ostentation of this assemblage of the great and good, the warbling and wobbling on stage of an ample soprano in long evening gown with sequins, the earnest backview head of Gerry, cocked seraphically a little to one side, the powder-blue-draped shoulders twinkling with imperial gems of the Queen Mother – neither of these two the least musical, but putting up a show of intense appreciation – provoked James to immediate giggles and then agonized shakes of laughter. Joan and I, likewise convulsed, were obliged to shove him, puce in the face and choking, out of the room before the disturbance made the front row turn in our direction. To James music was at the best of times anathema, usually reducing him to derision or tears of rage rather than laughter.

Being a weak character I too often fell victim to Jamesey's plausible persuasions, but not always. One weekend in wartime he called at my little house in Cheyne Walk to find me clearing up broken glass from windows and plaster from ceilings after a near miss by a bomb the previous night. It did not occur to him to offer help. Instead, clutching to his bosom some rare calf-bound volume which he had just bought ('at a marvellous bargain') he followed me nonchalantly round the rooms asking querulously whether it was really necessary for me to sweep. 'Other people's chores are a great bore,' he said in an aggrieved tone. 'Let's go out for luncheon.' 'No' was the answer.

If he was apt to brush aside disagreeable obligations which did not concern him, he could in moments of crisis be efficient as well as courageous, for example going to all lengths in helping and consoling Dame Una during some of the worst air raids. But his self-centredness was interpreted by his women adorers, of whom there were many, as a sort of fascinating affirmation of his genius. By their acceptance of his tiresome ways – chucking engagements at the last moment, insulting their friends who displeased him, or getting drunk – 'Dear little James is so attractive' – they positively encouraged his misdemeanours. Of the very few who endeavoured to restrain his excesses Lady Crewe was perhaps the foremost, in that she was patron as well as counsellor. This extraordinary woman, awkward and abrupt, exclusive and prone to devastating asides within range of her victims (a habit attributed by her relations to intense shyness), the daughter of the former Prime Minister, Lord Rosebery, once ambassadress to Paris and a political hostess of formidable presence, had commissioned James to write the biography of her father-in-law, Richard Monckton Milnes. She was the provider not only of money to the impecunious author, but of asylum in times of stringency. There was always her lovely and comfortable country house in Surrey with its library of Lord Crewe's rare books and historic papers for him to retire to. He was fond of her and totally

loyal. He also held her in some awe. It was in James's interest
to behave in her company. On the other hand, as a devious
intriguer herself she encouraged James's cynicism and
debunking of established persons and customs. At her grand
parties in Argyll House, Chelsea and at James's gatherings in
Ladbroke Grove, Peggy Crewe, swathed in furs, and he would
giggle covertly together at the expense of the guests. Generous
and supportive of James, she gave rather than lent him money,
for she valued his company too much to risk losing it by
becoming a creditor.

I was present at one of the Argyll House parties in 1943,
when James met Emerald Cunard for the first time. He was an
instant success and from that moment became an habitué of
her intimate dinner parties in the Dorchester Hotel, to which
she had returned from the United States in the middle of the
war. Their great link was Balzac's novels, which Emerald read
over and over again during sleepless nights, often telephoning
friends (on the assumption that they too would be awake at
two and three in the morning) to discuss characters and themes
of *La Comédie Humaine*. Emerald was inclined to treat James as
a responsive toy, giving him the nickname 'Bibelot' – and
indeed there was a faintly doll-like quality about him.

A macabre friend of Lady Crewe who played a sort of Rosa
Dartle rôle in James's life at this time was the whisky-sodden,
hiccuping Bridget Paget, a sad left-over of the Twenties and the
Prince of Wales's set. Incredibly slim, very chic and covered
with jangling bracelets, she had beautiful legs. Against a dead
white, over-lifted face a faint Mona Lisa smile flickered across
parched lips. She spoke in a dead-pan voice. She was funny in
an utterly hopeless way. When questioned about her love life
in her heyday she would release a delusive sigh and murmur,
'Darlings, it was always the same old up and down.' Tormented
by lack of money and unhappy children she was dependent
upon Peggy Crewe, to whom she acted as unofficial lady-in-
waiting. She became madly in love with James and, I imagine,
suffered agonies, like Peter Beckford's wife Louisa who doted
on and was kept at arm's length by her husband's cousin

William Beckford of Fonthill. Bridget provided James with light relief entertainment, but also further incited him to drink and drugs.

Riette Lamington was another older woman who likewise had a *schwärmerei* for James. The childless and disappointed wife of a Scottish peer, she was some sort of niece-in-law of Emerald and often to be encountered at her table. Intensely musical, she was a good pianist and nurtured intellectual aspirations. She too provided a comfortable haven in her luxury flat with cosy little têtes-à-tête. But Jamesey, who was naïve in some ways, let time slip by before becoming wary of her intentions. Seated close to her one evening on a deep sofa he took fright, and dexterously set fire with his cigarette to a cushion. Having alerted the fire brigade and helped put things back to normal, he made his escape.

Rose Macaulay, an intimate of Dame Una and like her moving not in the social but the literary world, was in the nature of a much esteemed and loved aunt. The influence of this eminently wise and cerebral writer, unsought as it was unproffered, was nevertheless considerably towards the good. Although Rose had, unknown to the world, a long affair with a married man, she appeared a dried-up old spinster. Only a handful of intimates, including the Pope-Hennessys, was privy to her lover's existence. James was greatly impressed by her stoic restraint and the secret she maintained. Rose was devoted to James no more and no less than to his mother and brother.

Doreen Colston-Baynes was a much loved friend of James and mine, having been a childhood companion of Dame Una. She was the author, under the pen name Dormer Creston, of several deservedly popular biographies. She was saintly and sweet, and could be a trifle silly. Was fey and sometimes whimsy. 'Precious Baynes', James called her. She saw visions of friends, alive and dead, and of herself, floating around her drawing-room cornice. She was quiveringly sensitive, and after reading an uncharacteristically sharp review, headed 'Artful Prattle', of her really excellent book *The Young Queen Victoria*, by Harold Nicolson who mistook the author for some perky female graduate of London University in need of being taken down a peg, she never wrote another line. James, in spite of his devotion, treated her in her old age in an off-hand manner. She complained to me that he would drink her sweet sherry without speaking a word, and looking bored: yet added in her forgiving way that she was grateful for his mere presence.

In the category of old ladies Mrs Betty was on the periphery. A splendid character, widow of a General W.E. Montgomery and daughter of Queen Victoria's most eminent private secretary, Sir Henry Ponsonby, she was christened Alberta Victoria, names which speak volumes of what was expected of her. Outspoken and of froglike plainness, she loathed Queen Victoria for a tyrannical spoilsport who in her bad moods kept the Royal Household in stony silence during meals. She loved to recount how dismal life was at Windsor Castle for a young girl of spirit. It is not difficult to guess that the infant Mrs Betty was not the kind of child with winning manners calculated to melt the heart of the ancient Sovereign who, herself mother of nine, not all brilliant or beautiful, yet liked the children of her dependents to be ornamental and deferential. The young woman who bore her and beloved Albert's names was neither deferential nor pretty. On the contrary, she was boisterous and rather rebellious, as well as plain. Nevertheless in widowhood Mrs Betty enjoyed the privilege of a grace-and-favour residence, albeit of portentous Victorian stuffiness, within a stone's throw of the Castle gates.

Mrs Betty, politically inclined to the left, belonged to that somewhat precious clique of superannuated Souls, of whom Lady Desborough and Logan Pearsall Smith were favoured survivors. With the latter, who lived in St Leonard's Terrace, Chelsea she was in regular telephonic communication. To all and sundry she spoke in a language of the clique's own, which it was often hard for non-members to catch hold of. She was much addicted to proverbs, such as 'A bird in the hand is worth a feather in the cap', the noun 'dewdrop' for pat-on-the-back, adjectives such as 'dank' and 'pointful', and the verb 'carp', for scandalizing about friends. Attributes of the word 'carpet', viz., an Aubusson, a Kidderminster and a 'velvet pile', denoted the rising degrees of boringness in friends and acquaintances. All of these and many other quaint expressions found frequent use in James's vocabulary.

Mrs Betty was another lady to be so fascinated by James that she hung on his every word; she sat in her gloomy house waiting for the telephone to announce his imminent visit to Windsor. I too became towards the end of her life a favourite, although I never superseded James, to whom she pointedly referred as James I. Once only, owing to some temporary backsliding of his, I was promoted from James II. I soon lapsed back. My introduction to Mrs Betty happened after I had been invalided from the army. She remarked to James that she supposed I was still an Eton boy, too young to be in the services. James did not like this and replied, 'On the contrary, he is too old.' We became fast friends and I relished her memories of Oscar Wilde, who referred to her as 'so deliciously morbid', and of Bosie Douglas, whom at the height of his beautiful infamy she pronounced to have been a pasty and spotty youth.

Among the more constant of James's woman friends, Joan Moore, later Drogheda, reigned the longest. And even then she was not deposed. She abdicated. Her quick mind, wide reading, and professional talent as a pianist (which without appreciating it, James respected), allied to ethereal beauty and elegance, greatly appealed. Moreover, she had an advantage in his eyes that overtopped those of his other society-women friends, in that her background had been fraught with penury and want, a fact which to her credit she never forgot or glossed over after marriage to Garrett had brought her security and comparative affluence. Her history touched the tender-hearted side of James, ever ready to champion the underprivileged and downtrodden especially when they were lovely to look upon.

To nearly all these ladies – possibly not Mrs Betty, who would not have understood what he was talking about – young and old, James in the most candid manner would disclose the

arcane secrets of his sex life, a habit against which I cautioned
him, especially in the case of the young ones, some of whom
he fell romantically in love with, even pledging eternal troth;
and I quoted the well-worn phrase about hell having no fury
like a woman scorned, all to no avail. He managed just in time
to worm his way out of an engagement to Anne Ebury, who
was to remain a firm friend to the end of her days. To another,
'a paragon of a girl', he fancied he was engaged without being
absolutely sure, although she held a quite definite opinion.
When he discovered that she was engaged elsewhere he was
stricken, so he asserted, to the earth.

He also rose to tentative essays at love-making with women,
none of which came to fruition, and some to grief. In fact his
escapades into heterosexuality often had a comic twist. He
professed to yearn for consummation, usually after he had had
a good deal to drink, while expressing misgivings. Once when
fascinated by an unremembered female he complained to me,
not for the first time, that he feared she wished to lure him into
her bed. 'But isn't that just what you are wanting?' I asked.
'Don't be so disgusting', came the pious retort. Another time
he announced in fear and dread that his seduction, or
induction, had been fixed for the following evening. 'Think of
me and pray for me, Jimmy, at 10.45 p.m.', he pleaded
piteously; and the next morning telephoned, 'I am still alive. It
was quite easy, but not riotous.'

As I have already said, his women friends nearly all forgave
his transgressions; his men friends not so readily. Of the latter,
apart from Harold who occupied a special place as merciful
father-figure, Ralph Dutton and Paul Wallraf were steadfast
rocks of tolerance. Ralph, rich owner of a large Hampshire
estate, country house and fine contents, greatly admired
James's talent and came to the rescue, like Lady Crewe, with
gifts, not loans, of money. When he sensed that James was in
financial straits he would pay large sums into his bank account
without telling him. James would be profuse with his thanks
and write Ralph letters of heart-melting gratitude – that is to
say, whenever he realized these benefactions had been made.

His bank manager did not hurry to impart the good news, which he feared might induce the benefacted to spend immediately on something he coveted in a book or antique shop. Paul Wallraf, Prussian refugee from Hitler's Germany and dealer in rare works of art, found himself in 1939 interned on the Isle of Man, where he was given rough treatment. His children in Germany were unable to get in touch with him and most of his English friends were too busy to be interested. But James took up his cause with fervour, badgering the authorities in London to release him. He was successful. Paul never forgot this loyalty. When peace returned he resumed his old trade and with extraordinary flair and knowledge managed to retrieve a fortune. He also married a second rich wife, Muriel Ezra. Both Wallrafs were ever ready to bail James out of recurrent money troubles and have him to stay with them in Venice and elsewhere, especially when he was in the throes of a book.

Guy Burgess and Cecil Beaton mentioned in the same breath sound incompatible companions, the one a vagabond fellow-traveller, squalid in his habits, the other a superfine artist, fastidious and dandy. Each must have found the other intensely distasteful when they met, which was seldom. But both were intimates of James. The first did him no good. For a few brief months after the war they shared a flat. Pernicketty James did not relish the chaos of unmade beds, unwashed dishes and unwashed Guy, whereas Guy laughed at James's dapper little habits and the orderly way in which he arranged his writing table and books. And although James pronounced Guy to be 'an old windbag; but I am fond of him, instructive and negative though he be', Guy's vicious iconoclasm definitely encouraged the other's assumed anti-authoritarianism. As for Cecil, James greatly admired his ready wit and repartee, sophisticated talk and links with the famous, and also his chameleon-like ability to adapt to social polarities, to move from Lady Cunard's drawing-room straight to the control room of Bomber Command, identifying himself with the gallant fighter pilots. James eventually went further than this. He

positively delighted in the game of switching from the exquisite
to the *louche* and back again within a matter of hours.

Now Len Adams ('my precious Lennie'), from a different
walk of life from his, had a particular place in James's domestic
scenario. He was to become his familiar, on whose absolute
loyalty and horse-sense James relied. By trade a house painter
in battle dress released from National Service, straightforward,
tough, butch, one hundred per cent normal, he and James
hitched up in the late Forties. I cannot do better than quote
from Peter Quennell's vivid vignette in *A Lonely Business*. Of
James's staunch friends, Peter wrote, 'the best, staunchest and
most resolutely patient was that Homeric figure Len Adams, a
native of Sheffield, one-time paratrooper and prisoner-of-war,
whom he had happened to meet in a lift in Holland Park
underground station...' He had the virtue of keeping James in
order by his mere presence, even to the extent of withholding
James's own money when he suspected him of overspending.
The slight minus to Len's quiverful of pluses was a tendency
to provoke brawls with officious customers and total strangers
in public places. I am sure James secretly relished the scrapes
Len got into; he showed little concern over their consequences.
In his diary of June 1950 he wrote 'at eleven-thirty [Len] came
in with his arm bandaged: he had been stabbed by a drunken
negro at Hyde Park Corner', as though such an incident was of
nightly occurrence. Would that the steadfast Len had been
present on the dreadful day when a criminal gang broke into
James's flat and murdered him in the most brutal fashion.

James's masochism flourished on drama and risk. A well
known 'cellist, having threatened suicide on James's account,
thought better of it and threw his cut-throat razors into the
Seine. He then made a start in the Place de la Concorde on
butchering James, but satisfied himself, and James, by merely
knocking him down. A Swiss companion, with whom James
spent a night smoking marijuana in an establishment called
Charly's Tearoom in Gstaad, behaved so badly, keeping the
other visitors and staff awake until four in the morning, that
the proprietor all but threw James out. The Swiss companion

was indeed hurled, and forbidden to return to Gstaad. James boasted that he and the Swiss had made thirty trips on three cigarettes, 'one of them into the Toledo countryside through a colour print I have of a Greco landscape – it all came to life.' He was dynamized by balancing on knife edges, and would take taxi drivers into his flat at midnight, persuading them to discuss their girl friends with him. He lost his heart to a pugilist – 'I am having boxing lessons now'. Then he was in love with a Communist Pole, so became a fervent Stalinist. Abandoned by the Pole, he became a fervent anti-Stalinist. Madly in love with a Norwegian, he became a fanatical champion of Scandinavia's depressed status among the world powers. And so it went on.

James was affectionate and generous to a fault. He was always bestowing presents on his friends. I have a Pugin water-colour of Manchester Cathedral, given me when he cannot have had a penny to his name. True, he informed me that he had been obliged to sell the painting of an eighteenth-century country house which he had left me in his will, but wrote down the address of the shop which had just bought it from him. 'If you are quick, Jimmy, you can buy it back for yourself.'

When war came I saw little of him at first. In July 1940 he wrote me a letter criticizing, not without justice, my 'collapse from pacifism into the class convention of the Guards ... Your point of view about the war amuses me; it is exactly between mine [downright opposition] and Mummy's [acceptance]; but I have before noticed this about your points of view. They form a bridge from the pre-1914 to the pre-1940. Which is natural.' Caustic perhaps, but pointful. When the National Trust returned to its London office and I with it, in January 1943, he suggested that we share a flat. But I had the sense to decline, although our friendship was then running as smoothly as silk. Indeed, we were together very often between intervals when he was despatched to Washington on the British Military Staff for brief visits.

My recollections of our meetings at this period are halcyon because devoid of any emotional tension, and vivid but not chronological. They come to me like gusts of refreshing breezes towards the end of a torrid afternoon. I am sitting next to him at Emerald's little round table in the Dorchester and Field Marshal Archie Wavell is the chief guest. Such is our empathy that we have nothing whatsoever to say to each other. Besides, têtes-à-tête are not permitted by Emerald. Nor does the Field Marshal, who looks like a man in deep water, have much to disclose. Another evening we are drinking Pimm's together in Rules' restaurant. We are as one. Jamesey expatiates on the nature of our close relationship, which could never have existed in a previous age, and did not even between Byron and John Cam Hobhouse. We stroll down to the Embankment and cross Lambeth Bridge in the blackout. By moonlight the river is silver and soundless. Nothing seems to stir and London is probably quieter than it was when Wordsworth's earth had not anything to show more fair. Yet a rain of bombs on such a clear night seems to us almost inevitable. On Cardinal's Wharf, within the shadow of the dome across the water, James declares that for him life is so momentously joyful that he can never die. He is twenty-six, and it is, he emphasises, a pity that I am already in decline. We cross the river again by London Bridge and he kicks aside a crumpled beer tin, saying, 'It is sobering to conjecture that this tin may outlive you and me.' Then I give a birthday dinner party for myself at Boulestin's and Harold Nicolson, who is present, mutters, 'What worries me is how Jim can afford to pay for it,' and Jamesey says brightly, 'That's all right. I can see to it.' Then I am sitting beside him in a pew in the Jesuits' Farm Street church waiting for Princess Winnie de Polignac's Requiem Mass to begin. We arrange that he shall accompany me on a National Trust jaunt to Suffolk; and he says, 'Being with you is like being with myself, only nicer.' In Suffolk we agree we must both marry simple, unsophisticated, submissive yeowomen.

He of course did nothing of the sort, and nine years were to pass before I married someone who was *not* a simple, unsophisticated or submissive yeowoman. When I did tell him about Alvilde, he was delighted. He advised, as though his advice were a prerequisite, that come what may I must marry her. Well, I did so. He and she became very attached, which pleased me inordinately. He often stayed with her at Roque-brune during those sad months when she and I had to be separated by her inexorable French domicile. Soon he became almost proprietary, as though he were married to her and not I. He nagged and hectored me to either give up my work for the National Trust and live with her totally in France, or clear out and leave her – it was tantamount to that, if it were not too fanciful to contemplate – to him. In fact, he took what I can only call liberties.

When I was perforce in London on my own, James would occasionally invite himself to dinner which my old house-keeper Emily cooked for us. Emily lived at a distance and I did not like keeping her late in the evenings, but James might arrive two hours late – and without any money to pay the driver of the taxi he had hired that morning. The fare had to be settled by someone. I found that pretty steep. Gulping down what food he thought fit to eat and wine to drink, he would suddenly announce that he had a date elsewhere and must reluctantly rush off. And if it suited him for some reason to stay the night, he might arrive at three o'clock in the morning.

His addiction to alcohol, cigarettes and drugs was soon equalled only by his hankering for mud, as the French so delicately put it. The deterioration set in while Dame Una was still alive. She knew of course all about his propensity to mud, but took his frailties in her stride. Strait-laced though she naturally was, she harboured no moral prejudices where her sons were concerned. She was more worried about the effect the mudlarks were having on James's health than disapproving of them as companions in his dissipations. They could not have been concealed from her watchful eyes even if James had wanted it: after he broke away from number 28 Lansdowne Road she telephoned him every morning for an account of what he was about to do and whom to see that day. In the evening he would telephone her with all (or nearly all) the particulars of what had passed. Towards the larks, when she met them, she behaved with an old-fashioned courtesy that was lost on the majority of the yahoo sort. I don't suppose she actually launched into a discussion about the inspiration behind Lamartine's sonnets; but she would graciously enquire, in between a series of little coughs, about their mothers, and ask if they thought the mothers would like a visit from her. This seemed to scare them considerably. Whenever James was out of sorts she summoned him to her house immediately and put him to bed. She once asked me to meet him at Heathrow and bring him to number 28. He was practically a stretcher case, clearly ill, and emitting an appalling smell which I could only assume to be the lingering miasma from prolonged orgies. When I delivered him at her door the Dame expressed no sign of anxiety, at least before me, nor did she upbraid him. She merely spared me a perfunctory nod of thanks and dismissed me. It was a signal that she was upset.

Dame Una's death in August 1949 was a knock-out blow to both the brothers. For James it meant the removal of the main prop of his well-being and self-respect. Her severe illness with pneumonia in the spring had plunged him into a dread so terrible that he funked the issue and would not come home from abroad when asked by John to do so. On the Dame's slight recovery he returned. But she soon had another relapse. And when it became clear that she was going to die he pulled himself together, although he was suffering from alcoholic poisoning, not to mention other sinister afflictions. He was determined, he promised his mother, to amend. John by this time was in Italy. Left alone with his mother and their old nanny, whom both boys adored, James acted bravely and sensibly. He insisted that John should remain away. In later years John termed it an act of expiation on James's part for his absence in the spring. James told me that the deathbed scene was the most awful experience of his life: that Dame Una's hopeless struggle to survive was a devastating commentary on the purposelessness of man's existence on earth. Having watched aghast her abandonment of the struggle, all he could think of doing was to collect every book she had written and raise a pyramid of them on the table beside her.

At least the Dame died with faith in her beloved Benjamin intact. To the last she still believed he was to be what she had ordained from his birth, a very great writer. His brother John, on the other hand, had come to acknowledge that James's character was so flawed he would not be a great writer. He wearied of receiving the same parrot-like retort to his remonstrances: 'Of course I change at the impress of some strong encounter – what artist doesn't? They will not understand that I gradually return to normal' – he might have added, 'by sponging on my poor friends' pockets and good nature'. He simply could not understand how much his excuse that his bad conduct was due to his being an artist exasperated these friends. He *was* an artist, which John was not, but the repeated declamation did not assuage his creditors. Eventually he was so unreliable in chucking dates at the drop of a hat that it was impossible to make plans with him. Even Joan Drogheda and Cecil Beaton washed their hands of him. He went on writing, seemingly little the worse for the dissipations. Yet I do not believe that *The Sins of the Fathers*, *Anthony Trollope* and *Robert Louis Stevenson* surpassed the early books about Monckton Milnes, or *Queen Mary* and *Verandah*.

Our friendship soured. We saw less and less of each other. Intervals between positive hostility (he took grave offence at any whisper of reproach) and half-hearted pledges of renewed affection were prolonged. Also, the pledges became meaningless. The worm in me was bored by his repeated turnings. He was patently bored by me. After a longish interval Alvilde and I had him to stay for a weekend in the country in January 1967. On the first evening he and I fell out. It was my fault for minding his disparagement of everything and everyone save those benighted members of society who sleep in cardboard boxes under arches. Many of them may be highly worthy citizens, but they do not hold a monopoly of the cardinal virtues and graces, as he maintained. The following morning he left; and I have felt guilty ever since. I do not think we met again.

I certainly saw him once more, from the top of a bus in Trafalgar Square. My bus was stationary in a traffic jam. Jamesey was walking rapidly in his rolling gait past the National Gallery steps. What first struck me before I recognized him were the arms flailing in gesticulation. He was alone. His head was tilted upwards and his long, rather shaggy locks, now grey, were being tossed from side to side. He was talking to himself and laughing over – who can say? – a memory or a project, maybe some fancied getting the better of a discarded friend? There was exultation in the laughter. But the face! He could not see me through the smudged window of the upper deck. The expression was absolutely terrifying – lined, creased, furrowed by anguish and hidden forces like a mountain rock scored by aeons of glaciers. It was not a face such as I imagine Mr Hyde's to have been like, that of a man giving rein to his evil impulses. No, it was – I didn't think so at the time, but I do now in retrospect – the pre-ordained image, imposed by some outside power, of a madman. It was like the picture of Dorian Gray Oscar Wilde described, just before that anti-hero took up the knife that had stabbed his great admirer and protagonist, the artist Basil Hallward, to slash the canvas on which his likeness had over the years assumed the physical effects of progressive dissipation and appalling apathy. Only James had never yet been intentionally cruel, any more than I or other close friends that I knew of had been his victims, as Sybil and Jim Vane were Dorian Gray's in Wilde's story. Nor had there been a Basil Hallward in his life unless, perish the thought, it had been Dame Una all along. That was a possibility which I could never bring myself to investigate.

Acknowledgements

PAUL METHUEN: I am beholden to Kenneth Rose for access to some private records of his visits to Corsham Court.

VITA SACKVILLE-WEST: Throughout I have been much indebted to Victoria Glendinning's *Vita, The Life of V. Sackville-West*, Weidenfeld and Nicolson, 1983.

SACHEVERELL SITWELL: Taken from my obituary of him in the *Independent*, 2 October 1988, and amplified.

ROSAMOND LEHMANN: Taken from my obituary of Rosamond Lehmann in the *Independent*, 14 March 1990, and slightly amplified.

HENRY YORKE and HENRY GREEN: The substance of this sketch was written for *Twentieth Century Literature* in 1984. Sebastian Yorke's *Memoir*, included in *Surviving* (1992), tells within sixteen pages all there is need to know about his father's life. It is a model for every literary biographer. I am particularly indebted to it for my last paragraph.

JOHN FOWLER: Based on an address I gave at John Fowler's memorial service at St George's Church, Hanover Square, 1977, but altered and expanded. This sketch also owes much to John Cornforth's invaluable book, *The Inspiration of the Past: Country House Taste in the Twentieth Century* (1985), in which John Fowler's work and influence are assessed.

EVERARD RADCLIFFE: I am indebted to Lady Mary Hesketh for some biographical particulars.

RICHARD STEWART-JONES: My contribution to *Richard Llewellyn Stewart-Jones as remembered by his friends*. Privately printed 1980.

I wish to thank the following for the loan of photographs and for permission to reproduce them: James Methuen-Campbell and *The Bath*

231

Chronicle (Lord and Lady Methuen); Jane Bown (Vita Sackville-West); the National Portrait Gallery (Sacheverell Sitwell); Alan Ross (William Plomer); Sotheby's, London (Henry Yorke); Mrs (Lucy) Rohan Butler (Robert Byron); John Murray (Osbert Lancaster); Mrs Mary Selwyn (Everard Radcliffe); and Mrs Elizabeth Pulford (Richard Stewart-Jones). I have again been privileged in having Douglas Matthews as indexer.

I am also more than grateful to my friends at John Murray's, especially my editors Grant McIntyre and Gail Pirkis for their constant help, patience and kindness; and also to Elizabeth Robinson for reading through my typescript with lynx-like eyes. Without them where would I have got to?

J.L.-M., 1996

Index

Aarons, Dr, 22
Aberdeen, George Hamilton Gordon, 4th
    Earl of, 182
Acton, Sir Harold, 103, 105, 138, 142, 150,
    156
Adam, Robert, 70
Adams, Len, 224
Addleshaw, Canon G.W.O., 110
Alexander, Peter, 96
Ancaster, Phyllis Louise, Countess of (née
    Astor; 'Wissy'), 162–3
Arthur, Michael, 211
Asquith, Herbert Henry, 1st Earl of
    Oxford and Asquith, 2, 8
Asquith, Raymond, 21
Athos, Mount, 145, 147
Auden, W.H., 52, 64
Avon, Clarissa, Countess of (née Churchill),
    206

Baird, Sandy, 211
Baldwin, Stanley (later 1st Earl), 51
Balfour, Patrick see Kinross, 3rd Baron
Baring, Maurice, 105
Barrie, Sir James Matthew, 2, 8
Bath Academy of Art, 28–9, 38
Baynes, Doreen, see Colston-Baynes,
    Doreen
Beanacre Manor, Wiltshire, 23–5
Beaton, Cecil, 202, 213, 223, 229
Beauchamp, William Lygon, 7th Earl,
    137–40
Beaverbrook, William Maxwell Aitken, 1st
    Baron, 111, 175
Beckford, Peter and Louisa, 218
Beerbohm, Sir Max, 2, 8, 169–70

Bell, Clive, 46, 62
Bellamy, Thomas, 28
Beresford, Lord John de la Poer, 159
Berkeley, Lennox, 18, 117
Betjeman, (Sir) John: at Café Royal, 52;
    poem to Kinross, 105–6; on
    estrangement from parents, 108–9;
    mocks Etchells, 110; and Kinross's
    death, 121; and Henry Yorke, 123; and
    Osbert Lancaster, 172
Betty, Mrs see Montgomery, Alberta
    Victoria
Birch, Sir Arthur, 203
Blake, William, 12
Blakiston, Noel, 105–7
Bloomsbury Group: on Vita Sackville-West,
    46, 48; welcomes Rosamond Lehmann,
    83; and Plomer, 96; Robert Byron's
    hostility to, 142
Bonnard, Professor Pierre, 39
Borenius, Tancred, 27
Bowers, Henry R. ('Birdie'), 3
Bowra, Sir Maurice, 83, 105, 172
Britten, Benjamin, 97–8
Brooke, Rupert, 41, 79
Brooks's Club, London SW1, 88, 202
Brown, Lancelot ('Capability'), 19, 27
Bullock, Sir Malcolm, 15
Burgess, Guy, 211, 223
Butler, Lucy (née Byron), 139
Butts, Anthony, 97
Byron, Daisy (Robert's mother), 136–40,
    157
Byron, Eric (Robert's father), 136–7, 139
Byron, George Gordon, 6th Baron, 89,
    226; Don Juan, 69

Byron, Robert: travels and writings, 117, 134–6, 139–41, 143–51; and Henry Yorke, 123; death, 132, 134; values and prejudices, 132–3, 141–4; background and upbringing, 136–8; relations with mother, 138–40, 157; appearance, 140–1; and Desmond Parsons, 149–52; friendship with author, 149; political activities, 152–3; attachment to Horton Park Menagerie, 154; and outbreak of war, 154–7; argumentativeness, 155–6; *An Essay on India*, 148; *How We Celebrate the Coronation*, 152; *The Road to Oxiana*, 135, 143, 149–50; *The Station*, 143–4

Café Royal, London, 52
Campbell, Mary, 57
Campbell, Roy, 57, 64, 92–3
Campbell, Victor (Captain RN), 1–2
Cape, Jonathan (publishing house), 100
Carnock, Frederick Nicolson, 2nd Baron, 53
Cavendish, Lady Elizabeth, 121
Chagford *see* Easton Court
Chambers, Robert, 80–1; *Vestiges of the Natural History of Creation*, 80
Chambers, William, publisher, 80
Chambers's Edinburgh Journal, 80
Chantrell, Robert Dennis, 183
Chapman, Hester, 81
Charles Edward Stuart, Prince (Bonnie Prince Charlie), 81
Chatwin, Bruce, 135, 143
Cherry-Garrard, Apsley, 3
Churchill, Clarissa *see* Avon, Clarissa, Countess of
Churchill, John G., 113
Churchill, Randolph, 172
Churchill, Sir Winston, 214
Clark, Jane, Lady, 105
Clark, Kenneth (*later* Baron), 105
Claude Lorrain, 183
Clonmore, William, Baron (*later* 8th Earl of Wicklow; 'Cracky'), 137–8
Cobb, Carolyn Postlethwaite, 115
Cobbe, Alec, 186
Cockerell, Sir Sydney, 10, 13
Cocteau, Jean, 142
Coghill, Nevill, 123
Colefax & Fowler Ltd, 160–1, 166
Colefax, Sibyl, Lady, 7, 59, 160, 162
Colston-Baynes, Doreen ('Dormer Creston'), 59, 219–20
Connolly, Cyril, 52, 103, 105–7
Cook, Herbert, 23
Cooper, Alfred Duff (*later* 1st Viscount Norwich), 21
Cooper, Lady Diana, 55, 117

Cornforth, John, 160
Corsham Court (estate), Wiltshire, 19–24, 26–9, 36, 38–9
Country Life (magazine), 132, 148
Crawley, D.J.C., 212–13
Crewe, Margaret, Marchioness of (née Primrose), 59, 217–18
Croft-Murray, Edward, 27, 31
Cunard, Maud Alice (Emerald), Lady, 67, 136, 218–19, 223, 226
Cuninghame, Doreen, 1

Daily Express: Osbert Lancaster with, 174–5
Darwin, Charles: *Origin of Species*, 80
d'Avigdor-Goldsmid, Harry (*later* Sir Henry), 172, 210
Day-Lewis, Cecil, 84
Dean Paul *see* Paul
Degas, Edgar, 31
Demeures Historiques, Les (France and Belgium), 29
Derwentwater, James Radcliffe, 3rd Earl of, 180
Desborough, Ethel, Lady, 220
de Vesci, Frances Lois, Viscountess, 151
Devonshire, Deborah, Duchess of, 164
Dickens, Catherine, 82
Dickens, Charles, 82
Ditchley Park, Oxfordshire, 163, 167
Douglas, Lord Alfred ('Bosie'), 221
Drogheda, Garrett Moore, 11th Earl of, 221
Drogheda, Joan Moore, Countess of, 216, 221, 229
Drogheda, Kathleen, Countess of, 9
Dugdale, Michael A. S., 211
Duncan, Isadora, 2
Dutton, Ralph, 222
Duveen, Joseph, Baron, 23

Easton Court, Chagford, Devon, 115
Ebury, Anne, Lady, 222
Eliot, T.S., 52, 64, 97; *The Waste Land*, 41
Elizabeth the Queen Mother, 216
Epstein, Sir Jacob, 16
Erskine, Hamish St Clair, 55
Esher, Oliver Brett, 3rd Viscount, 37
Etchells, Frederick, 110
Etchells, Hester, 110
Evans, Ted, 3
Evans, Sammy and Sidney, 20

Fedden, Robin, 190–3
Federal Union Club, 134, 152–3
Field, Henry, 163
Firdausi (Persian poet), 149
Fisher, Geoffrey, Archbishop of Canterbury (*later* Baron), 216

Fisher, Ros, 121
Fleming, Ian, 101
Forster, E.M., 96
Forthampton Court, Worcestershire/
    Gloucestershire, 122, 128, 131
Fowler, John: friendship with author,
    158–9; qualities, 158; background, 159;
    and cousin Una, 159; decorating and
    restoration work, 160–1, 163–7;
    relations with staff and clients, 161–3,
    165; appearance, 164; financial
    indifference, 166; observation and
    expertise, 166–7; cancer, 168
Fox, Charles James, 51
Fritton Hythe, near Yarmouth, 5, 12

Garnett, Edward, 101
Georgian Group, 134, 152, 203, 210
Gibbs, James (architect), 70
Giotto, 145
Glasgow Art Gallery, 43
Glendinning, Victoria, 46, 60; *Vita: The Life
    of V. Sackville-West*, 61
Goncourt, Edmond and Jules, 209
Gordon, William, 182–3
Graig, Edward Gordon, 2
Greco, El (Domenico Theotocopoulos),
    145, 147
Greece: Osbert Lancaster and, 175–7
Green, Henry *see* Yorke, Henry
Grenfell brothers, 20
Grimsthorpe Castle, Lincolnshire, 162
Gwynn, Stephen, 9

Hamilton, Sir Ian, 39
Hardwick Hall, Derbyshire, 70–1
Harris, Cara, Lady, 173
Harris, Honey, 174
Harris, Sir Austen, 173
Hatchlands Park, Surrey, 186
Hawksmoor, Nicholas, 70
Henderson, Gavin, 136, 140
Hennessy, W.J., 21
Hess, Dame Myra, 12
Hobhouse, Christopher, 51, 115,
    134
Hobhouse, John Cam, 37, 216
Hogarth, Georgina, 82
Holland-Martin, Robert, 13
Holmes, Sir Charles, 20
Hopkins, Gerard Manley, 126
Horton Park, near Northampton:
    Menagerie, 154
Houghton, Richard Monckton Milnes,
    Baron, 207, 217, 229
House, Colonel Edward Mandell, 8
Howard family, 26

Howard, Elizabeth Jane (*formerly* Scott;
    Peter's first wife), 7
Howard, Geoffrey, 26

India: Robert Byron on, 147–8

Japan: Plomer in, 93, 95–6
John, Augustus, 4, 52
Jones, Inigo, 70
Jones, Keith Miller, 8, 13
Jones, Peter (London store), 160
Jourdain, Margaret, 27
Joyce, James, 54

Kavanagh, P.J., 85
Kavanagh, Sally (née Philipps; Rosamond
    Lehmann's daughter), 84–5
Kelly, Sir Gerald, 39
Kendall, Diana, 38
Kennet, Edward Hilton Young, 1st Baron
    ('Bill'), 1, 4–6
Kennet, Kathleen, Lady (*formerly* Scott):
    marriage to Captain Scott, 1–3;
    appearance, 2; sculpting, 2, 10, 15–16;
    sons, 4–5; character and qualities, 6–8,
    15; vanity, 8–9; obituary details, 9–10;
    friendship with author, 10–13, 16–17,
    29; skating and dancing, 11; decline in
    health, 16
Kennet, Wayland Young, 2nd Baron, 5
Kilvert, Revd Francis: Plomer and,
    100–2
Kinross, Angela, Lady (née Culme-
    Seymour; Patrick's wife), 112–16
Kinross, Caroline, Lady (née
    Johnstone-Douglas; Patrick's mother),
    104, 109–10
Kinross, Patrick Balfour, 3rd Baron: at
    Café Royal, 52; family background,
    103–4; education, 104–5; social life,
    105–9, 119–20; journalistic career, 106,
    111, 117; clumsiness, 111–12; travels,
    111–12, 117; marriage, 112–13; succeeds
    to title, 113–14; war service, 114–15;
    appearance, 115–16, 119; domestic
    life, 116; cooking, 119; cancer and
    death, 120–1; and Henry Yorke, 131;
    Atatürk, 118, 120; *Between Two Seas*, 117;
    Europa Minor, 112; *Grand Tour*, 112;
    Lords of the Equator, 112; *The Orphaned
    Realm*, 112; *The Ottoman Centuries*,
    120–2; *The Ruthless Innocent*, 115; *Society
    Racket*, 107–9, 111; *Within the
    Taurus*, 112
Knole Park, Kent, 43, 46–7, 60
Knollys, Eardley, 58, 115
Kormis, F.T., 37

Lambert, Constant, 52
Lamington, Riette, Lady, 219
Lancaster, Clare (Osbert's mother), 171
Lancaster, Colonel Claude, 162
Lancaster, Karen (née Harris; Osbert's
wife), 173–4
Lancaster, Nancy (*formerly* Tree), 162–3
Lancaster, Sir Osbert: at Café Royal, 52;
appearance and dress, 169–70, 174;
birth, 169; Edwardianism, 169;
background and upbringing, 171–2;
conversation, 172, 178; friendship with
author, 172–3; marriages, 173–4;
artistry, 174–7; fondness for Greece,
175–7; literary style, 177–8; *All Done
from Memory*, 178; *Classical Landscape with
Figures*, 176; *Drayneflete Revealed*, 176;
Homes, Sweet Homes, 174; *The
Littlehampton Bequest*, 176; *Pillar to Post*,
174; *Progress at Pelvis Bay*, 174; *Sailing to
Byzantium*, 176; *With an Eye to the Future*,
178
Lancaster, Sir William (Osbert's
grandfather), 171
Landsberg, Mrs Bertie, 179
Larkin, Philip, 88
Lawrence, D.H., 30; *Lady Chatterley's Lover*,
50
Lawrence, Thomas Edward, 2, 32
Lear, Edward, 31, 79
Le Corbusier (Charles Edouard Jeanneret),
110
Lees-Milne, Alvilde, 58, 61, 86, 89, 226–7,
229
Lehmann, Alice Marie (née Davis;
Rosamond's mother), 82
Lehmann, Amelia (née Chambers;
Rosamond's great-aunt), 81
Lehmann, Beatrix (Rosamond's sister), 79
Lehmann, Frederick (Rosamond's
grandfather), 80–2
Lehmann, Helen (Rosamond's sister), 79
Lehmann, John (Rosamond's brother),
79–80, 83; (ed.) *Ancestors and Friends*, 81
Lehmann, Nina (née Chambers;
Rosamond's grandmother), 81–2
Lehmann, Rosamond: character, 79–80,
86–7; family background and
upbringing, 79–82; appearance, 83;
marriages and love affairs, 83–5; and
daughter's death, 85–6; psychical
beliefs, 86; and Kinross, 105; *The Ballad
and the Source*, 85; *Dusty Answer*, 83, 105;
The Echoing Grove, 85; *No More Music*, 84;
A Note in Music, 84; *A Sea-Grape Tree*,
86; *The Swan in the Evening*, 86; *The
Weather in the Streets*, 84

Lehmann, Rudolph Chambers (Rosamond's
father), 81–2
Lehmann, Rudolph (Rosamond's
great-uncle), 81; *An Artist's Reminiscences*,
81
Lister, Edgar G., 37
Lloyd, George Ambrose Lloyd, 1st Baron,
2, 51, 148, 155
Lloyd George, David (*later* 1st Earl), 2, 51
Lothian, Philip Henry Kerr, 11th Marquess
of, 13
Lübeck, 213–14
Lutyens, Sir Edwin, 39, 148
Lygon, Hugh, 137, 139

Macaulay, Dame Rose, 219
McCarthy, (Sir) Desmond and Molly
(Lady), 105
Mackenzie, Sir Compton, 52
Madresfield Court, Worcestershire, 137–8
Manning, Cardinal Henry Edward, 185
Marsh, Sir Edward: *Georgian Poetry 1912–21*,
41
Mary, Queen of George V, 207, 216, 229
Mary, Queen of Scots, 71
Massingberd, Hugh (Montgomery-), 162
Matheson, Hilda, 57–8
Matheson, MacLeod, 58
Mathew, David, Archbishop of Apamea,
203
Maud, Queen of Norway, 1
Mellon, Mrs Paul, 166
Melvill, Harry, 156
Messel, Oliver, 154
Methuen family, 19–20
Methuen, Eleanor ('Norah'), Lady (née
Hennessy; Paul's wife): marriage, 21–2;
childlessness, 22–3; sewing, 22, 27; and
husband's financial problems and
career, 24–5; and maintenance and
improvements to Corsham, 27–8, 38;
French-speaking, 29; and husband's
work in wartime France, 34; death and
effigy, 37; and psychical research, 37
Methuen, Rt Hon. John, 19
Methuen, Mary Ethel, Lady (née Ayshford),
20
Methuen, Paul, 1st Baron, 20
Methuen, Paul, 4th Baron: qualities and
character, 18, 21, 25, 37–8; family
background, 19–20; education, 20;
marriage, 21; service in Great War,
21–2; financial anxieties, 23–5; relations
with father, 23–5; inherits title and
Corsham, 26–9; appearance and dress,
29–30, 36; painting and sketching, 30–2,
39–40; service in Second World War,

32–5; deafness and isolation, 36; interest in psychical research, 37; public duties and offices, 38–9; *Normandy Diary, 1944*, 52–5
Methuen, Sir Paul, 19
Methuen, Field Marshal Paul Sanford, 3rd Baron, 20–1, 23–6
Methuen Treaty (1703), 19
Milnes, Richard Monckton *see* Houghton, Baron
Mitford, Nancy: and Kathleen Kennet, 14–15; on Rosamond Lehmann's spiritualism, 86; on Henry Yorke, 123; letter-writing, 128; marriage to Rodd, 133; on Robert Byron, 156
Mitford, Unity, 15
Monro, Harold, 91–2
Montgomery, Alberta Victoria (née Ponsonby; 'Mrs Betty'), 220–1
Montgomery-Massingberd, Hugh *see* Massingberd, Hugh (Montgomery-)
Moore, Joan *see* Drogheda, Countess of
Mori, Captain, 93
Morris, William, 197
Mortimer, Raymond, 56
Mosley, Diana, Lady, 15
Mosley, Sir Oswald (Tom), 15, 50–1
Mossman, Jim, 87
Muggeridge, Malcolm, 117
Murray, John (Jock), 52

Nansen, Fridtjof, 8
Nash, Joseph: *Mansions of the Olden Times*, 70
National Trust: author's work with, 13–14, 58, 152, 190, 194–5, 197, 225; and Corsham, 27–8, 36; acquires Knole, 47; Radcliffe and, 189, 191–3
New Party, 50–1
New Writing (magazine), 80
Newman, Cardinal John Henry, 185
Nicolson, Ben (Vita Sackville-West's son), 48, 55
Nicolson, Sir Harold: marriage to Vita Sackville-West, 44, 49–50, 55–6, 63; honours, 63–4; views and manner, 63; literary reputation, 66; praises Rumbold's autobiography, 99; and Kinross, 105; letter-writing, 128; on Robert Byron's death, 134; on Pope-Hennessy's *Queen Mary*, 207; and Pope-Hennessy's anti-bombing views, 213; relations with Pope-Hennessy, 214–15, 222, 226; wartime political views, 214; reviews Colston-Baynes's *Young Queen Victoria*, 219; *Some People*, 69

Nicolson, Nigel (Vita Sackville-West's son), 43, 48, 55, 60, 214; (ed.) *Portrait of a Marriage*, 62
Niggeman, Elvira, 215

Oates, Captain Lawrence Edward Grace, 3
Observer (newspaper), 62, 64
Odiham, Hampshire, 162
Oswald, Arthur, 183

Paget (Bridget), Lady Victor, 218–19
Paget, Sir Richard, 13
Paris, 54
Parsons, Lady Bridget, 15
Parsons, Desmond, 122, 149–53; death, 132, 154
Paul, Brenda Dean, 107
Paul, Sir Brian Kenneth Dean ('Nappa'), 116
Peking, 150–1
Pelly, Elizabeth, 107
Pentland, Henry John Sinclair, 2nd Baron, 13
Persia: Robert Byron in, 148–9
Philipps, Hugo (Rosamond Lehmann's son), 84
Philipps, Wogan (*later* 2nd Baron Milford), 84
Phillimore, Claud, 179
Pius VII, Pope, 185
Playfair, Sir Nigel, 30
Plomer, Charles Campbell (William's father), 90–1, 93
Plomer, Edythe (William's mother), 90, 102
Plomer, William: edits Kilvert diaries, 10, 100–2; appearance, 88; friendship with author, 88–9, 101; character and qualities, 89; home life, 89–90; background and upbringing, 90–1; education, 90–1; literary career, 92–3; in Japan, 93, 95–6; in London, 96–7; love life, 96; writes Britten librettos, 97–8; edits Rumbold's diaries, 99–100; with Jonathan Cape, 100–1; beliefs, 101–2; *African Poems*, 93–4; *Ballads Abroad*, 98; *Country Ballads*, 98; 'The Heart of a King' (poem), 98; 'In a Bombed House' (poem), 97; *London Ballads*, 98; *Poems Written in Japan*, 95; 'A Transvaal Morning' (poem), 94; 'Tugela River' (poem), 93; *Turbott Wolfe*, 92–3
Plunkett, Sir Horace, 106
Polignac, Princess Edmond de (Winaretta; 'Winnie'), 226
Polunin, Vladimir, 173
Ponsonby, Elizabeth, 107
Pontifex, H., & Sons, 124, 130

Pope-Hennessy, James: at Sibyl Colefax's, 59; relations with Harold Nicolson, 60, 214–15, 222; and Henry Yorke, 128; background and upbringing, 201, 205; writing, 201, 205–8, 229; dislikes father, 202; relations with mother, 203, 205, 217, 230; sense of immortality, 204; war work, 205, 223, 225; works at Sheed & Ward, 206, 210–12; love-making, 208–9, 222; appearance and manner, 210, 215–16, 230; friendship with author, 210, 225–7; anti-colonialism, 212–13; in Sierra Leone, 212–13; in Trinidad, 212; character and behaviour, 215–17, 224–5, 229; extravagance and debts, 215, 222–3; social life and friendships, 217–25; relations with Len Adams, 224; deterioration, 227–8, 230; and mother's death, 228; rift with author, 229; *Anthony Trollope*, 229; *The Flight of Youth*, 207; *London Fabric*, 206; *Queen Mary*, 207, 216, 229; *Robert Louis Stevenson*, 229; *The Sins of the Fathers*, 212–13, 229; *Verandah*, 206–7, 229; *Years of Promise*, 207
Pope-Hennessy, Sir John (James's brother), 18, 39–40, 201–3, 205–6, 209, 228–9
Pope-Hennessy, Sir John (James's grandfather), 206, 210
Pope-Hennessy, Major-General Richard, 201–3
Pope-Hennessy, Dame Una (née Birch): relations with sons, 201–6, 210, 217, 219, 227–8, 230; death, 228–9
Powell, Anthony, 103
Powys, A.R., 197
Proust, Marcel, 72
Pryce-Jones, Alan, 52, 172, 211
Purdie, A.E., 184
Pyne, William Henry: *Royal Residences*, 186

Quennell, (Sir) Peter, 52, 103, 115, 206; *A Lonely Business*, 224

Radcliffe, Betty (née Butler), 181
Radcliffe, Charles (Everard's son), 189–91, 193
Radcliffe, Sir Everard: friendship with author, 179; background and upbringing, 180–1; Catholicism, 180–1, 185; unhappiness, 180; first marriage and children, 181, 189; inheritance, 181–2; military career, 181; and Rudding Park, 184–91; advises National Trust, 189; divorce, 190; second marriage and child, 190–1, 193; succeeds to baronetcy, 191; sells

Rudding, 192–3; move to Switzerland and death, 193
Radcliffe, Sir Joseph, 182–4
Radcliffe, Sir Percival, 184
Rees, Goronwy, 84, 123
Reid, Robert, 104
Rembrandt van Rijn, 141–2
Repton, Humphry, 182, 188, 191
Roach, Dot, 161
Rodd, Peter, 15, 133
Rodin, Auguste, 15
Rosse, Anne, Countess of, 127, 151, 154
Rosse, Michael Parsons, 6th Earl of, 127, 132, 136
Rothschild, Mrs James de, 165
Royal Tapestry and Carpet Factory, Madrid, 27
Rudding Park, Yorkshire: building, 181–6; art collection, 187–8; garden, 188–9; National Trust negotiates for, 190–2; sold, 192–3
Rugby School, 91
Rumbold, Richard: death, 88, 99; diaries edited by Plomer, 89, 99–100; *My Father's Son*, 99
Runciman, Sir Steven, 83
Runciman, Walter (*later* 2nd Viscount), 83
Ruskin, John, 145, 197
Russell, Bertrand, 139
Ryf, R.S., 125

Sackville, Charles Sackville-West, 4th Baron, 47
Sackville, Victoria, Lady, 43, 47–8
Sackville-West, Edward (*later* 5th Baron Sackville), 14, 47, 88
Sackville-West, Henry (Lady Sackville's brother), 48
Sackville-West, Vita: Strang portrait of, 43–4; tastes and standards, 46, 48–9; background, 47; affair with Violet Trefusis, 49–50, 55–6, 62; literary career and writings, 49–50, 62, 64–6; marriage, 49–50, 55–6; friendship with author, 52, 55, 58–60; appearance and voice, 55, 58; romantic entanglements, 57–8, 96; decline in health and withdrawal, 60–1; reputation, 61–2, 64–6; and honours, 64; final illness and death, 215; *All Passion Spent*, 44, 49; *The Dark Island*, 49; *The Dragon in Shallow Waters*, 49–50; *The Edwardians*, 44, 49; *The Garden*, 50, 64–5; *King's Daughter*, 41–4; *Knole and the Sackvilles*, 47; *The Land*, 44–6, 49–50, 64
St Levan, Gwendolen St Aubyn (née Nicolson), 53
Sandys, Cynthia, Lady, 86

Index

Sanford, Revd John, 20
Sargent, Sir Malcolm, 52
Scott, Geoffrey, 46, 57; *The Architecture of Humanism*, 69
Scott, (Sir) Peter, 1, 3–4, 6, 14
Scott, Captain Robert Falcon, 1, 3–4, 8, 14
Scott, Sir John Murray, 48
Scott, Sir Walter, 80
Scott-James, Anne (Lady Lancaster), 174
Selby-Lowndes, Diana, 116
Shackleton, Sir Ernest, 3
Shakespeare, William: Robert Byron's antipathy to, 141–2
Shaw, George Bernard, 2, 8
Shawe-Stewart, Patrick, 21
Sheed & Ward (publishers), 206, 210–12
Shelley, Percy Bysshe, 89
Sheridan, Margaret, 110
Shone, Richard, 30
Sickert, Walter, 30–1, 39
Sierra Leone, 212–13
Sissinghurst Castle, Kent, 50, 55, 57, 59–60, 64
Sitwell, Dame Edith, 41, 67, 72, 77–8, 105; *Façade*, 76
Sitwell, Sir George, 77
Sitwell, Georgia, Lady (née Doble; Sacheverell's wife)), 73–6, 78, 154
Sitwell, Lady Ida (née Denison), 77
Sitwell, Sir Osbert, 67–8, 76–8, 105
Sitwell, Sir Sacheverell: friendship with author, 67–8; manner, 68, 76; writings, 68, 72; architectural enthusiasms, 70–1; range of knowledge, 72; appearance, 73; romantic liaisons, 73; religious indifference, 74–5; travels, 74; marriage, 75–6; social life, 76; relations with family, 77–8; decline, 78; and Kinross, 105; rents house to Desmond Parsons, 152; at Weston Hall, 154; 'Agamemnon's Tomb' (poem), 74; *All Summer in a Day*, 73; *British Architects and Craftsmen*, 69; *Southern Baroque Art*, 69
Smith, H. Clifford, 27
Smith, Logan Pearsall, 85, 105, 220
Smith, Thornton (decorator), 159–60
Soane, Sir John, 183
Society for the Protection of Ancient Buildings, 194–5, 197, 203–4
South Africa: Plomer and, 90–4
Sparrow, John, 215
Spender, (Sir) Stephen, 52, 64, 98, 172
Squire, Sir John C., 52, 153
Stevenson, Robert Louis, 104
Stewart-Jones family, 152
Stewart-Jones, Richard: author meets, 194, 196–8; background, 197–8;

humanitarian work, 198; character and manner, 199–200
Stoke-on-Trent, 50–1
Stokes, Edward: *The Novels of Henry Green*, 125
Strang, Sir William: *Portrait of a Lady in a Red Hat* (painting), 43–4
Susterman, Joest, 187
Sutro, John, 109, 149, 153
Sykes, Christopher, 142–3, 147, 149–50, 155

Talbot-Rice, Professor David, 144, 147
Talman, William, 70
Ternan, Ellen, 205
Tonks, Henry, 15
Toynbee, Philip, 211
Tree, Nancy *see* Lancaster, Nancy
Tree, Ronald, 163
Trefusis, Denys, 57
Trefusis, Violet: and Vita Sackville-West, 49–50, 55–7, 62; leaves money to Kinross, 121
Tremblay, Château de, 35
Trevelyan, George Macaulay, 10
Trinidad, 212
Trollope, Anthony: *Phineas Finn*, 207
Turkey: Kinross's interest in, 117–18, 120–1

van der Post, (Sir) Laurens, 92–3
Victoria, Queen, 220
Vinson, Bill, 208
Voorslag (magazine), 92

Waddesdon Manor, Buckinghamshire, 165
Wallraf, Muriel, 223
Wallraf, Paul, 222–3
Walpole, Horace, 70
Walpole, Hugh, 2
Walton, Sir William, 52
Warren, Dorothy, 30
Watts, George Frederic, 171
Waugh, Evelyn: and Kinross, 103–5; at Chagford, 115; letter-writing, 128; at Lygon home, 138; xenophobia, 142
Wavell, Field Marshal Archibald, Earl, 226
Webb, Norman, 115
Welch, Denton, 80
Wellesley, Dorothy, 45, 57
Wellesley, Lord Gerald, 211, 216
Westmorland, Diana, Countess of, 55
Westwood Manor, Wiltshire, 37
Whistler, James Abbot McNeill, 31
White, Graham, 9
Wilde, Oscar, 221, 230
Willingdon, Freeman Freeman-Thomas, 1st Marquess of, 148

239

Wilson, Edward Adrian (Bill), 3
Woolf, Leonard, 96
Woolf, Virginia: Vita Sackville-West
   addresses verse to, 43; relations with
   Vita Sackville-West, 57, 96; letters, 81;
   and Plomer, 96–7; *Orlando*, 43
Woolley, Sir Leonard, 32–3, 35
Wren, Sir Christopher, 70

Yarmouth, 5
Yorke, Adelaide (Henry's wife; 'Dig'), 122,
   131
Yorke, Gerald (Henry's brother), 128
Yorke, Henry ('Henry Green'): friendship
   with author, 122–3, 130; literary
   achievements and style, 123–30;

business interests, 124, 130–1;
   broadcasts, 128; death, 131; isolation,
   131; friendship with Robert Byron,
   137–8; *Back*, 125; *Blindness*, 123; *Caught*,
   123–4; *Concluding*, 125; *Doting*, 125;
   Living, 124, 126, 129; *Loving*, 125–7;
   Nothing, 125; *Pack My Bag*, 125; *Party
   Going*, 125
Yorke, Vincent (Henry's father), 124, 130–1
Young, Edward Hilton *see* Kennet, 1st
   Baron
Young, Hilda, 88
Young, Sir Hubert, 212
Young, Louisa: *A Great Task of Happiness*,
   17n
Young, Wayland *see* Kennet, 2nd Baron